JAY MAISEL'S NEW YORK

JAY MAISEL'S NEW YORK

FIREFLY BOOKS

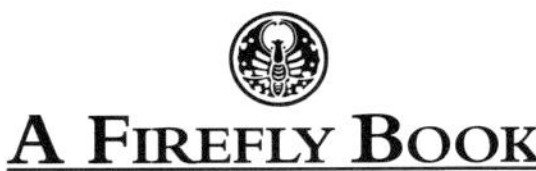

Published by Firefly Books Ltd. 2000

First Printing

U.S. Cataloging-in-Publication Data

Jay Maisel's New York / photography by Jay Maisel.
–1st ed.
[192]p. : col. ill. ; cm.
Summary: A master photographer's photographic essay on New York City.
ISBN 1-55209-496-0
1. New York (N.Y.) – Pictorial works. I. Title.
974.7/1 21 2000 CIP

Canadian Cataloguing in Publication Data

Maisel, Jay
Jay Maisel's New York

ISBN 1-55209-496-0

1. New York (N.Y.) – Pictorial works. I. Title.

F128.37.M44 2000 974.7'1'00222 C00-930880-6

Published in Canada in 2000 by
Firefly Books Ltd., 3680 Victoria Park Avenue
Willowdale, Ontario, Canada M2H 3K1

Published in the United States in 2000 by
Firefly Books (U.S.) Inc., P.O. Box 1338, Ellicott Station
Buffalo, New York 14205

Design by Bob Wilcox
Printed and bound in Canada by Friesens, Altona, Manitoba

The Publisher acknowledges the financial support of the Government of Canada through the Book Publishing Industry Development Program for its publishing activities.

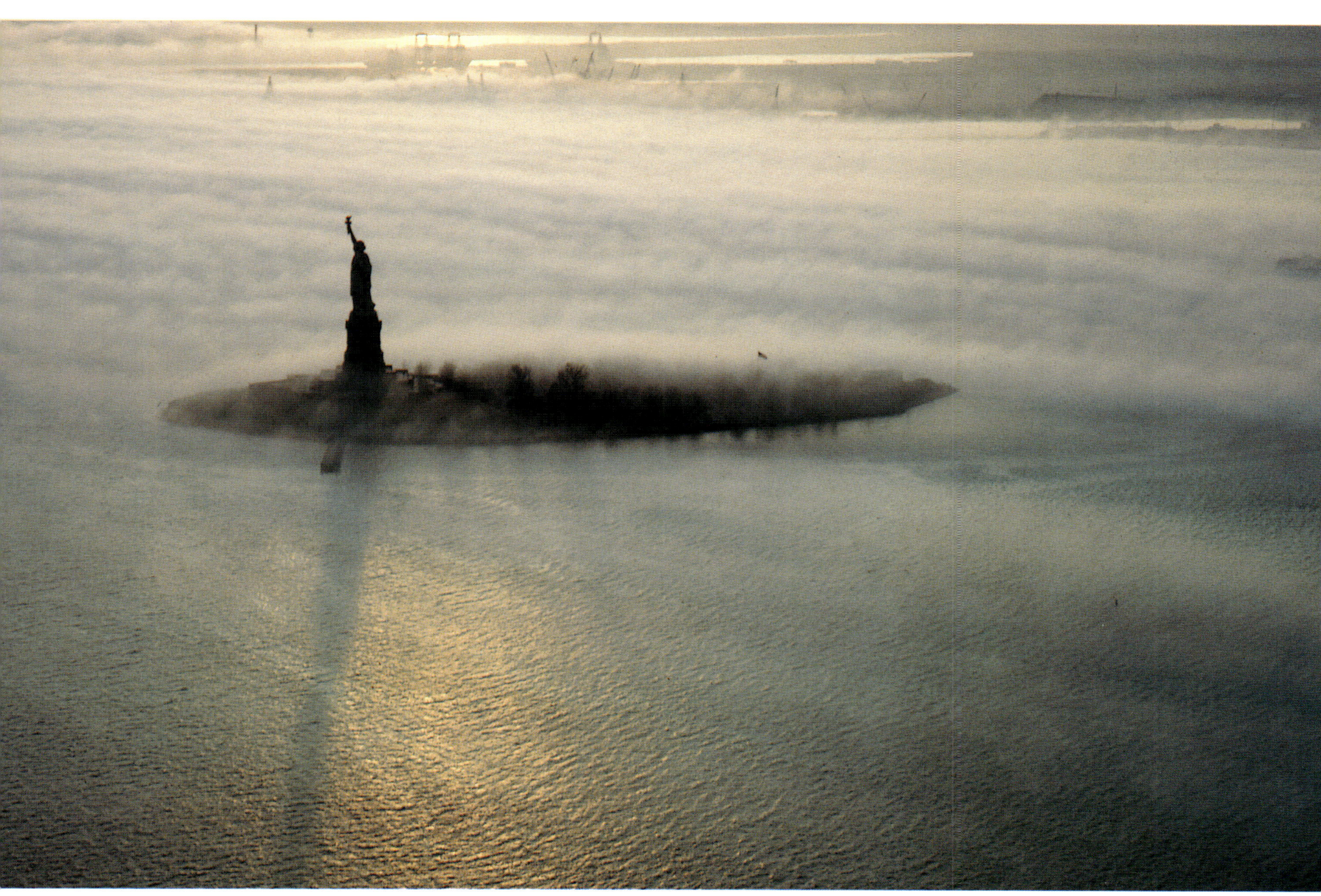

This book is dedicated to all the people who appear in it, and to the Nikon cameras with which it was made.

It is specifically dedicated with thanks to Jennifer Worth, Bryan Casebolt, Noelle Tan, Sam Garcia, John Thaxton and Gregory Heisler. They were in the forefront of those friends who nagged me to "do a book already."

Much credit goes to Joshua Hebert, who had to deal with my procrastination. I also want to express my appreciation to Geoff Green. Without his help and perseverance this book never would have happened.

I have been fortunate to work with Bob Wilcox, who has designed this book, and with the publisher, Lionel Koffler, whose calmness and expertise in the face of my equivocation were unnerving to say the least. Thank you both for your patience, trust and empathy.

Last, to the true powers behind the throne, I thank my wife L.A., who made me "pinkie swear to finally do a book *this year*." This is also for my seven-year-old daughter Amanda, who recently suggested that maybe I should get a second job.

Jay Maisel
New York City

MY WORD

After a visit to New York a tourist hails a taxi and asks the cabbie, "Can you take me to the airport, or should I just go to hell?"

New York is a tough city—too hot in summer, too cold in winter, crowded, noisy, expensive, and dangerous. I've never wanted to live anywhere else.

Its beauty lies in its vitality and diversity. The pace and the energy are staggering to me and I'm a native. I treasure a walk in my neighborhood; the view from my home is spectacular. I live in a city which has not only a downtown, but a midtown and an uptown—all different and all full of visual delights.

I've taken my camera worldwide, but New York is my first love. Photographing New York is like trying to take a bite out of an elephant. It's the one place that can truly be called larger than life. Into its physically tiny boundaries are packed spectacle and change unmatched anywhere.

Buildings disappear, new ones sprout; neighborhoods change quality, cabbies change nationality; senior citizens get older, cops get younger, and the rents always soar. The New Yorker, battle-scarred by strikes and blackouts, survives in the heartland of the cynic, the skeptic, and the paranoid. New Yorkers think they're sophisticated, but they still retain the awestruck wonder of children.

New York is dream and nightmare, beautiful and ugly, with thousands of wonderful special events and a totally decaying infrastructure. The light and the skyline can break your heart. The visual power is special, like no place on earth.

There are probably more photographers taking pictures in New York at any given moment than in any other place in the world. Even if all these images were put into use, we would never have a total comprehensive record of New York. Certainly this book makes no claim to be comprehensive. Rather, what you have in your hands is an idiosyncratic view of the city. A record of perennial meanderings, strolls, and wanderings. Some walks, some rides; some in the air, others on the ground; some planned images but, mostly, a series of random events. We all have heard the expression, "New York, New York. A town so nice they named it twice."

I don't think so!

The twinning is appropriate though because New York has more of everything you can think of. There are more museums, taxis, galleries, cops, theaters, cars, trucks, buses, wackos, arguments, fires, airplanes, helicopters, tourists, restaurants, hospitals—and more of anything else... except parking spaces.

New York is a joy and a terror, rich in details, events, density, and variety. It calls you to look and dares you to make sense of what you see. New York is the scariest place in the world to take pictures. New Yorkers challenge you verbally, philosophically, and physically. They rarely hide their passions behind a facade of good manners, so you know where you stand with them. I have witnessed all the emotions one can think of, positive and negative, on the streets of New York.

I have rarely seen the rudeness, coldness, and cruelty supposedly the hallmark of the New Yorker. I have, however, been moved to tears by the acts of warmth and kindness from the same New Yorkers who have a rightfully deserved reputation for abuse, profanity, and hostility. There's nothing consistent about this, which is just about how New York is. At times it is theater, stunning with its intensity and virtuosity. It rarely bores, but it can exhaust you with its constant flow of energy. You don't swallow New York—New York swallows you.

It's a dirty, dangerous, expensive place, but the only place to be. To a true New Yorker, no matter where you are in the world, if you're not in New York, you're "out of town."

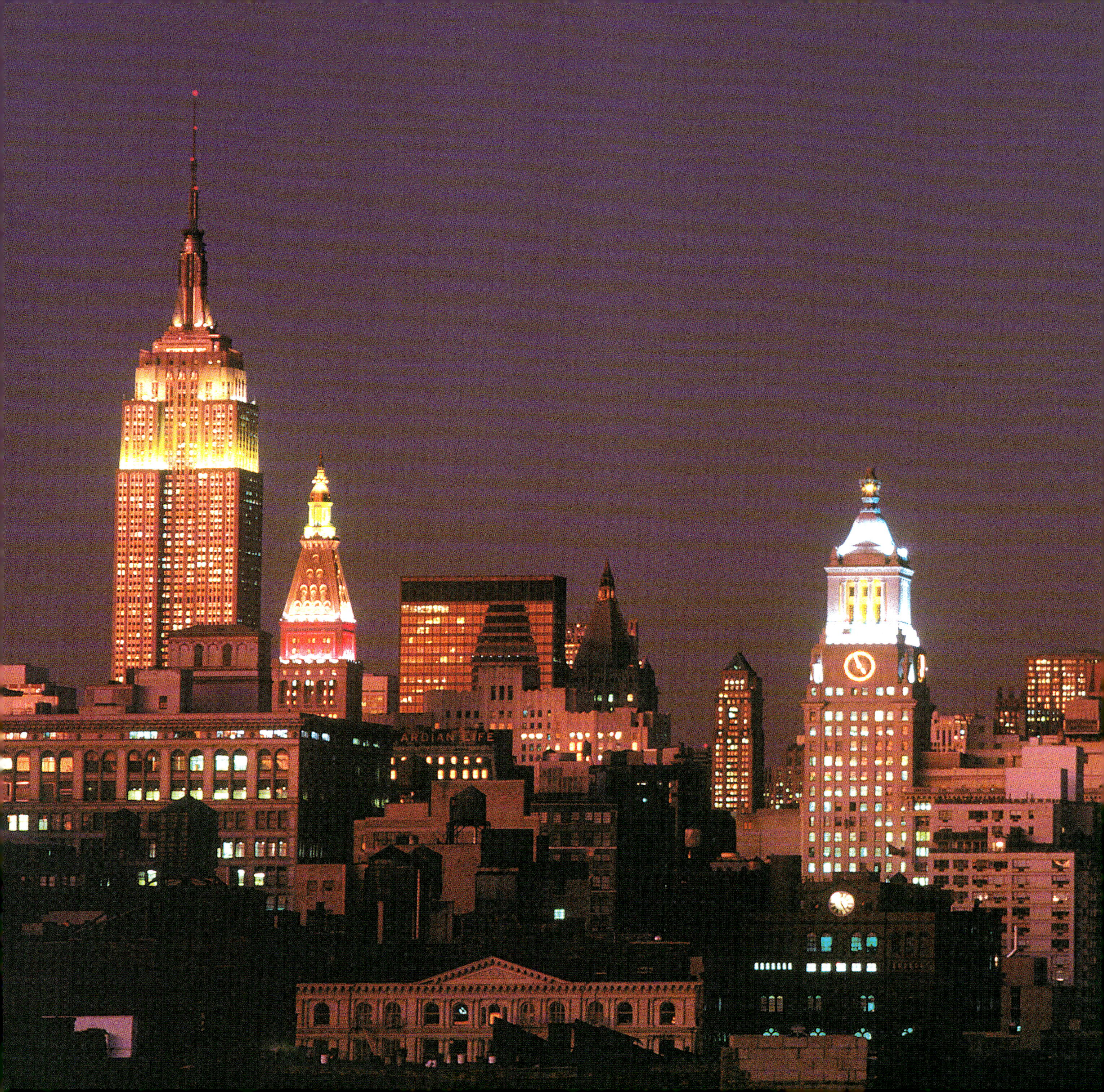
ARDIAN LIFE

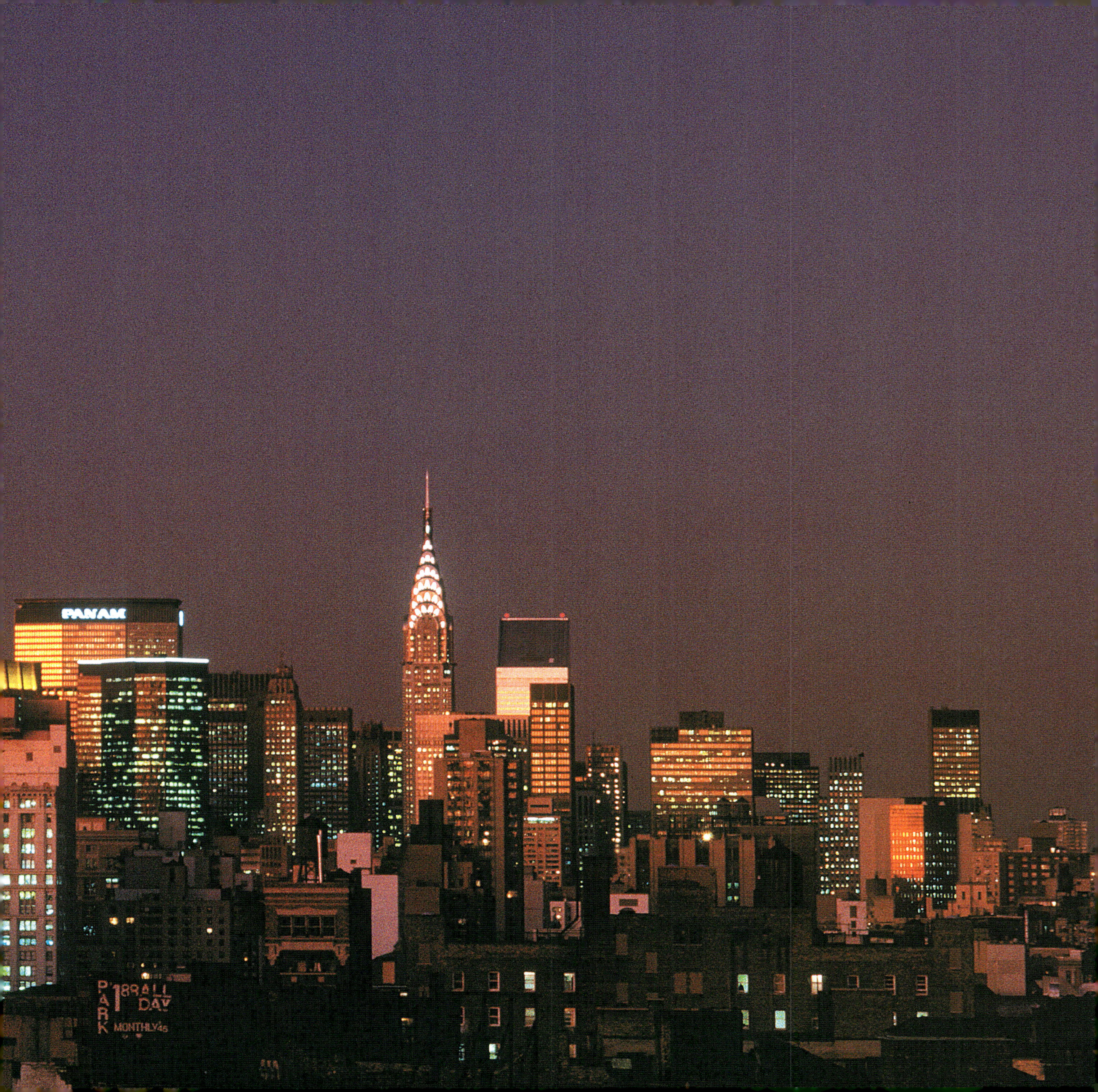
PANAM
PARK
ALL DAY
MONTHLY

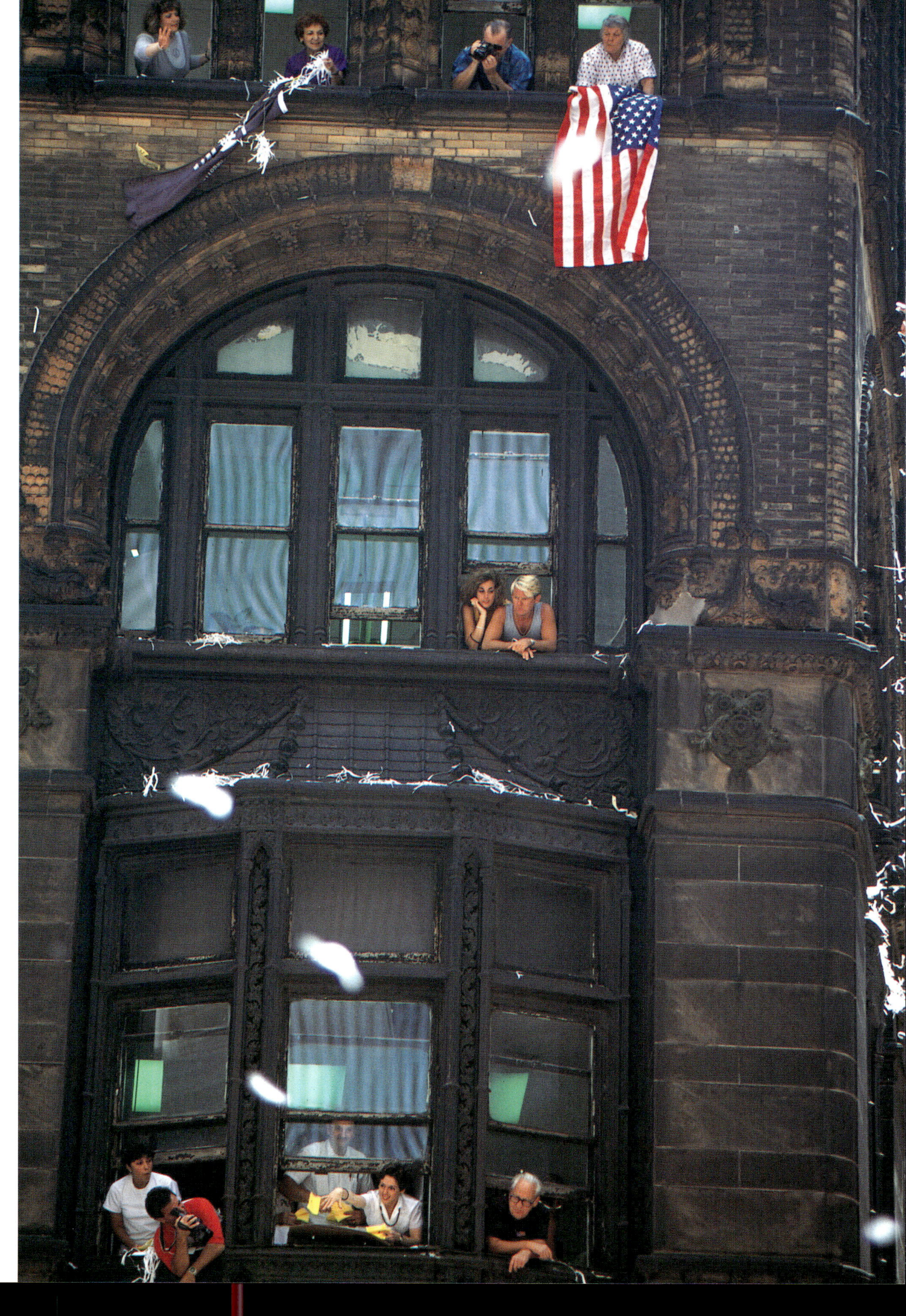

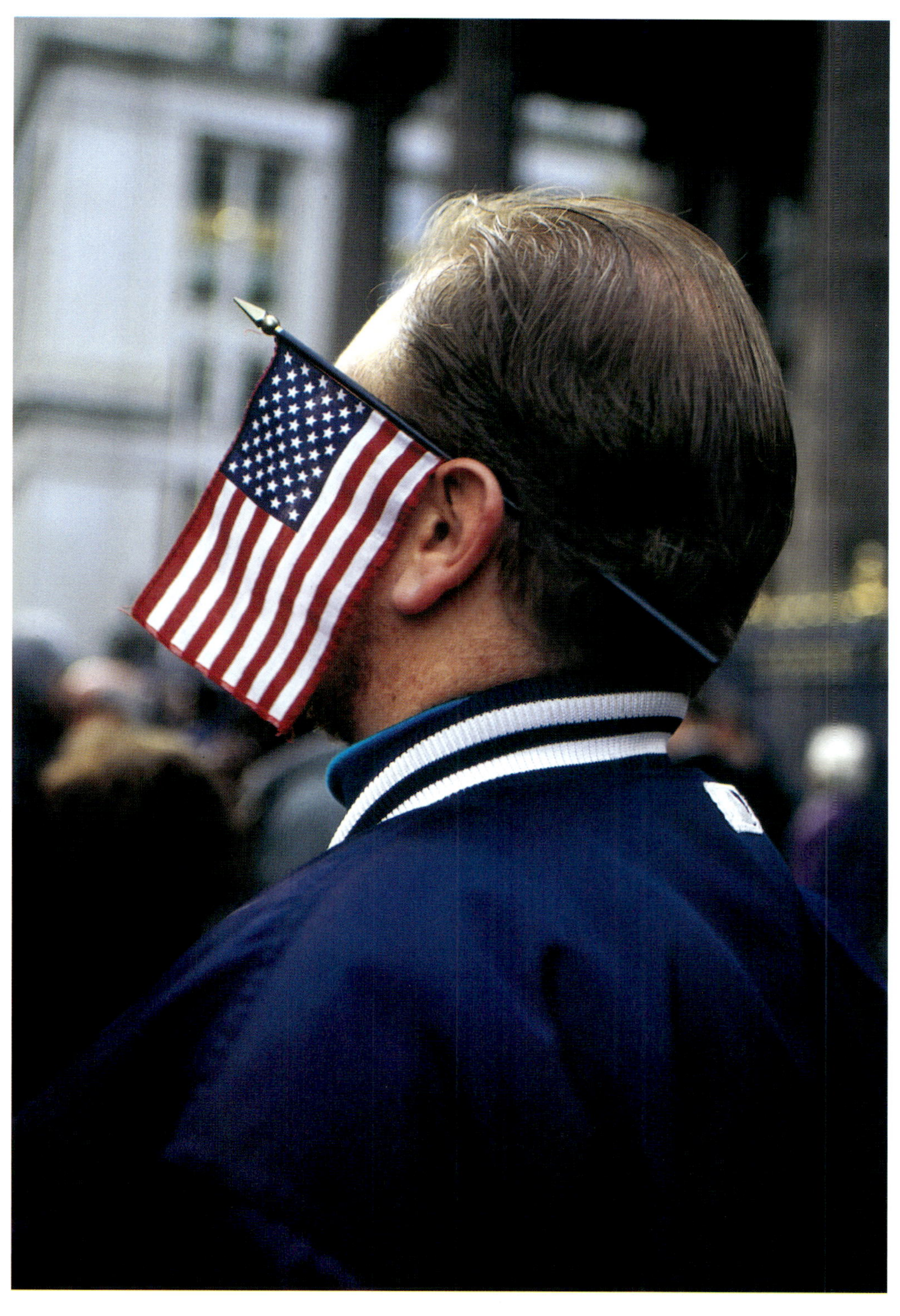

The icons of New York. I've been shooting the twin towers of the World Trade Center since they were half built.

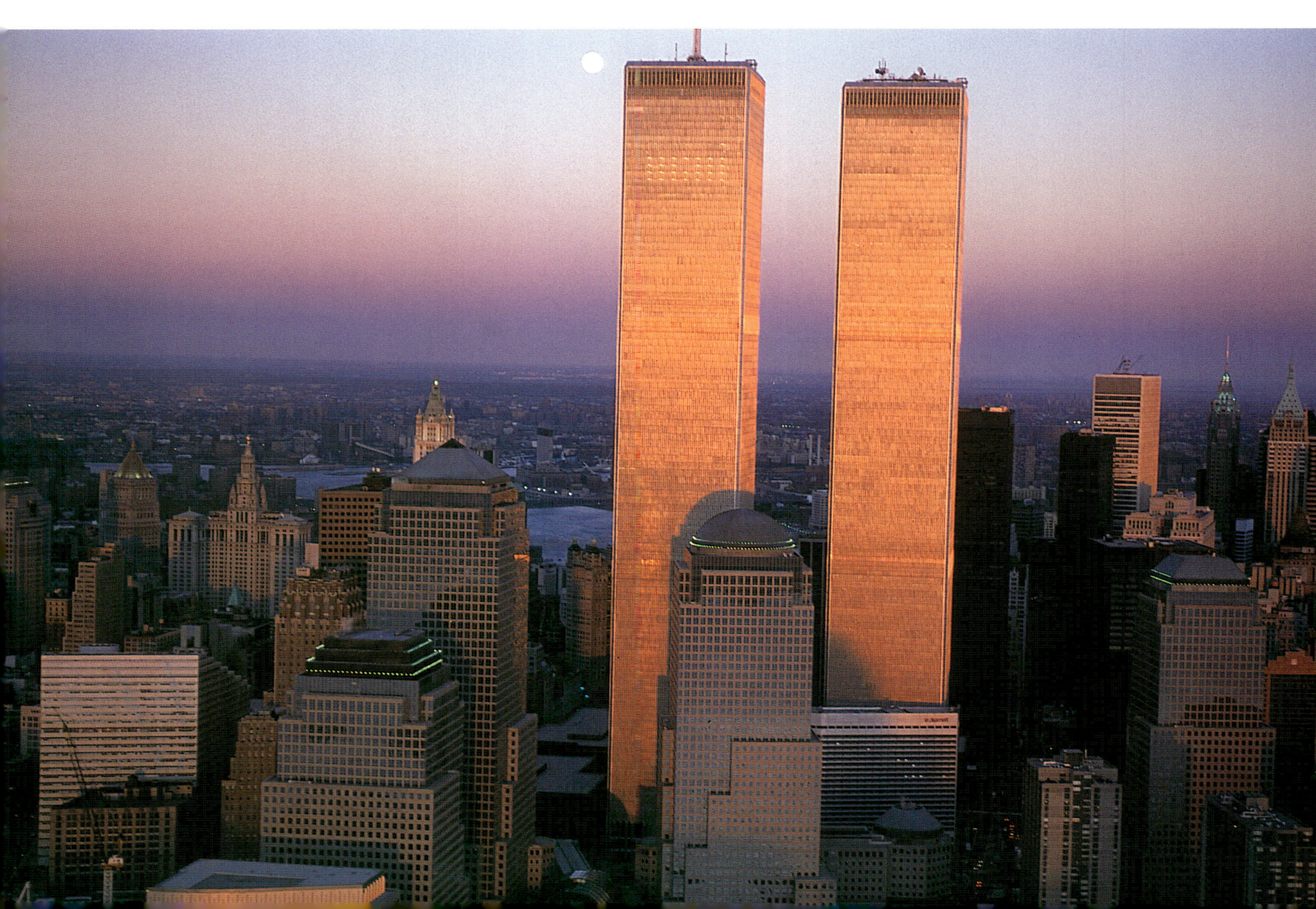

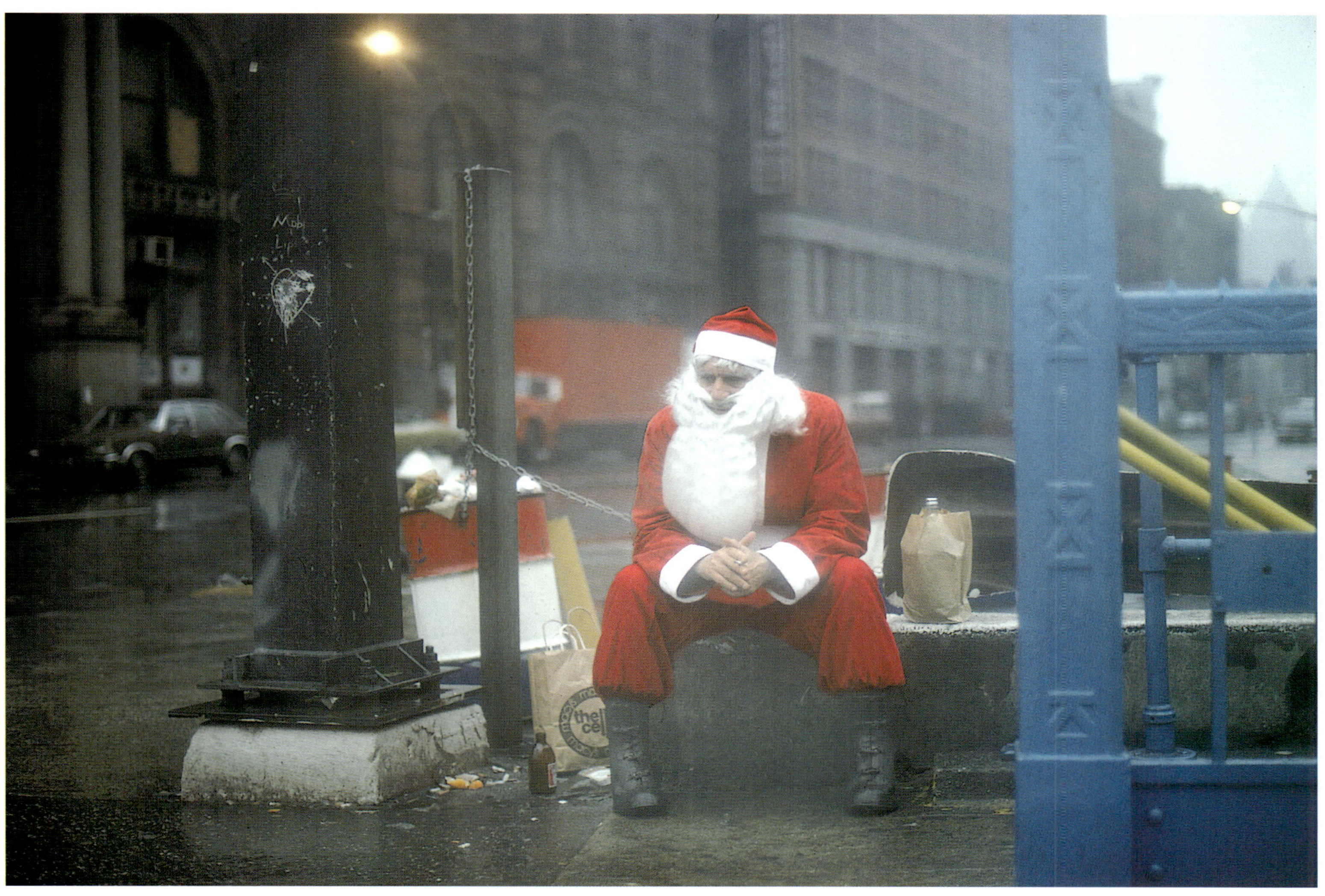

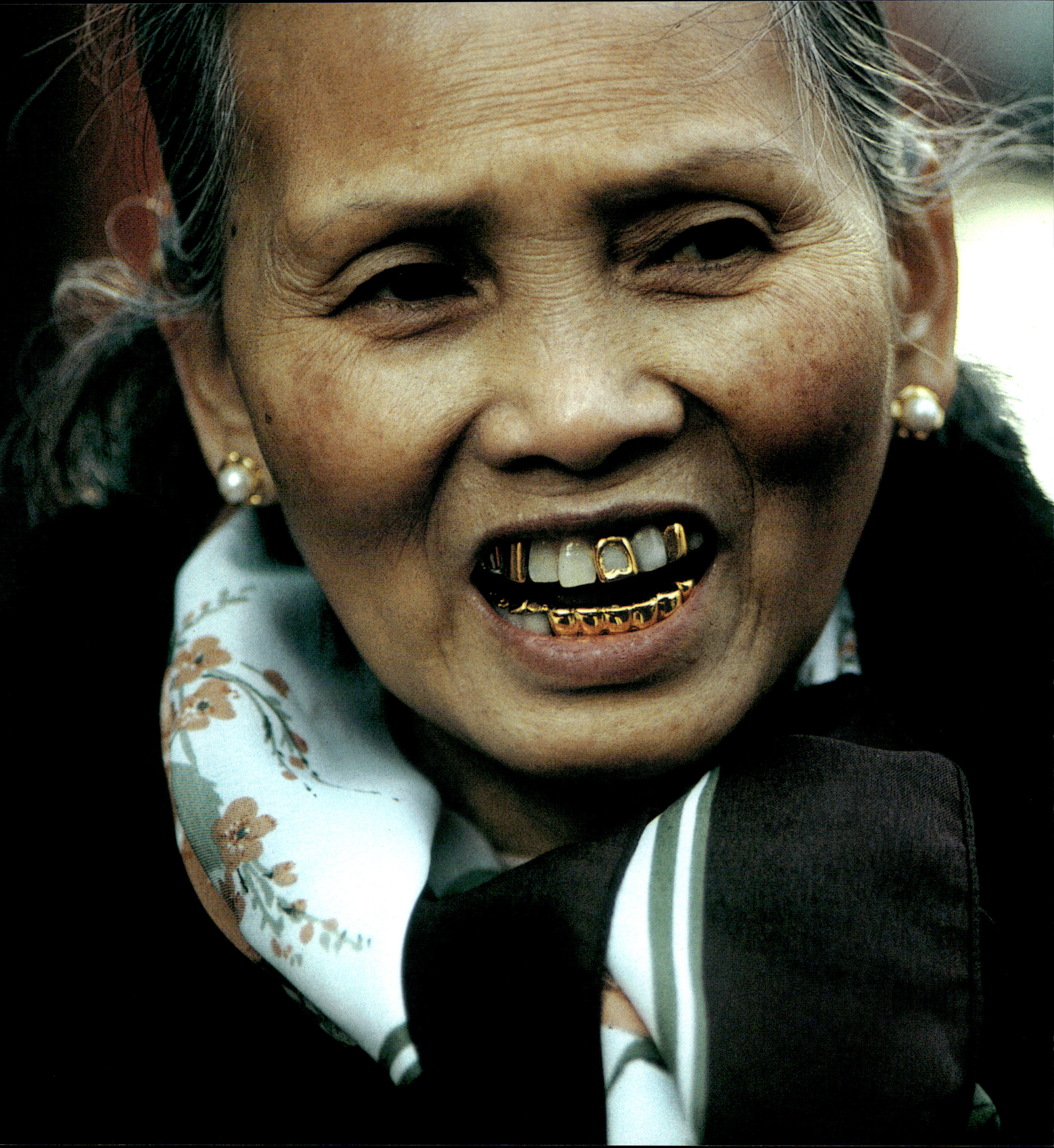

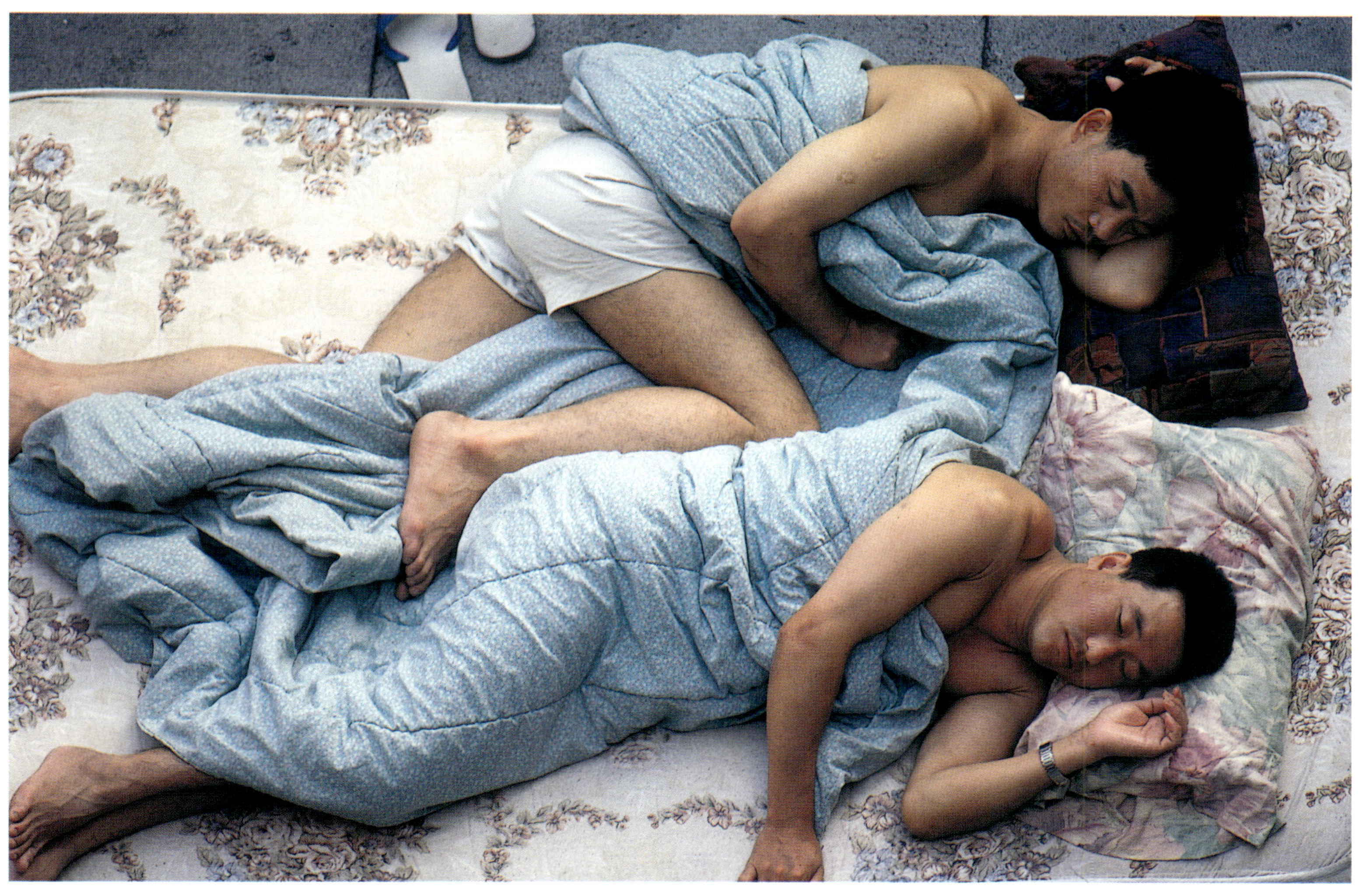

100 degree heat day and night, no air conditioning, small apartments.

These recent immigrants follow the example of those in the early 1900s.

They sleep on rooftops, hoping for relief from the humidity.

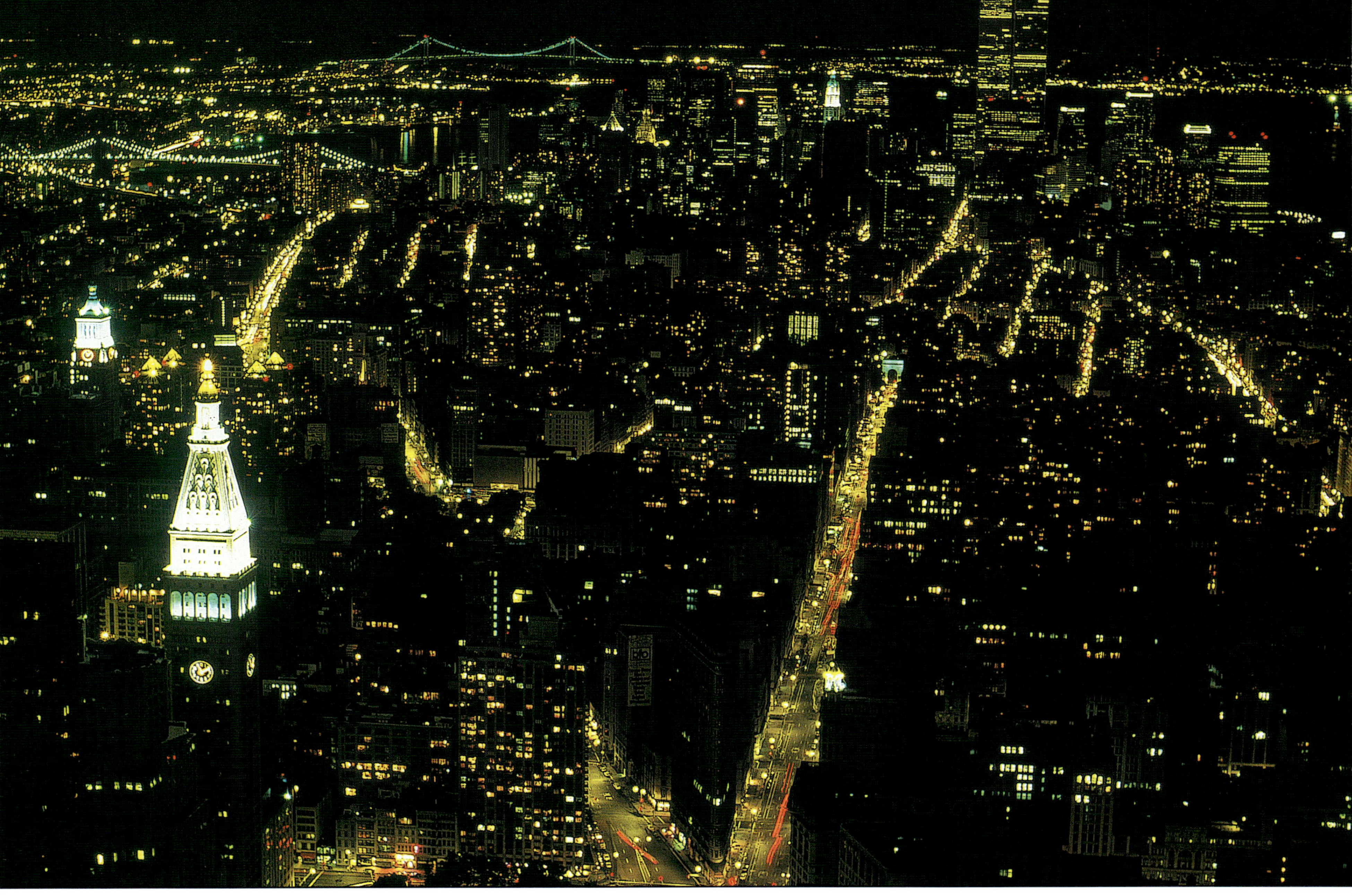

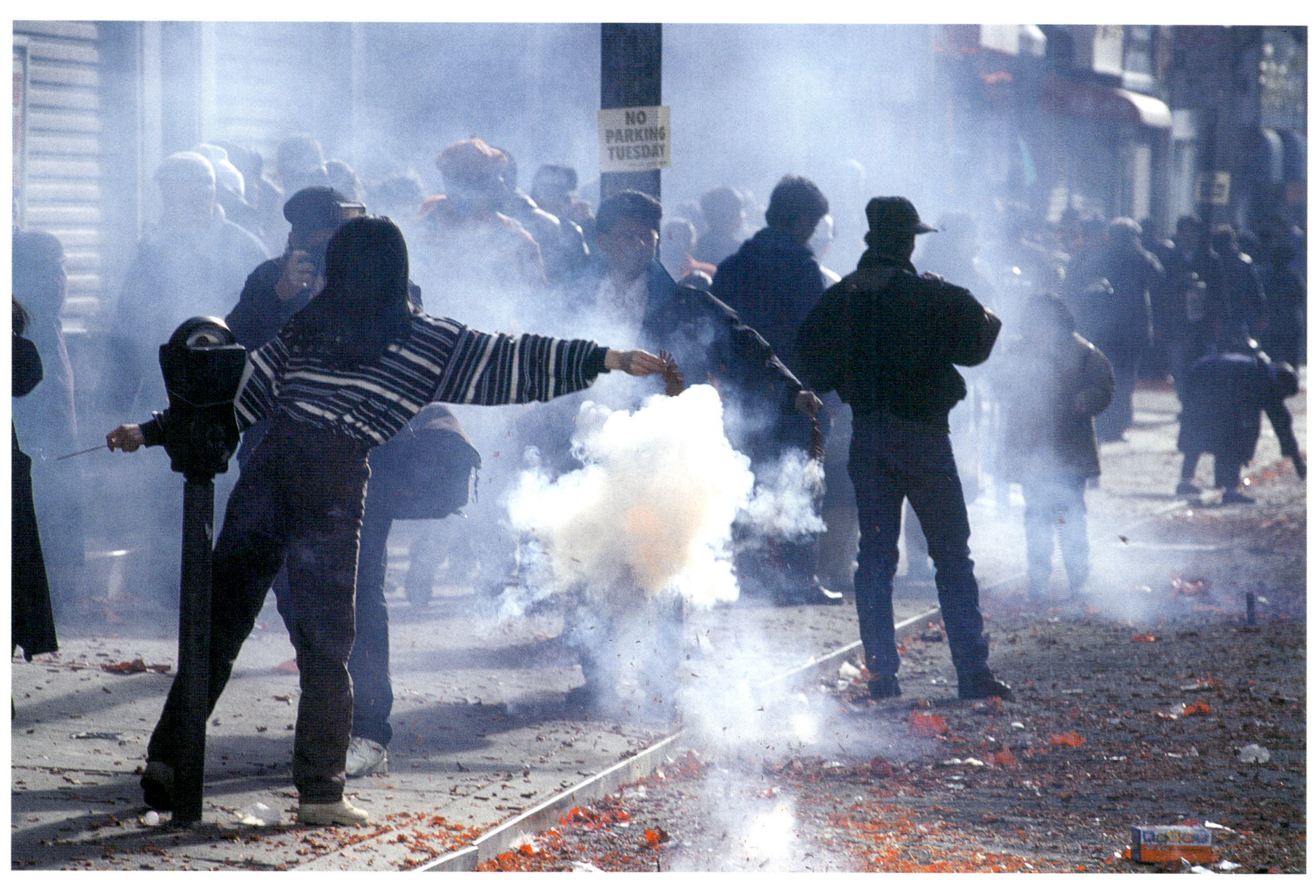
NO
PARKING
TUESDAY

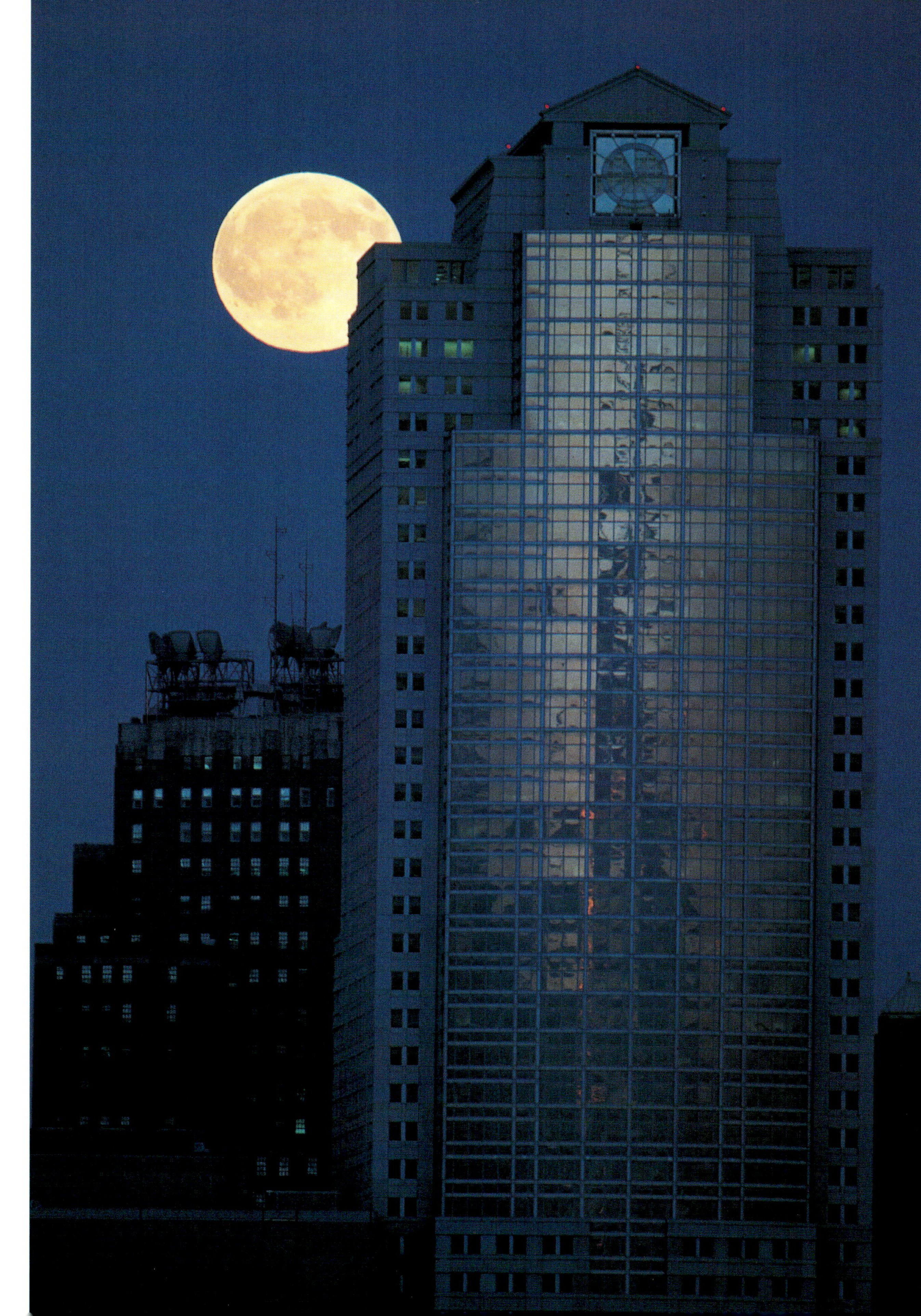

Probably the most photographed bakery window in New York.

This is Vesuvios, on Spring Street. The man is an artist.

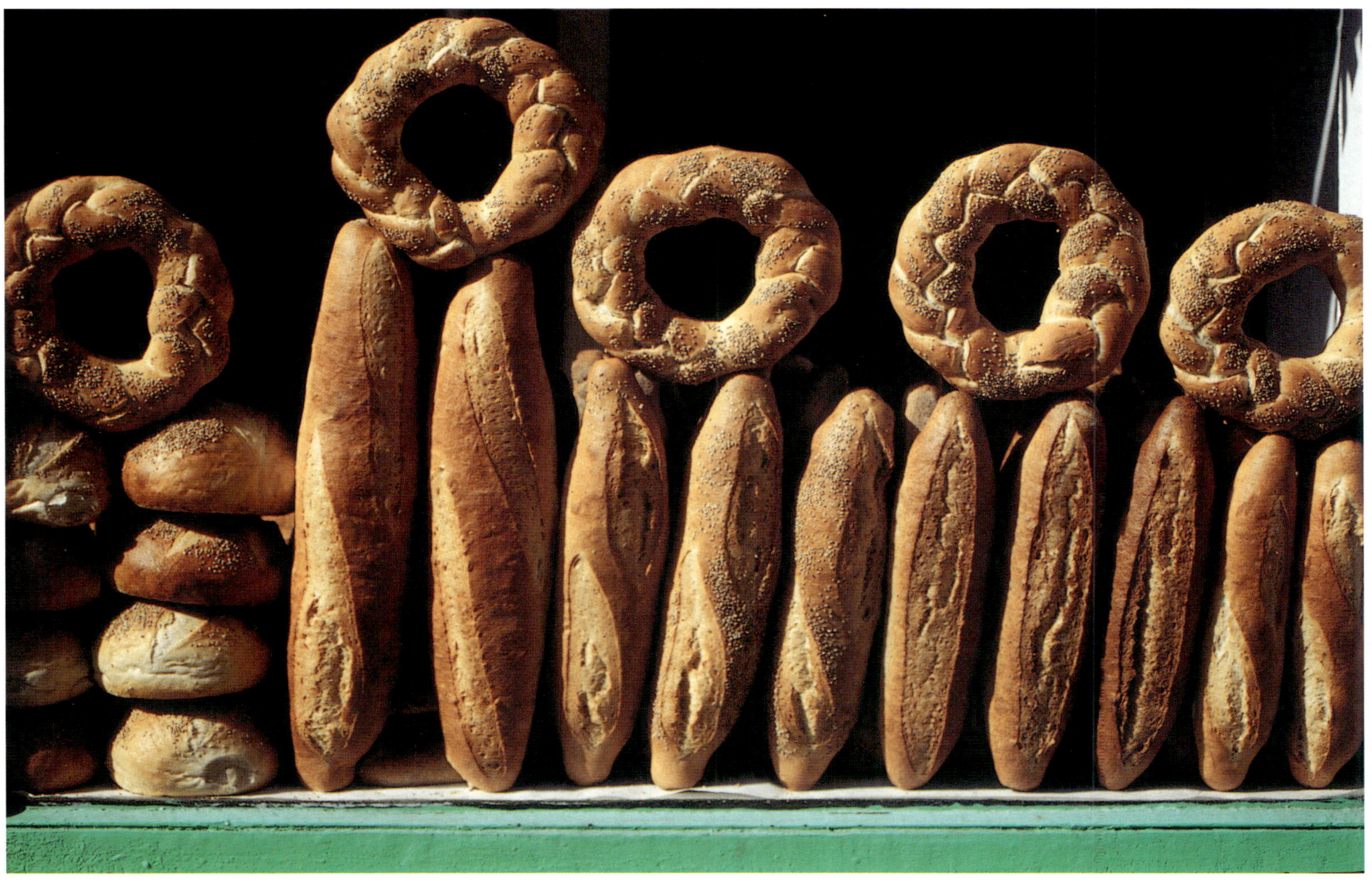

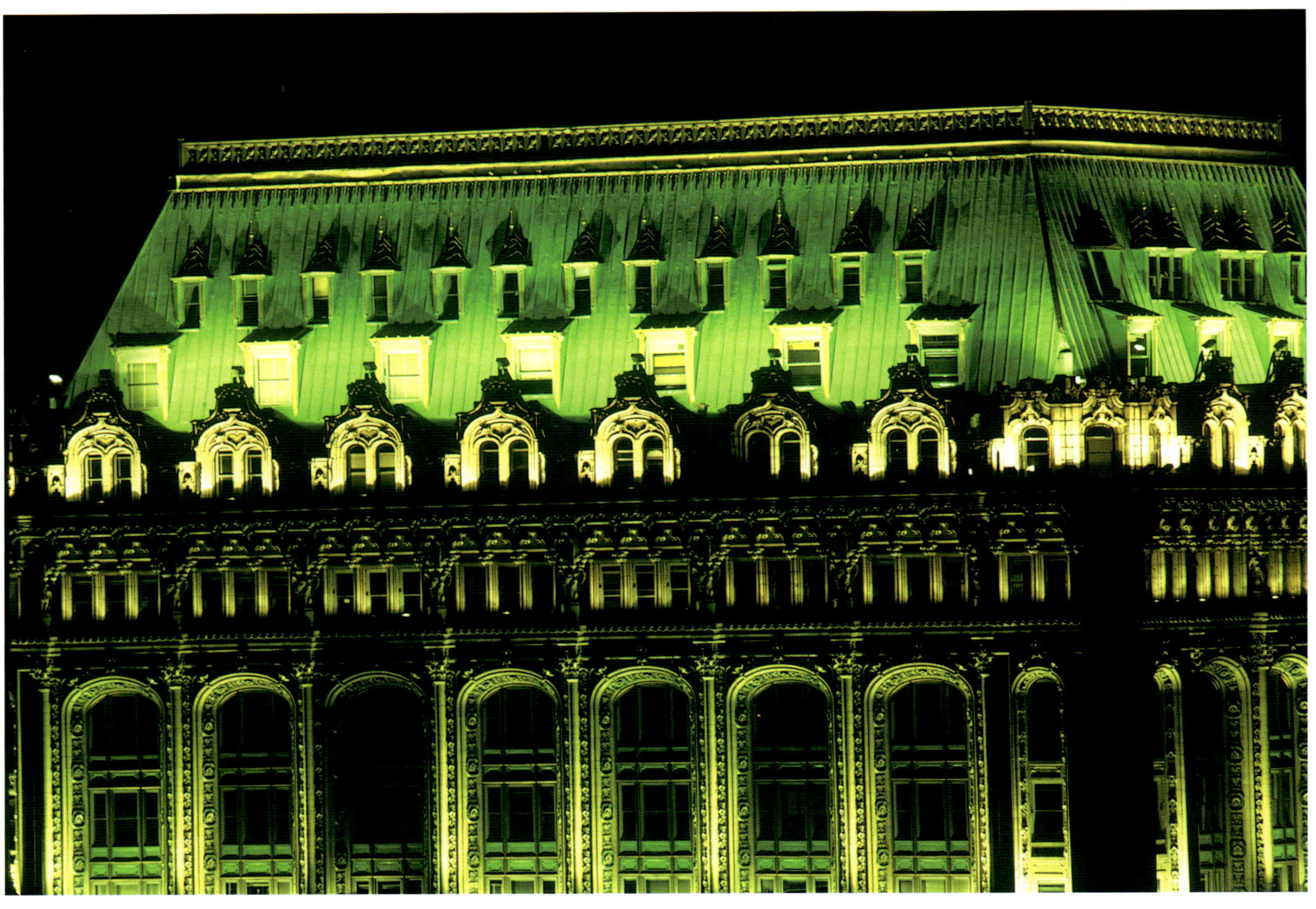

This building on the west side is much brighter than any other on the skyline, so it always just blows out. But it's lovely by itself.

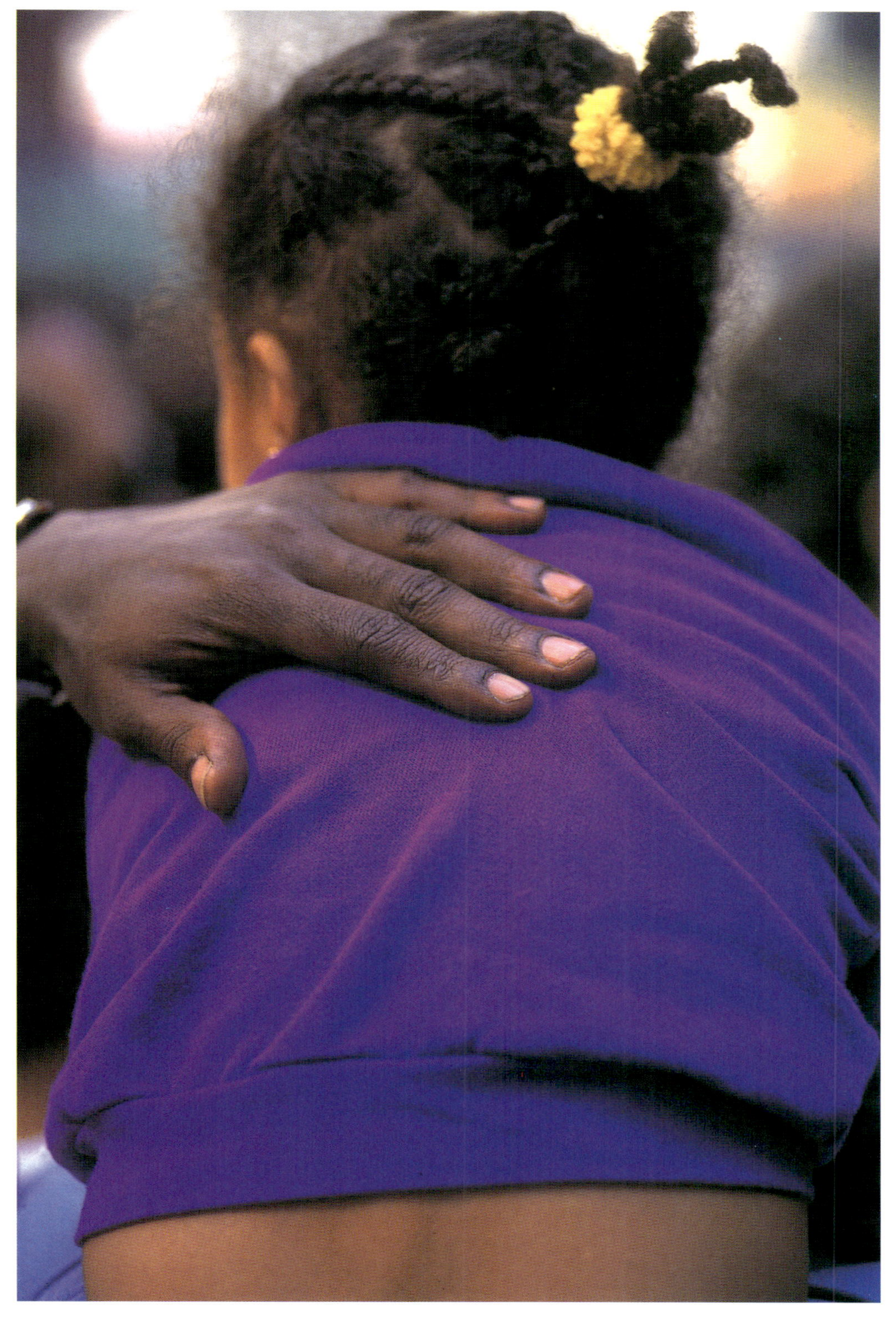

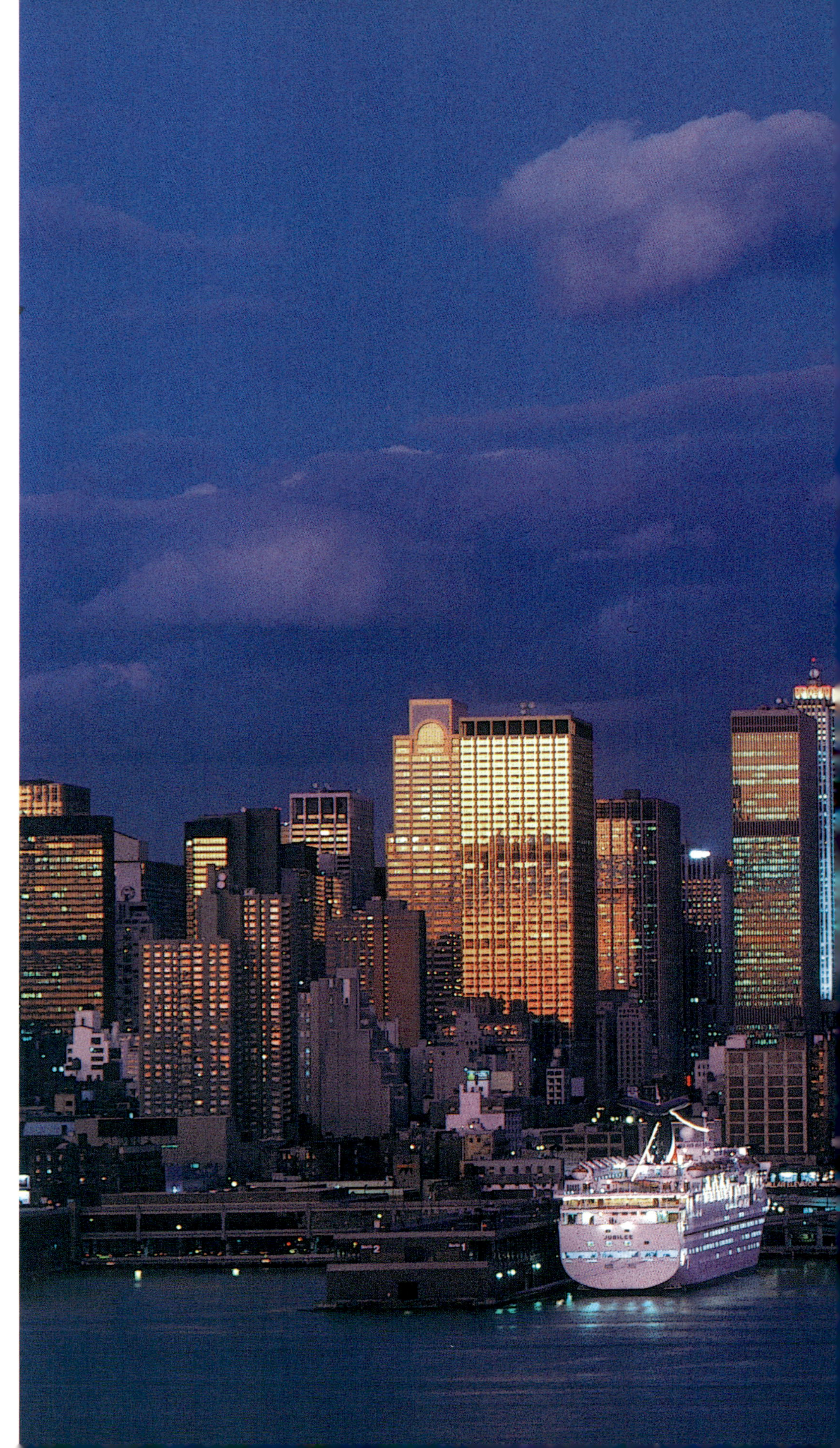

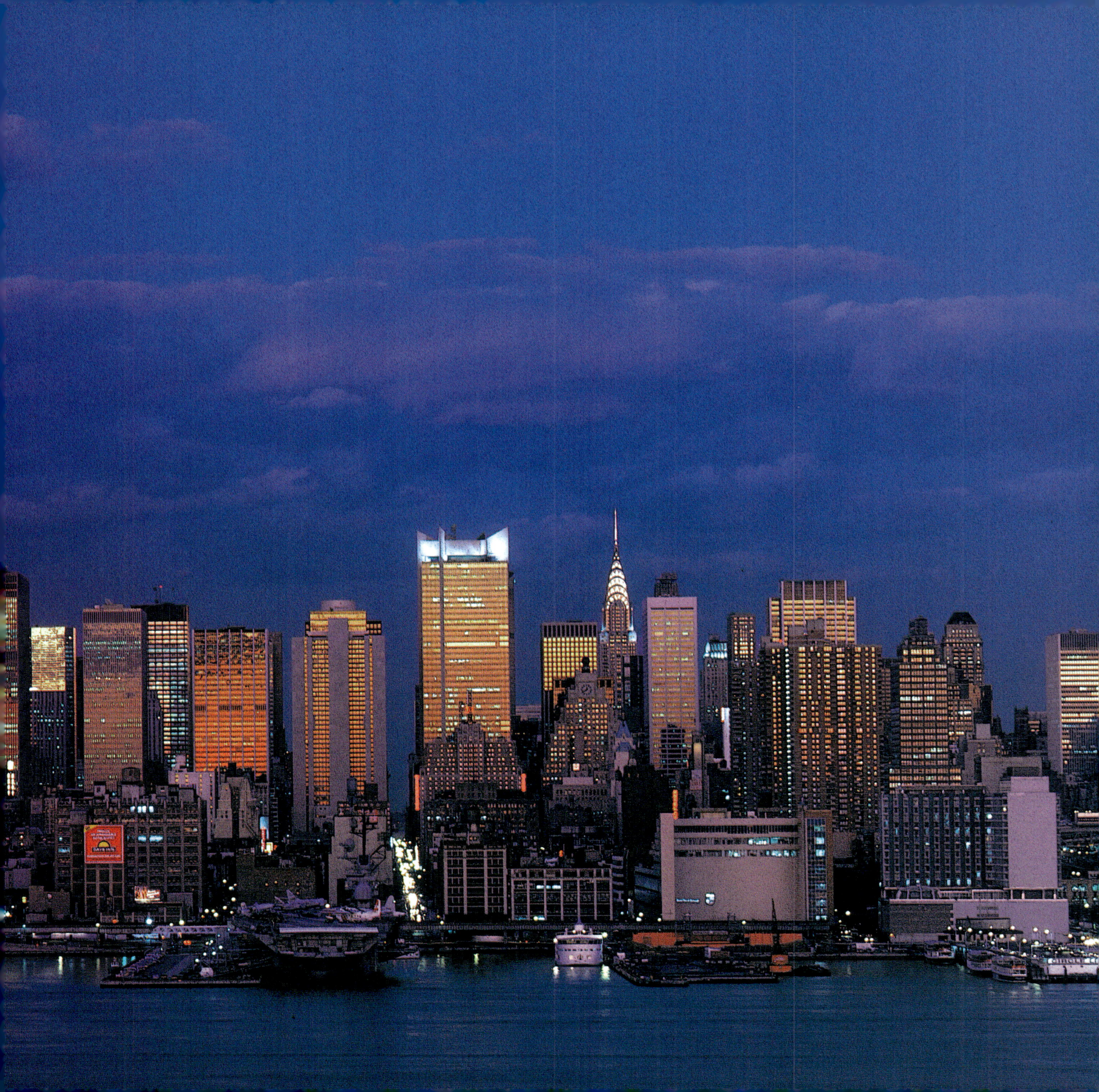

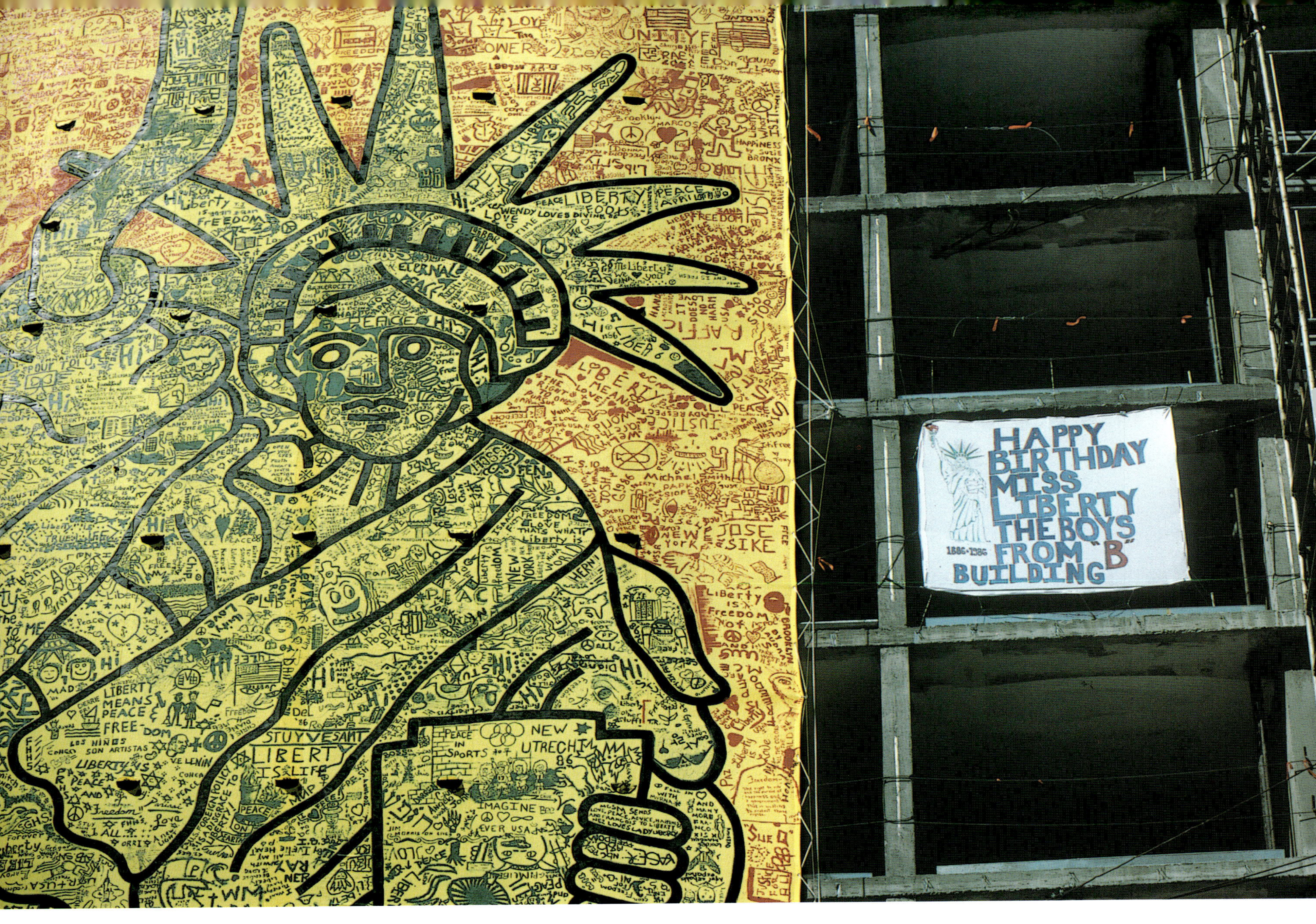
HAPPY
BIRTHDAY
MISS
LIBERTY
THE BOYS
FROM "B"
BUILDING
1886-1986

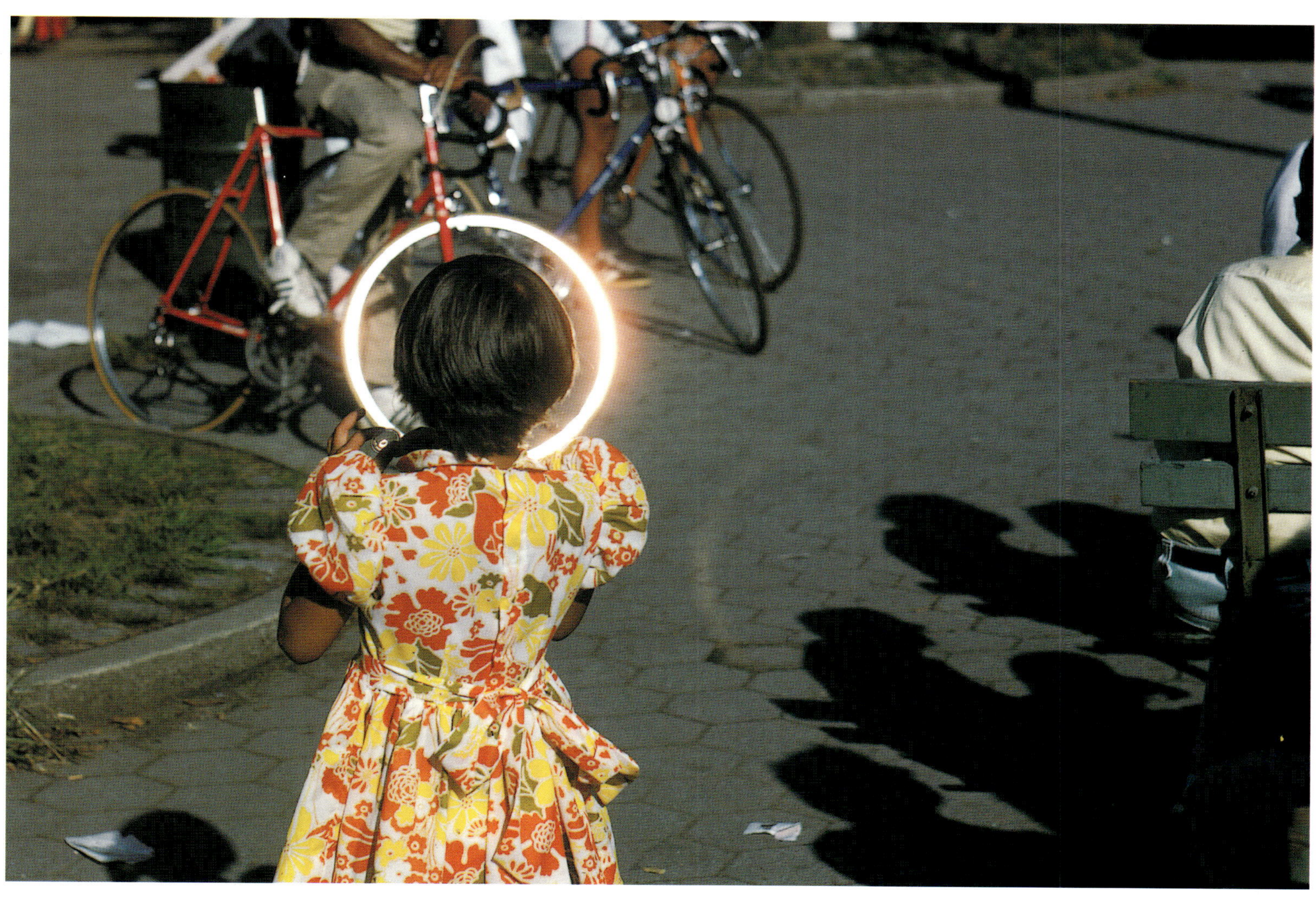

A fleeting moment of light in Central Park.

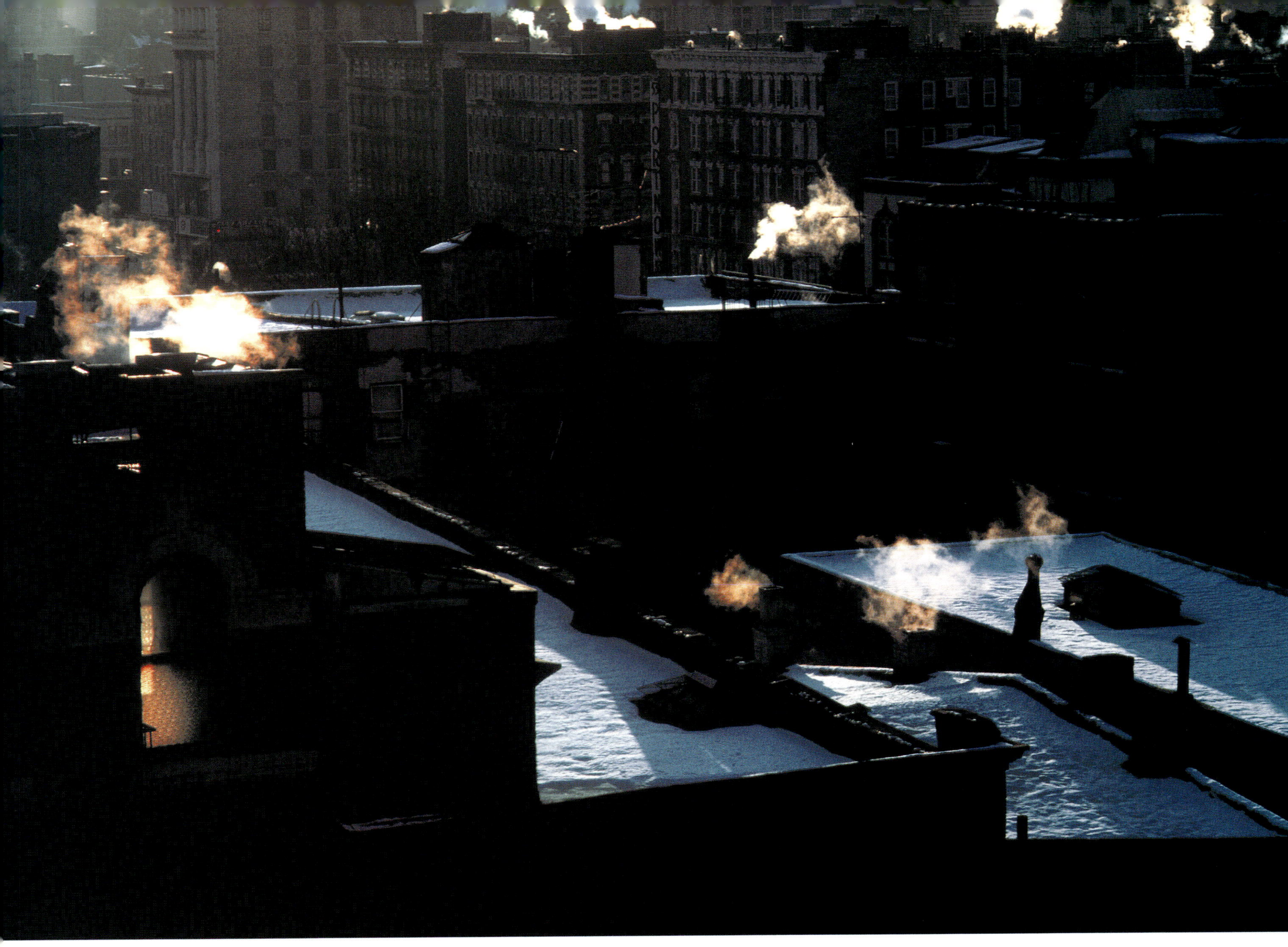

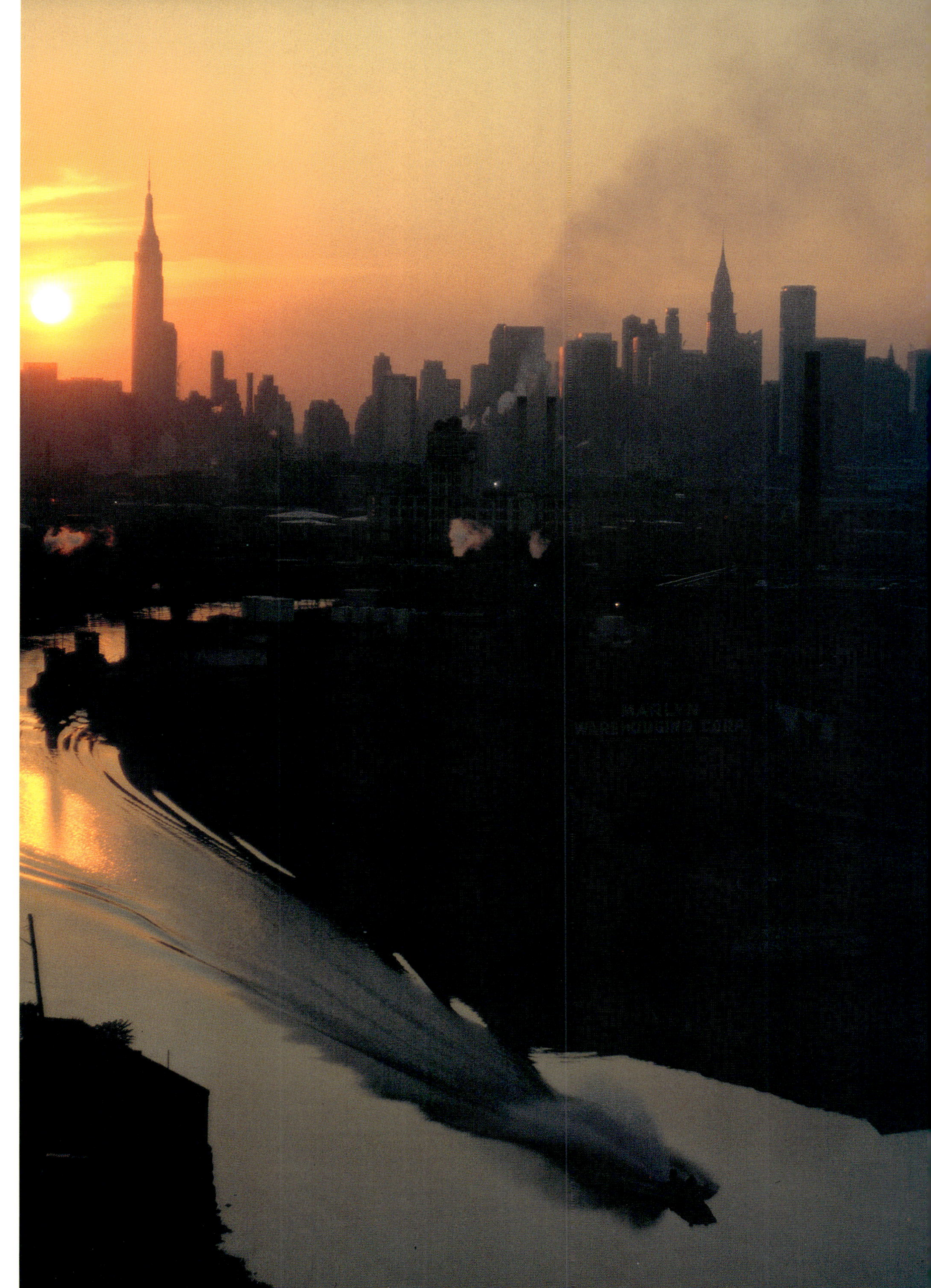

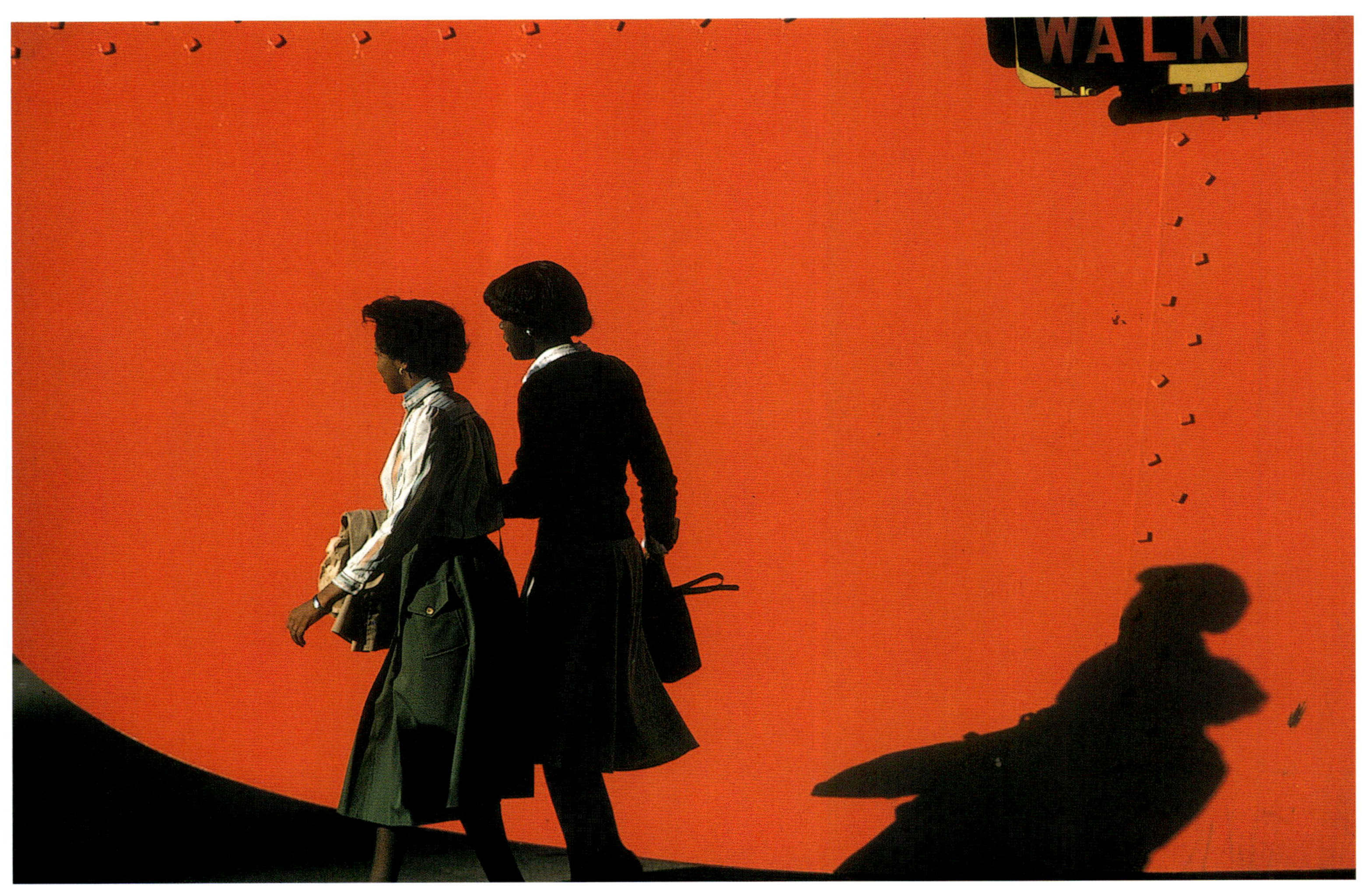
WALK

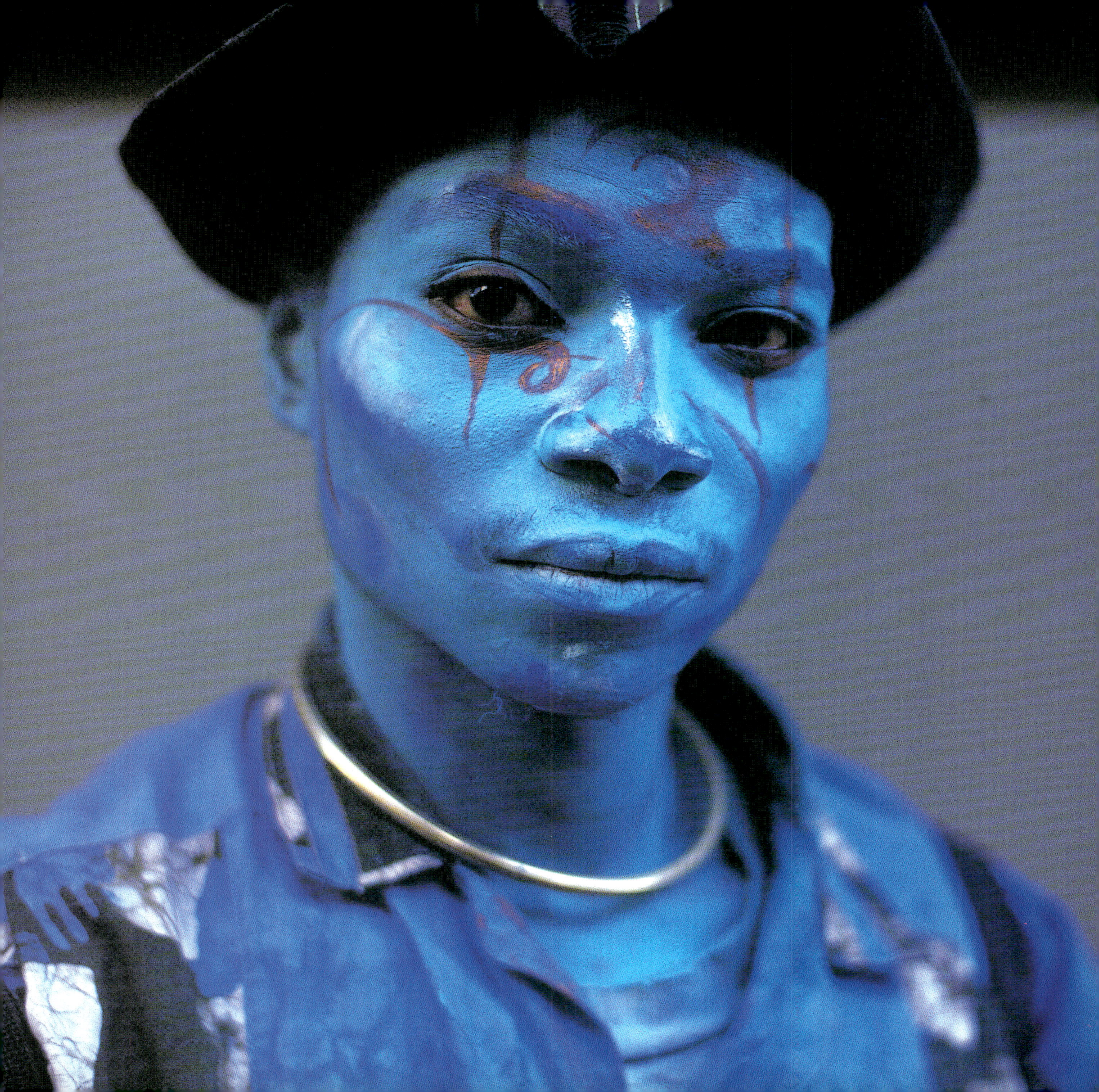

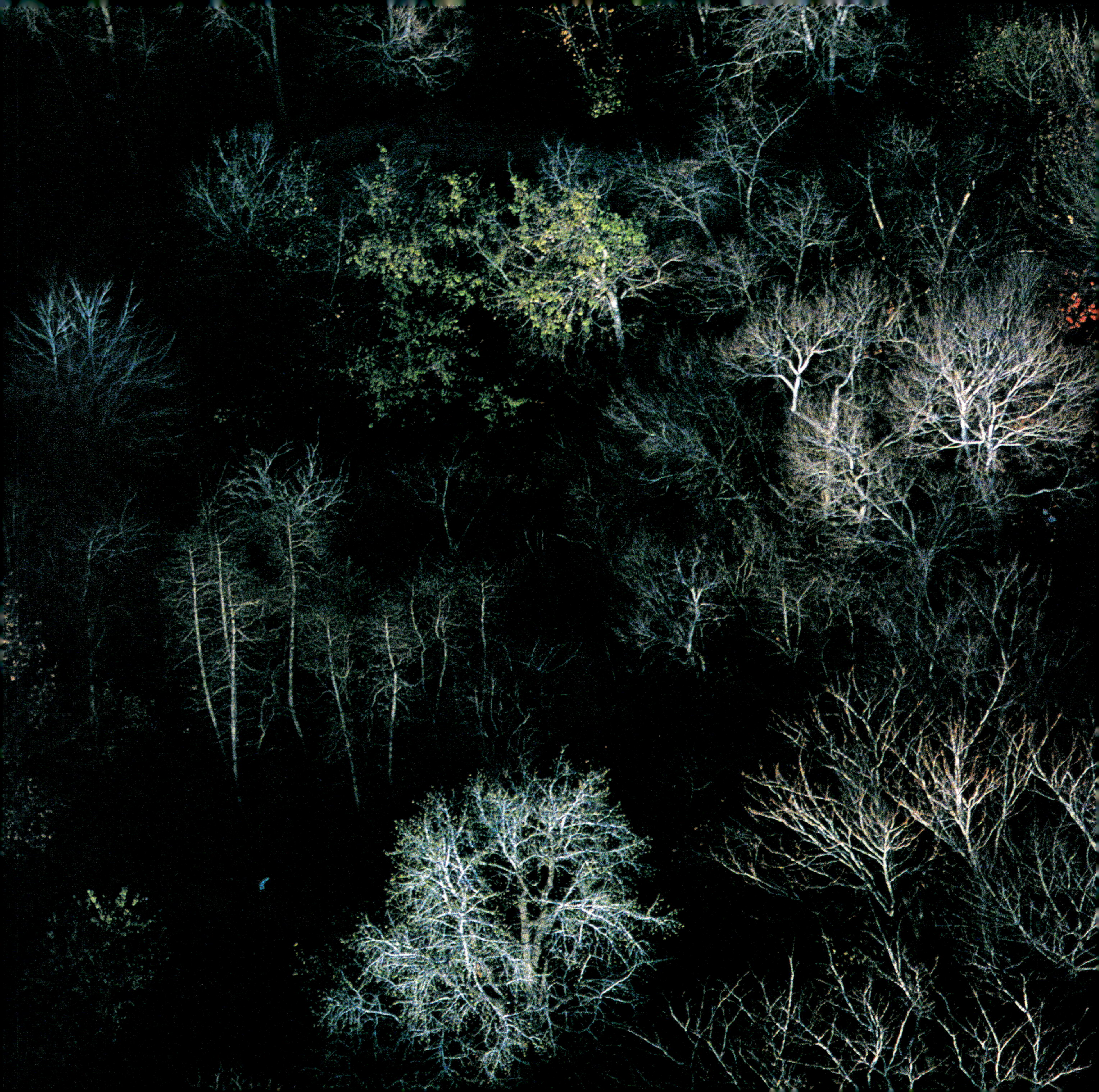

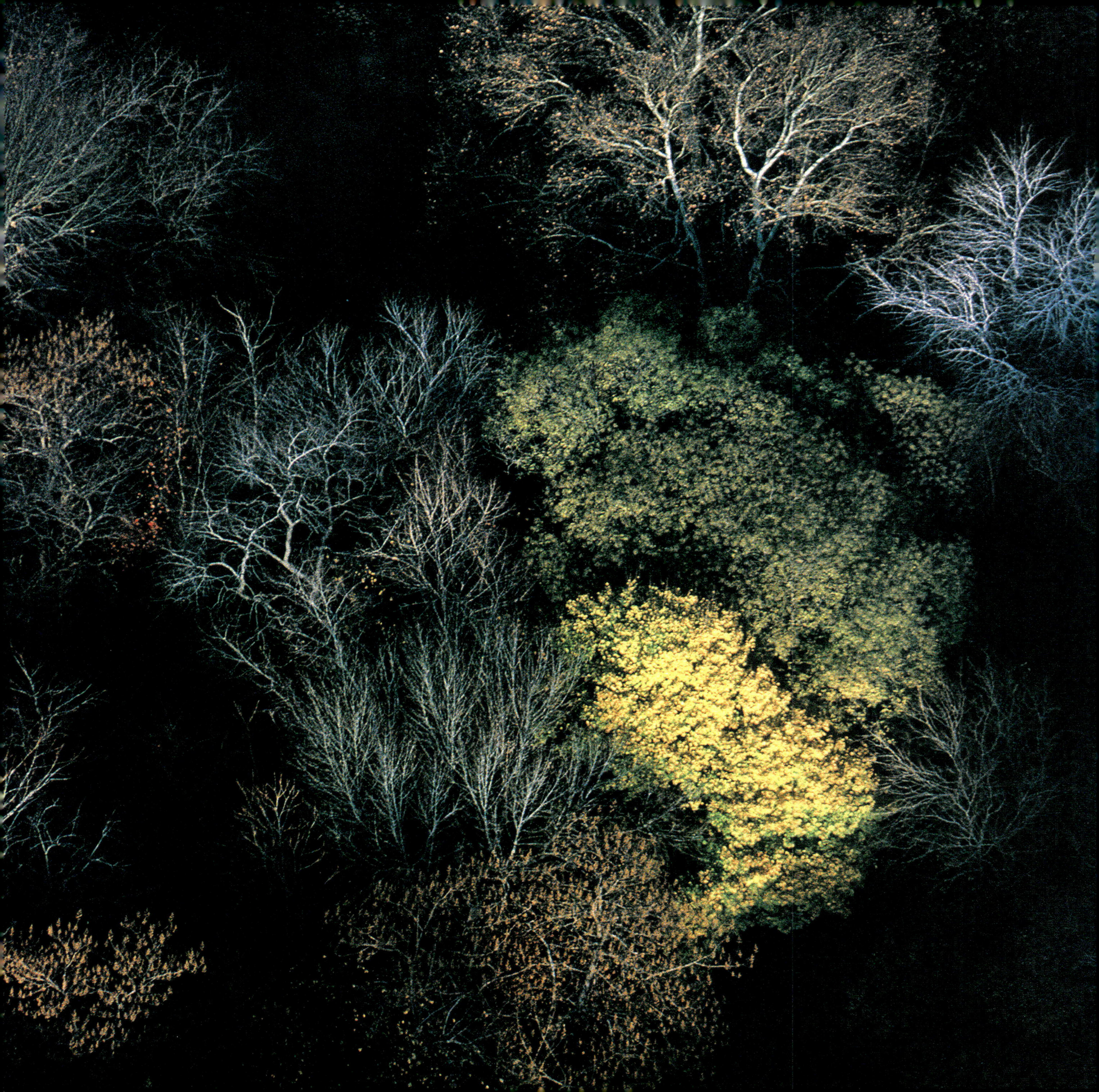

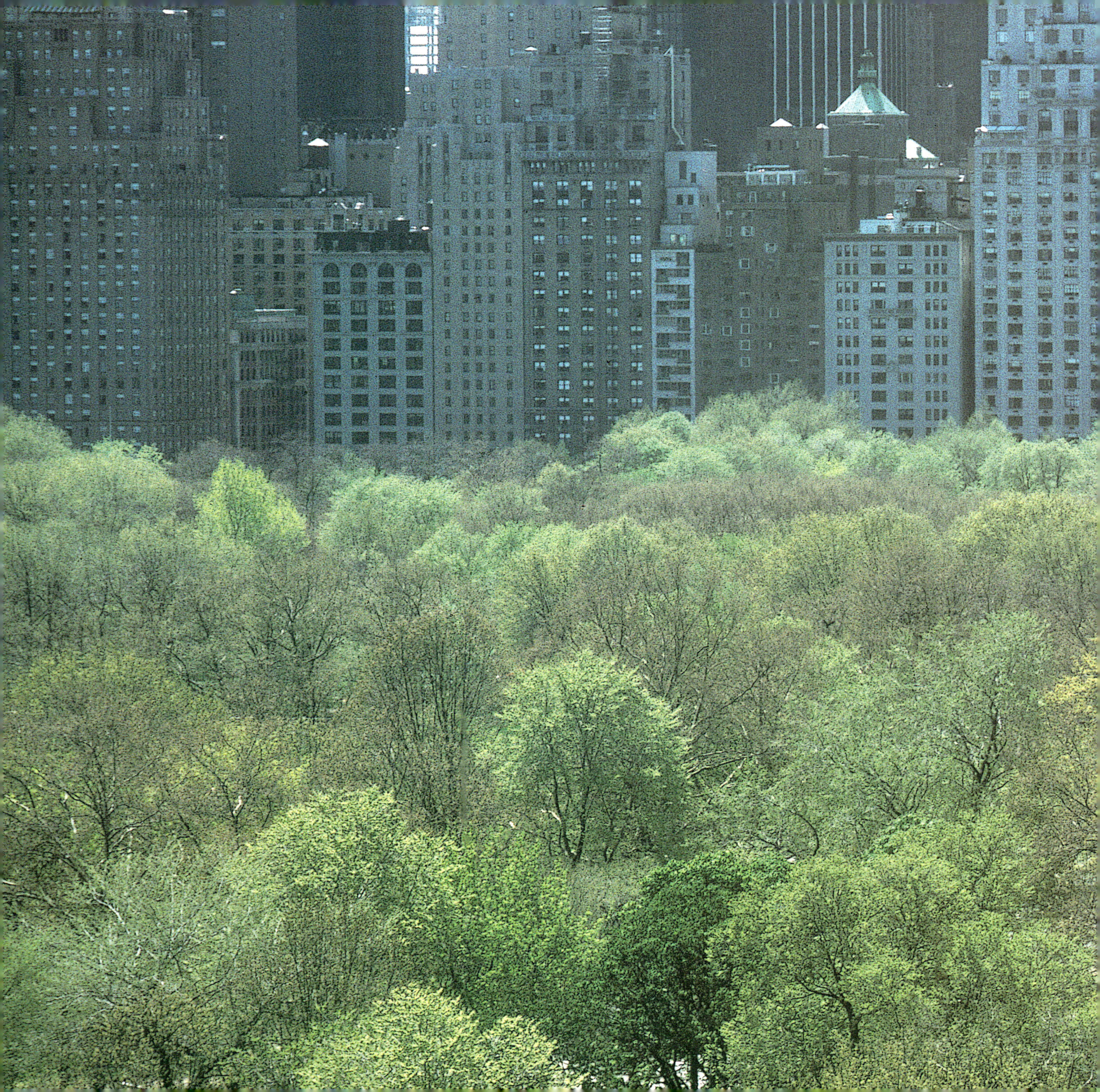

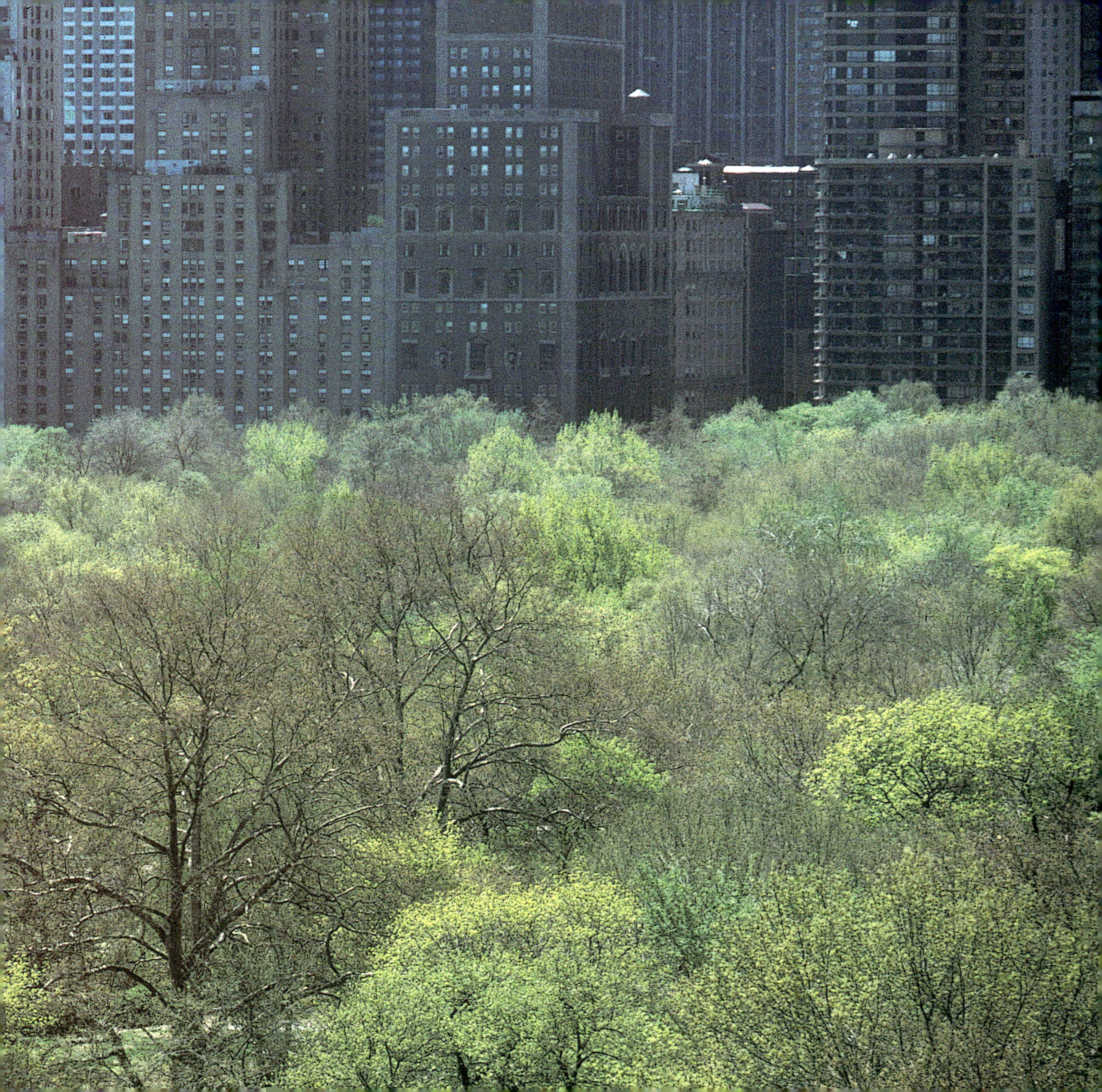

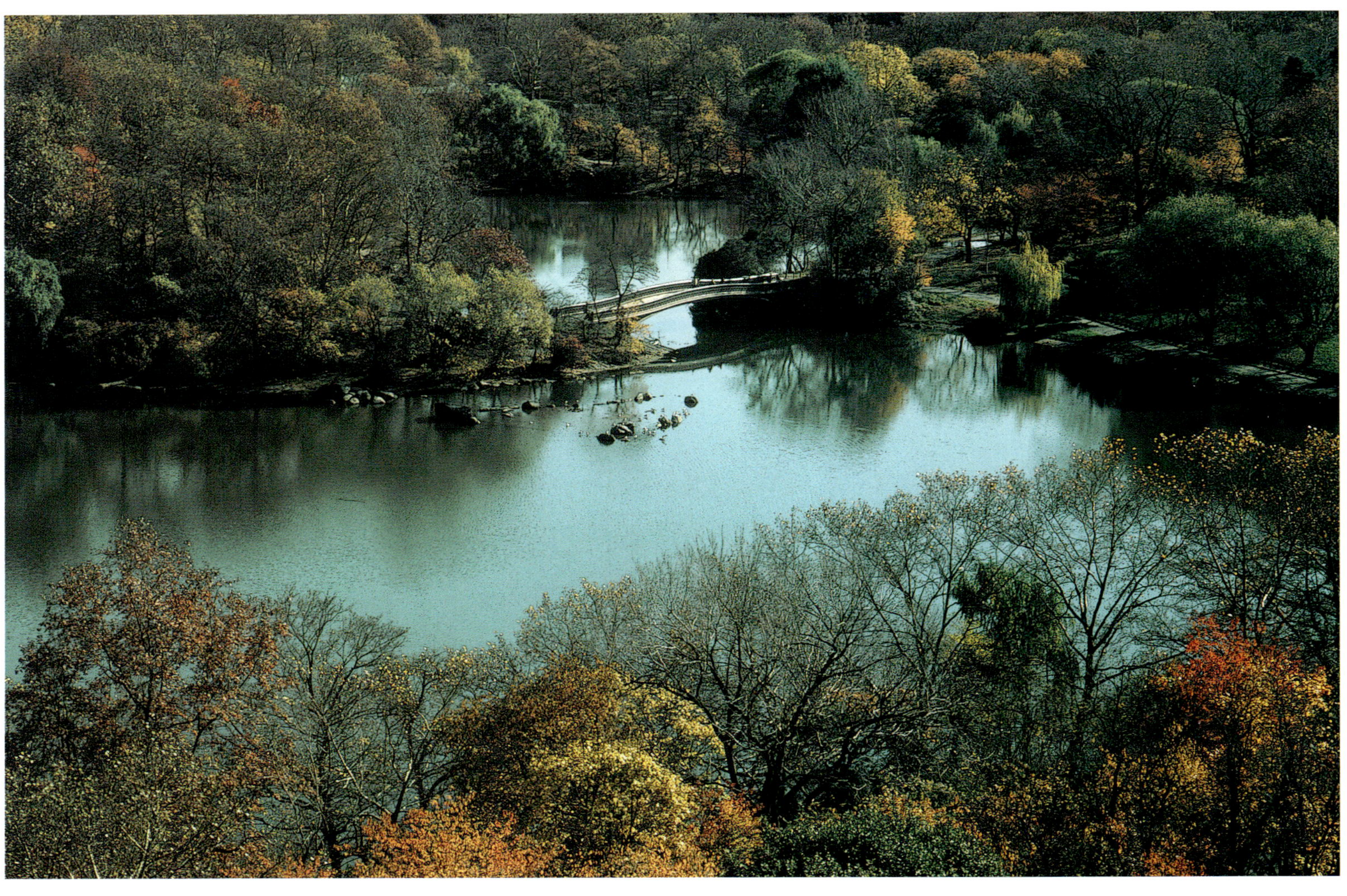

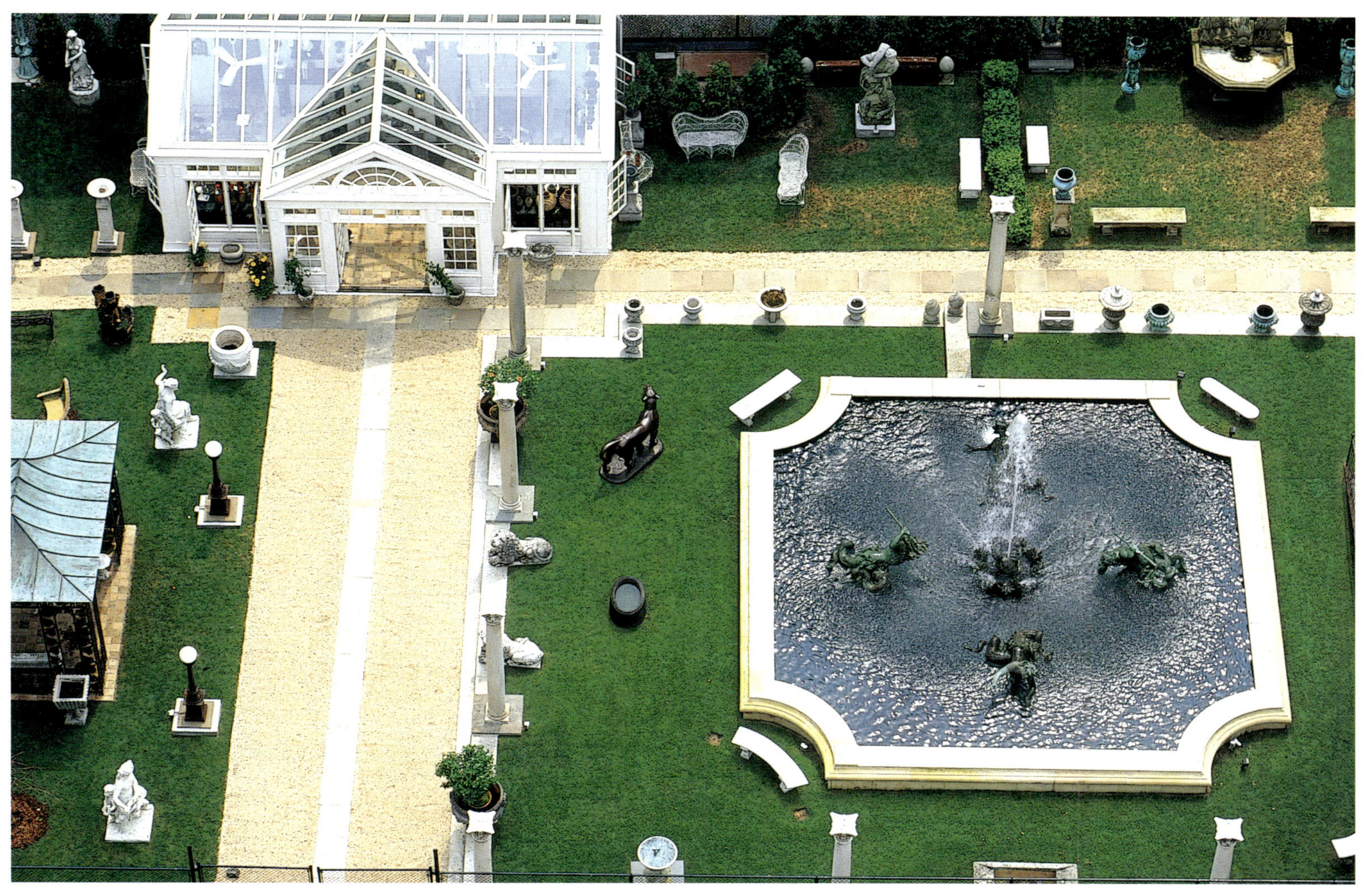

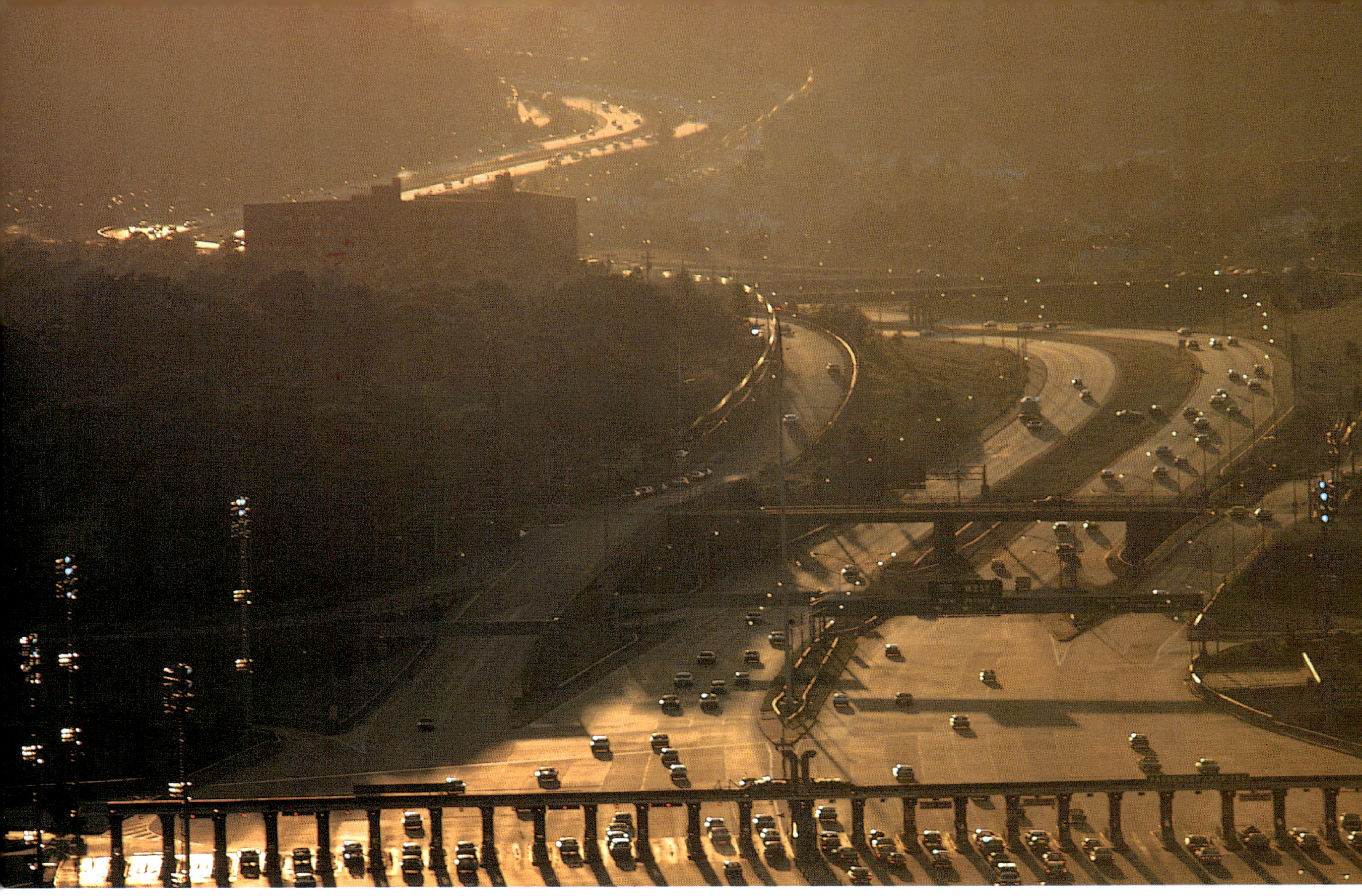

Staten Island. A helicopter view of the approach to the Verrazano Narrows toll gate.

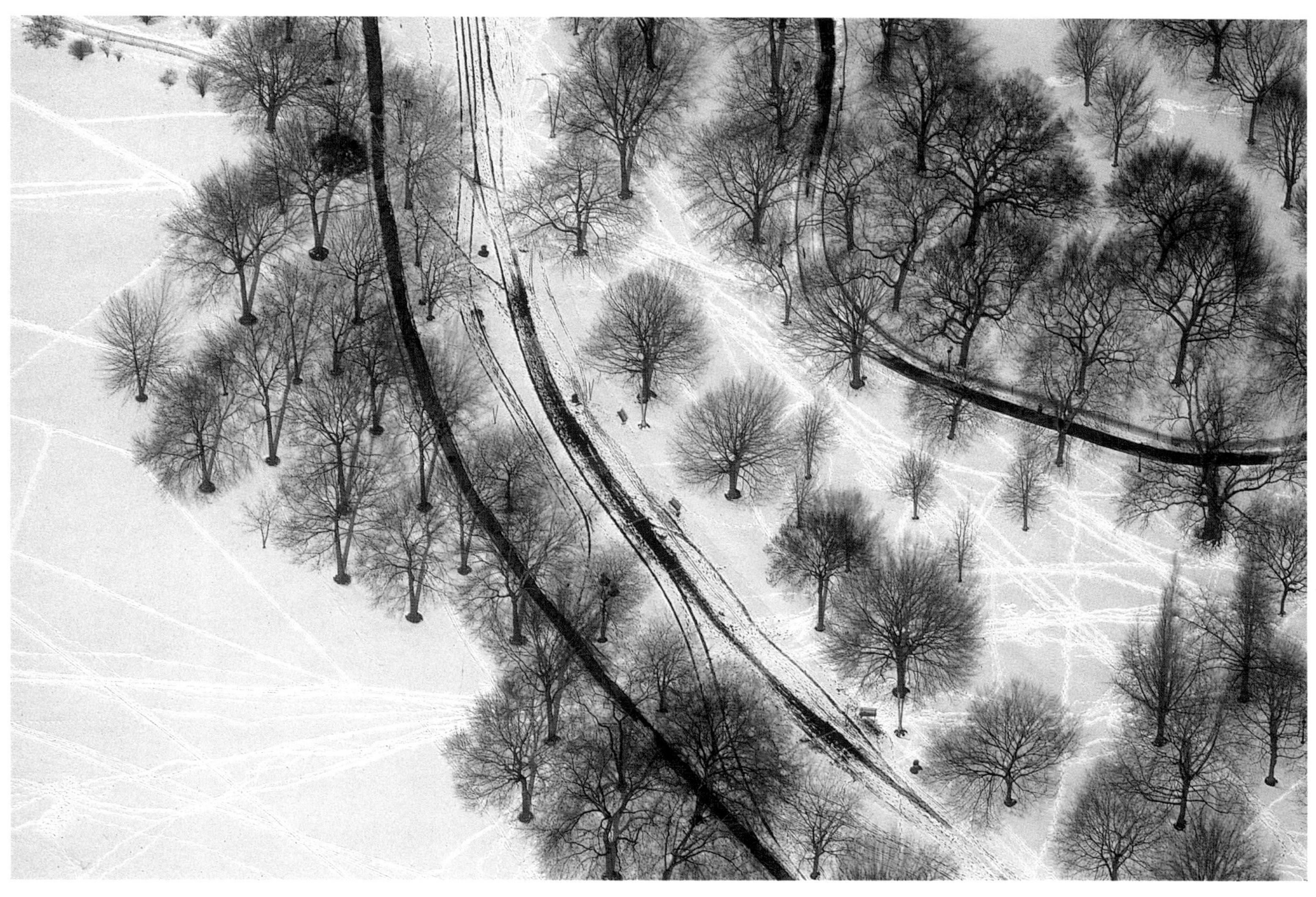

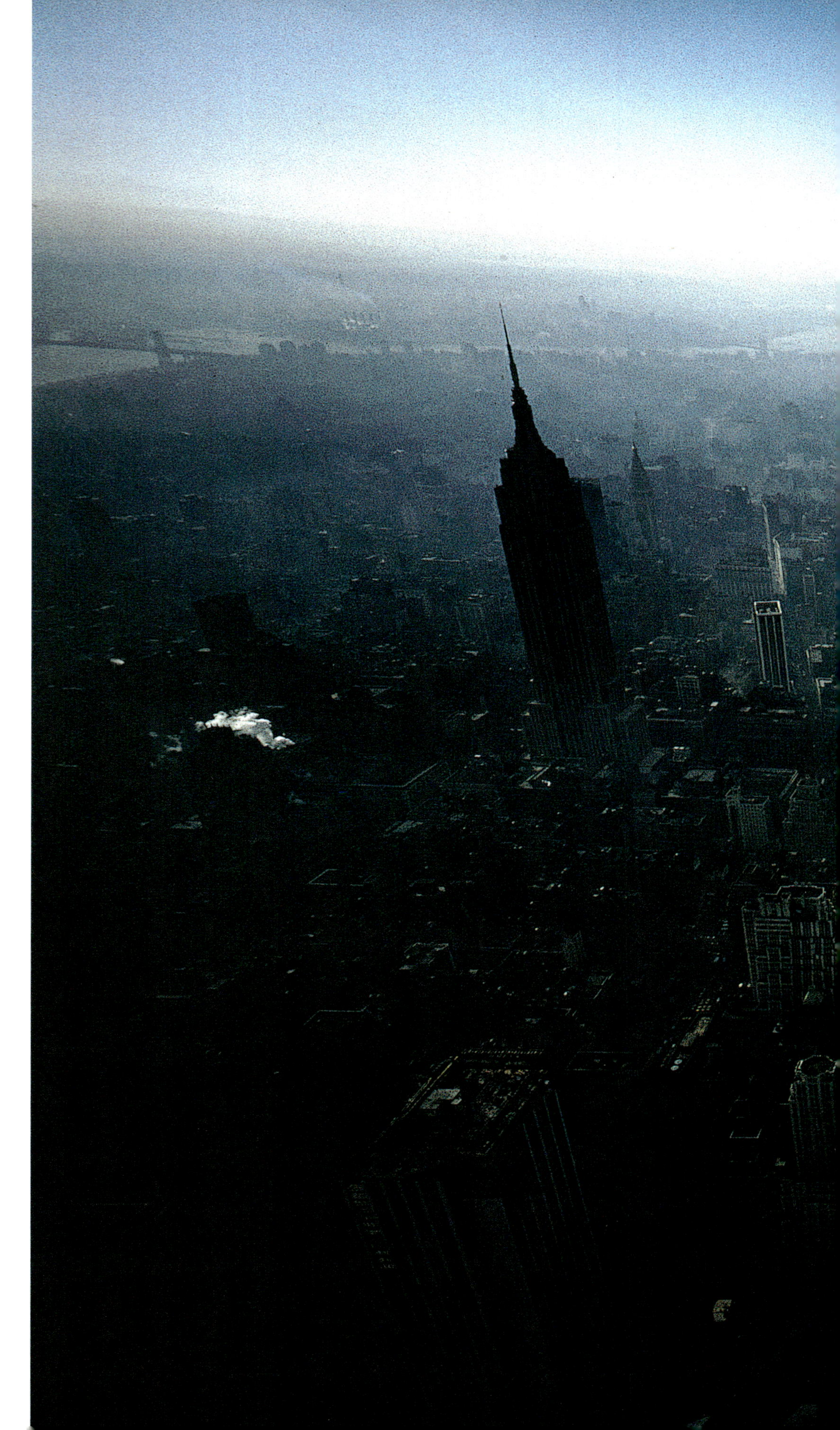

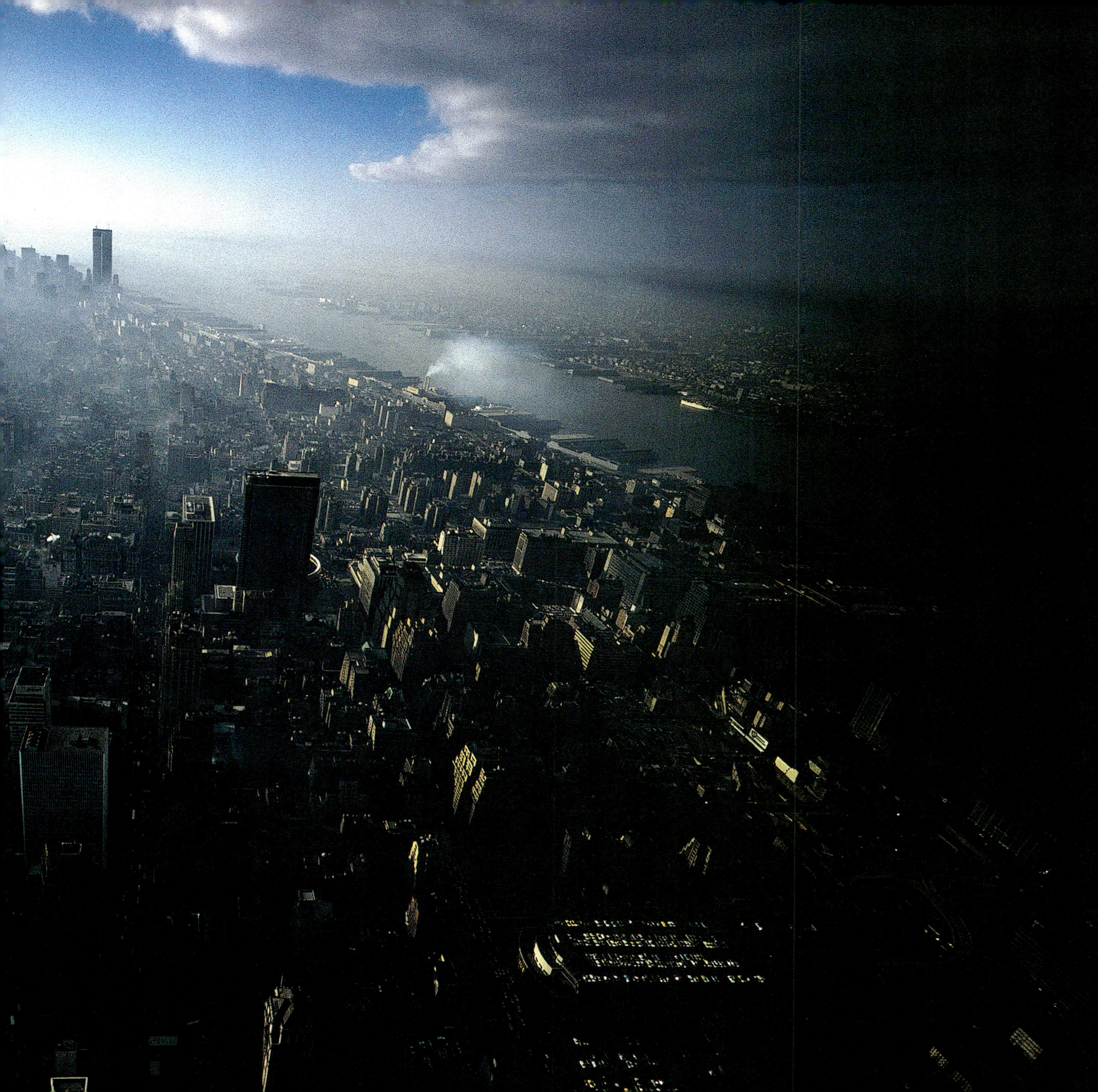

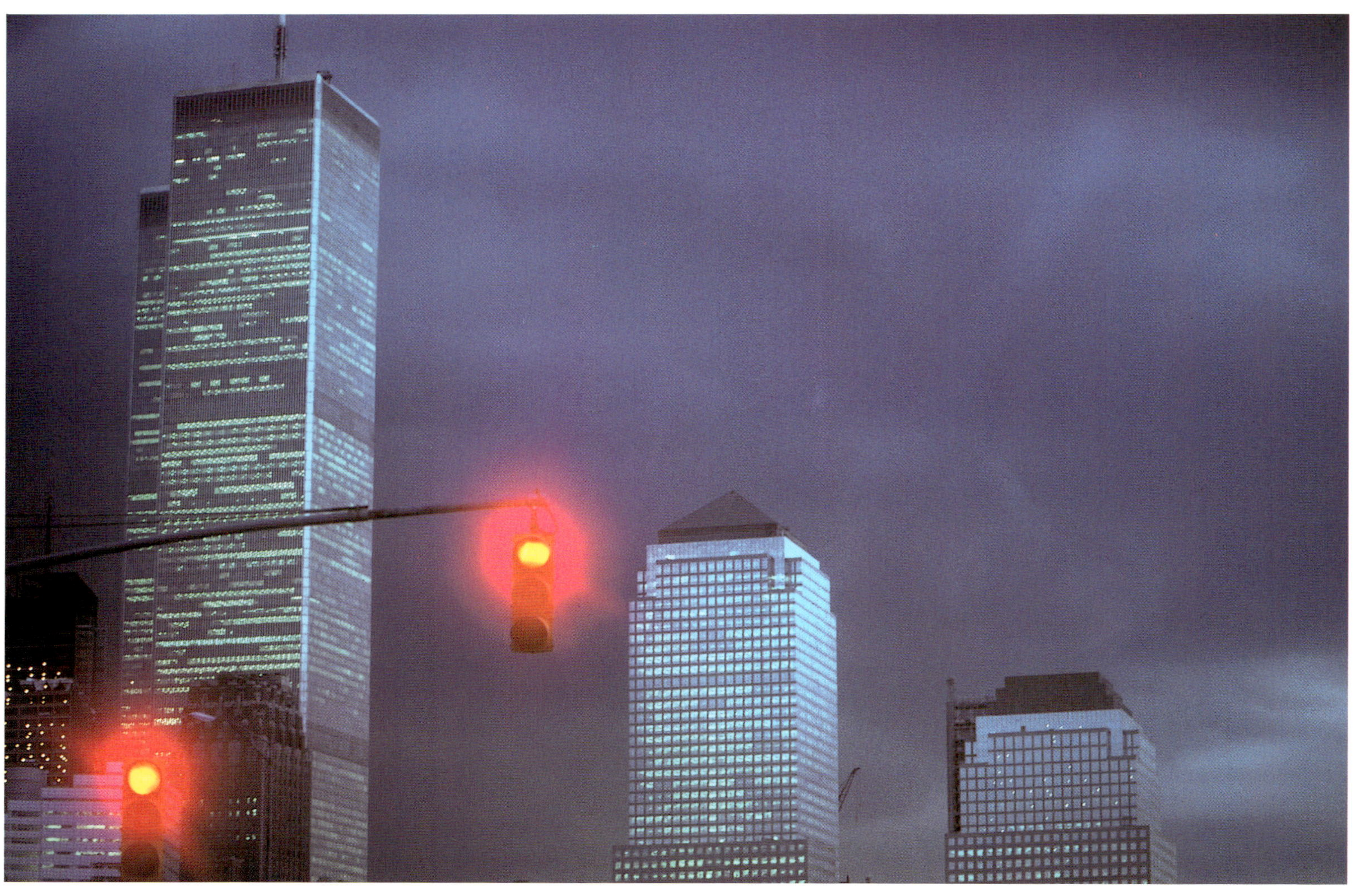

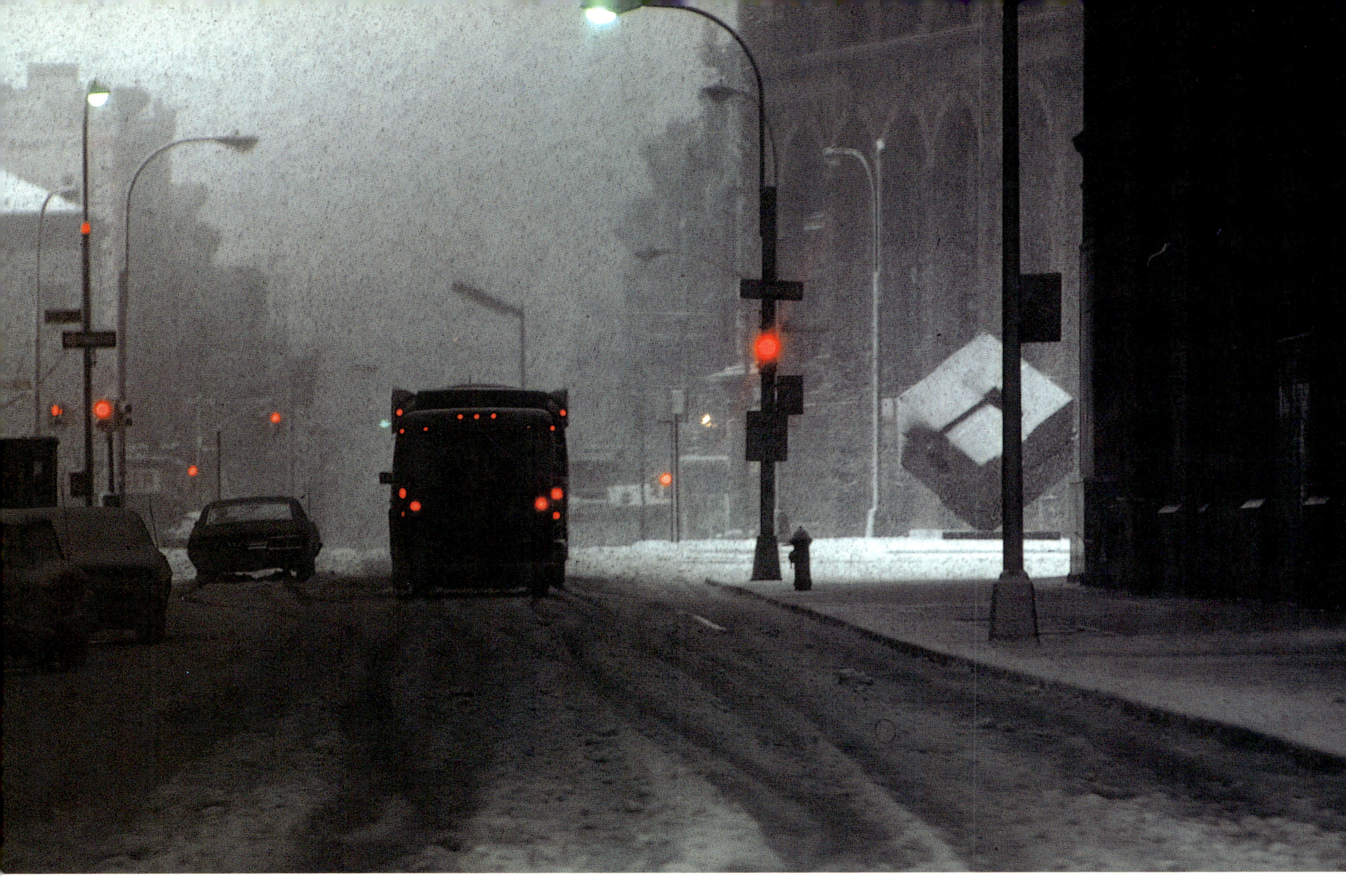

My daughter went to upstate New York and played in the fresh snow.

She came back and said, "Daddy, the snow is *white!*"

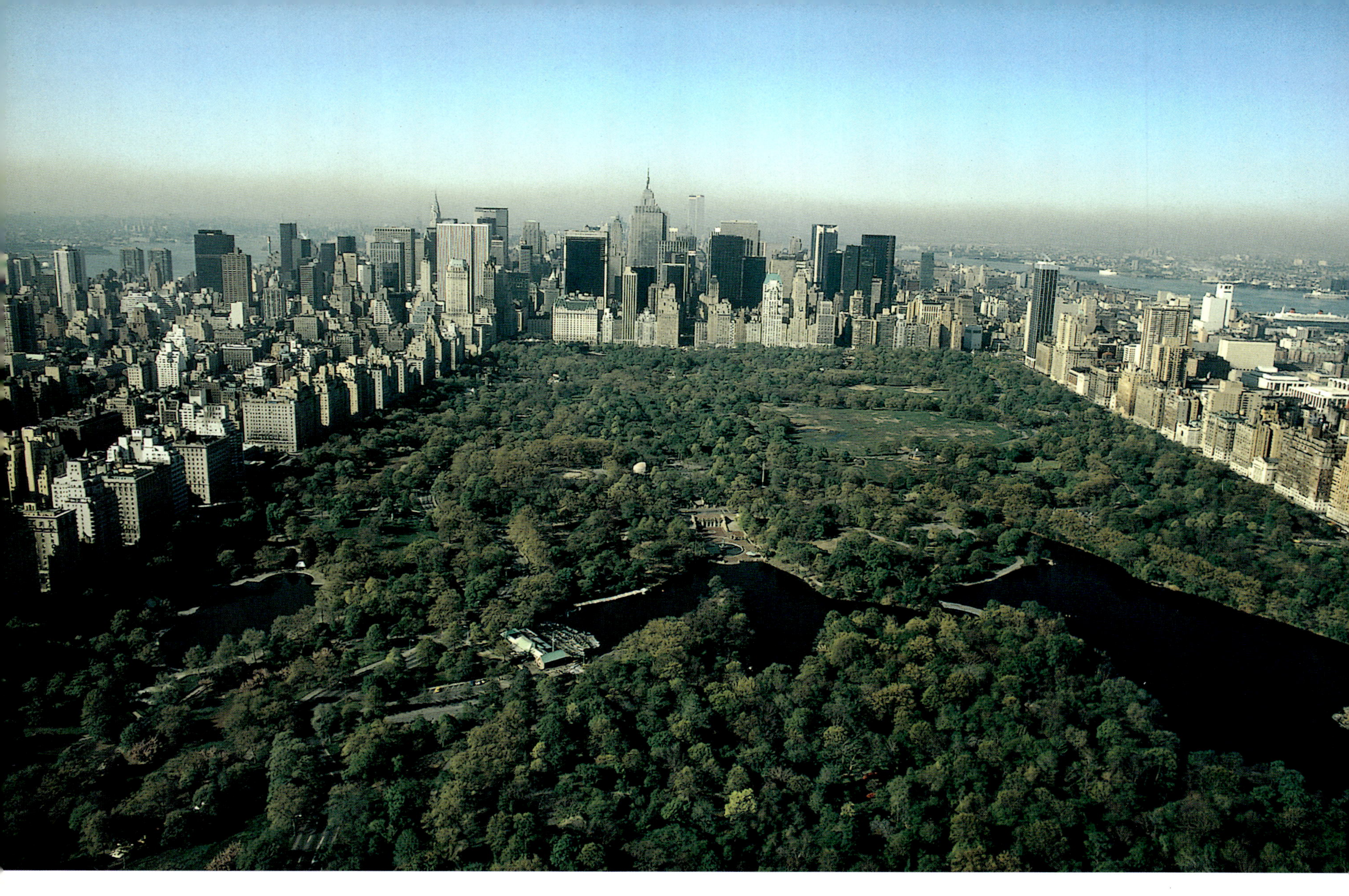

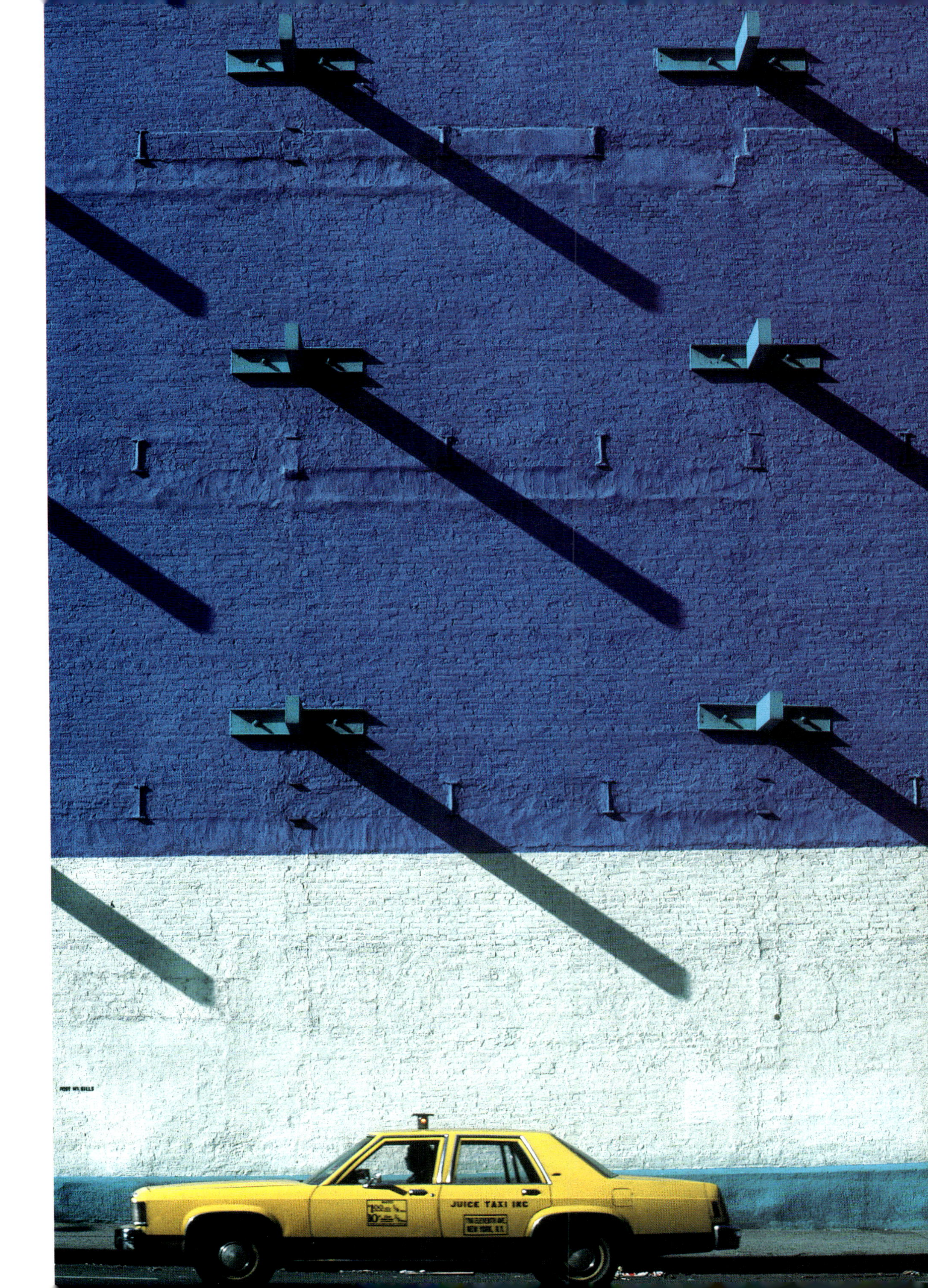
JUICE TAXI INC

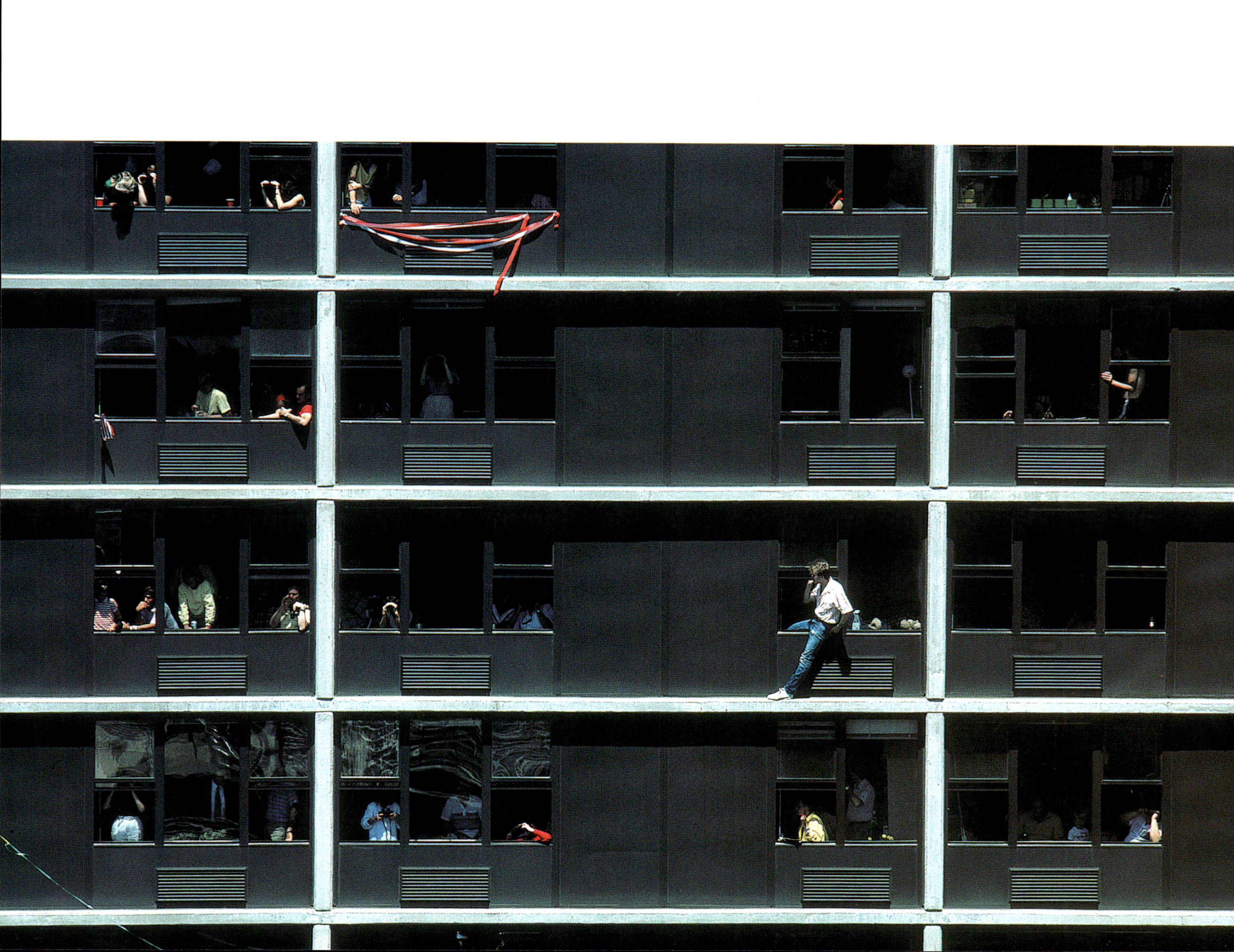

I've shot Fifth Avenue for years as a metaphor for New York itself. Such as the Bulgari diamond display and the straw in the cup.

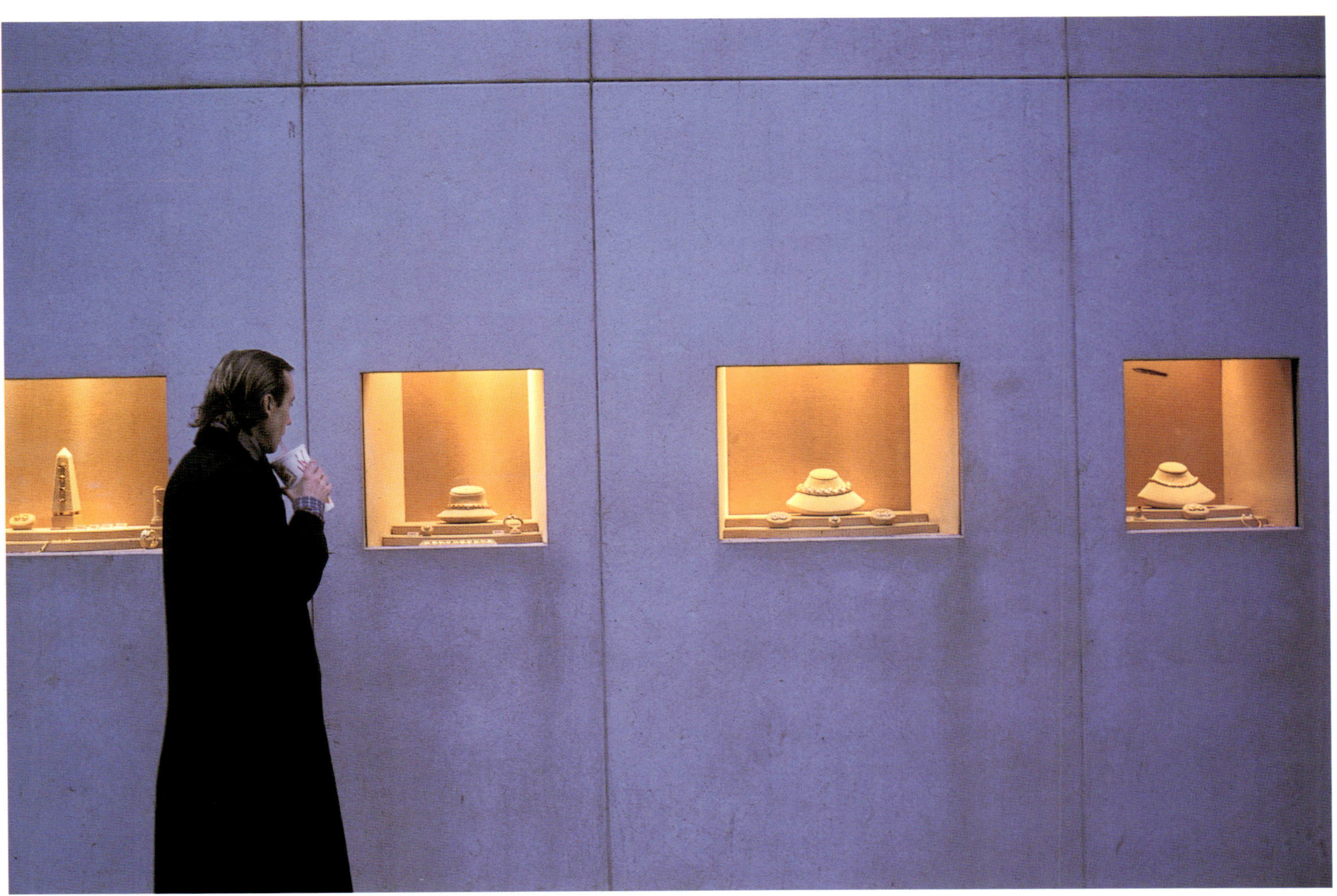

Just off the West Side Highway, a turn-of-the-century industrial building, now renovated for use by emerging companies and as possible residences.

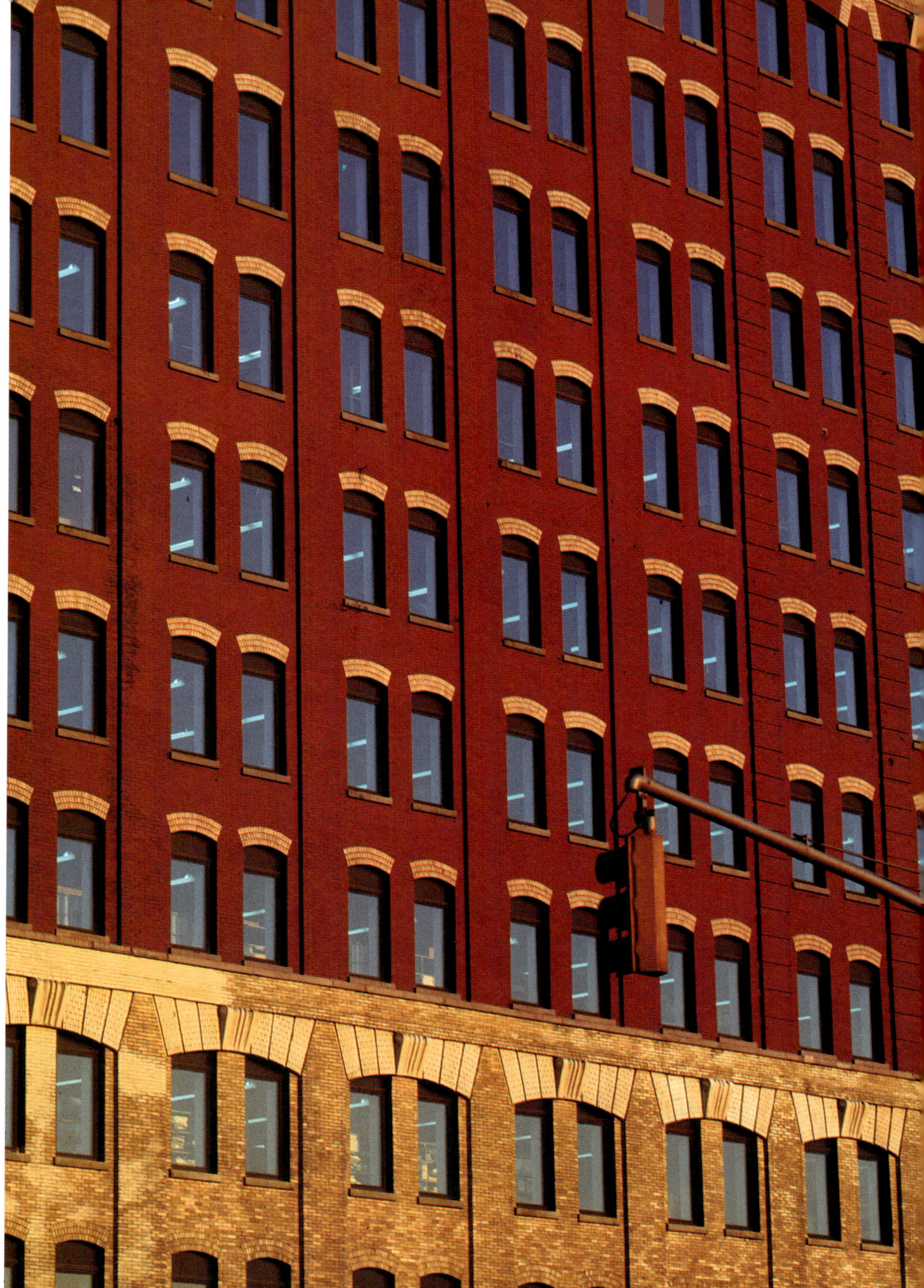

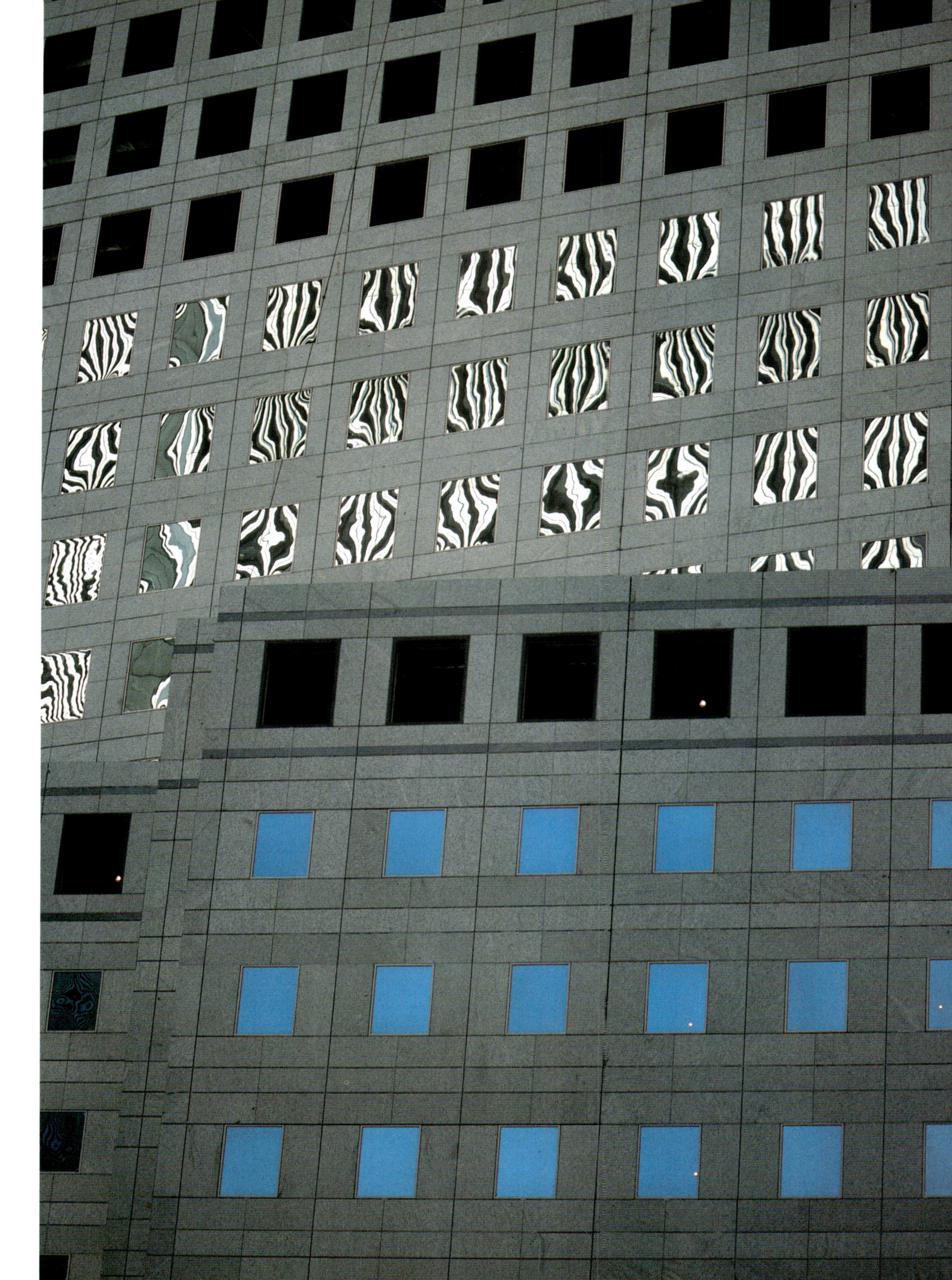

Midtown Manhattan

from Queens.

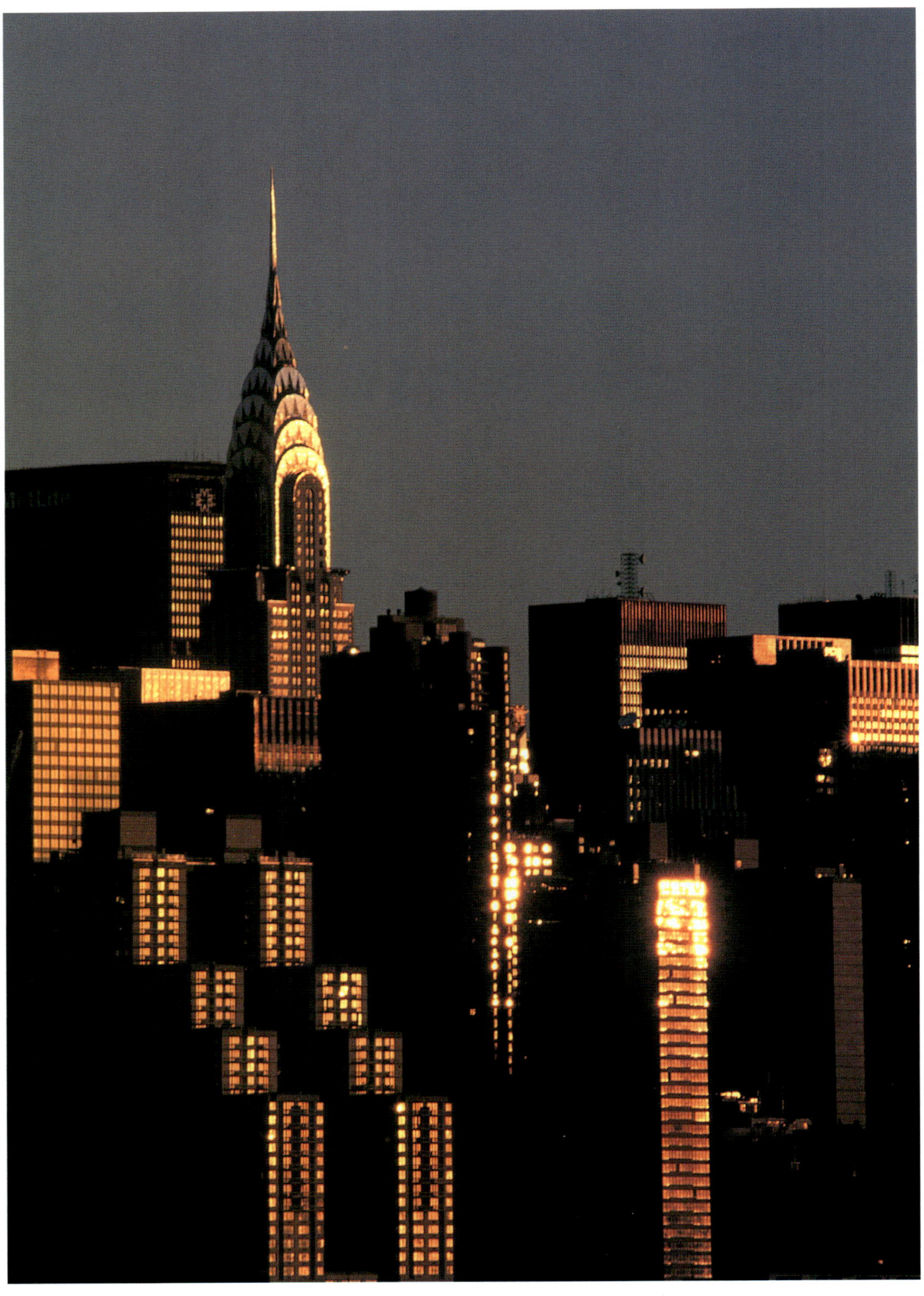

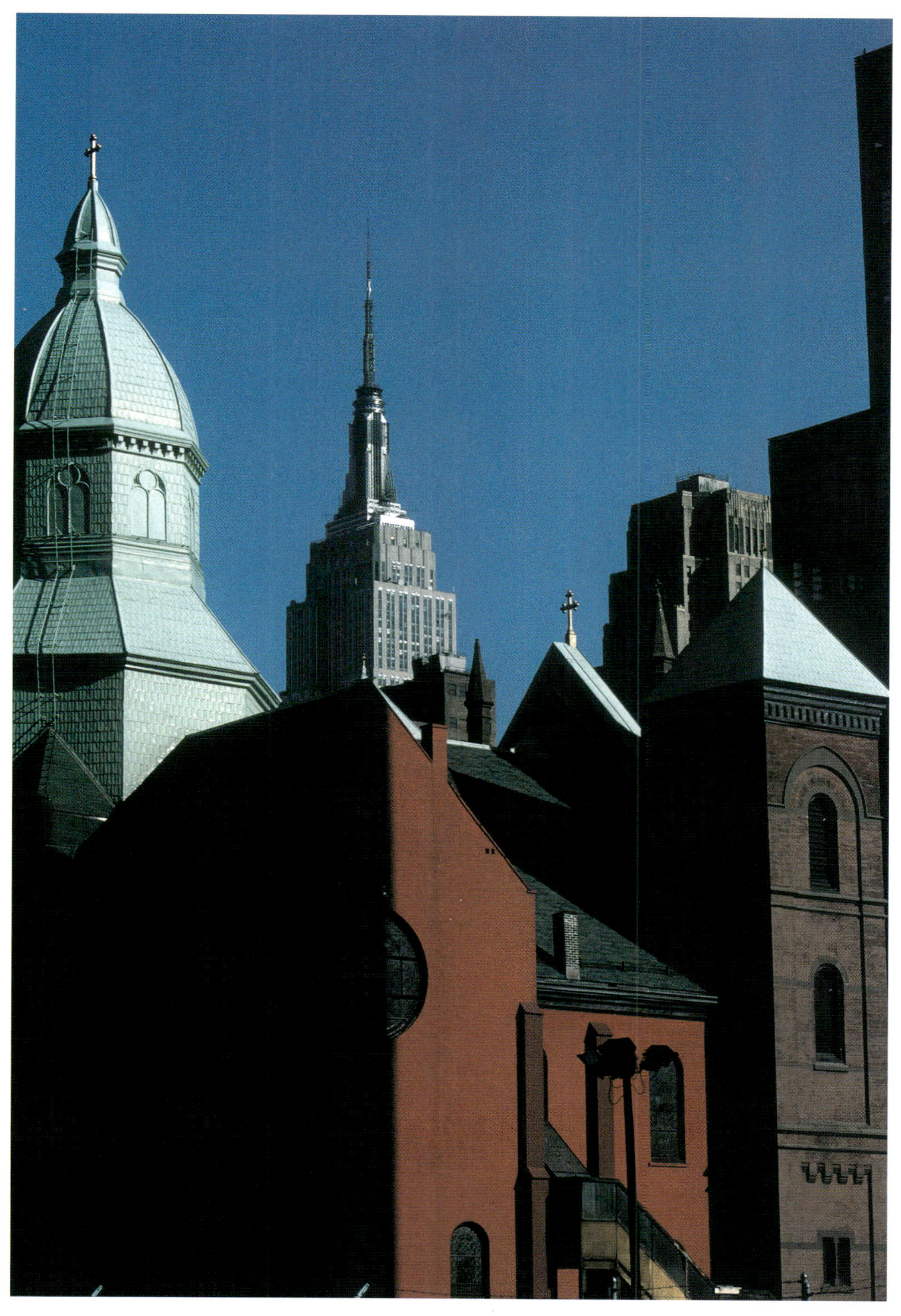

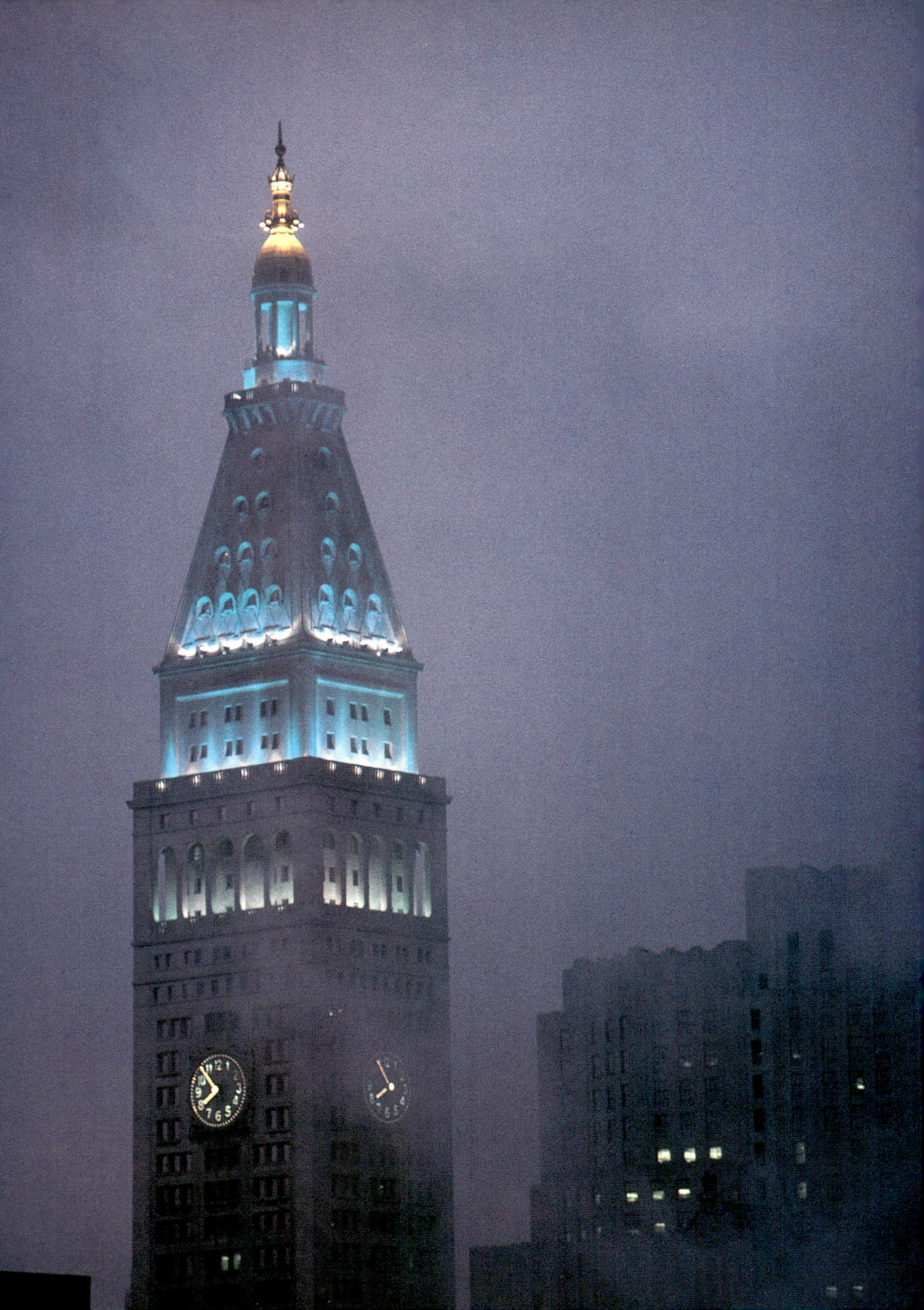

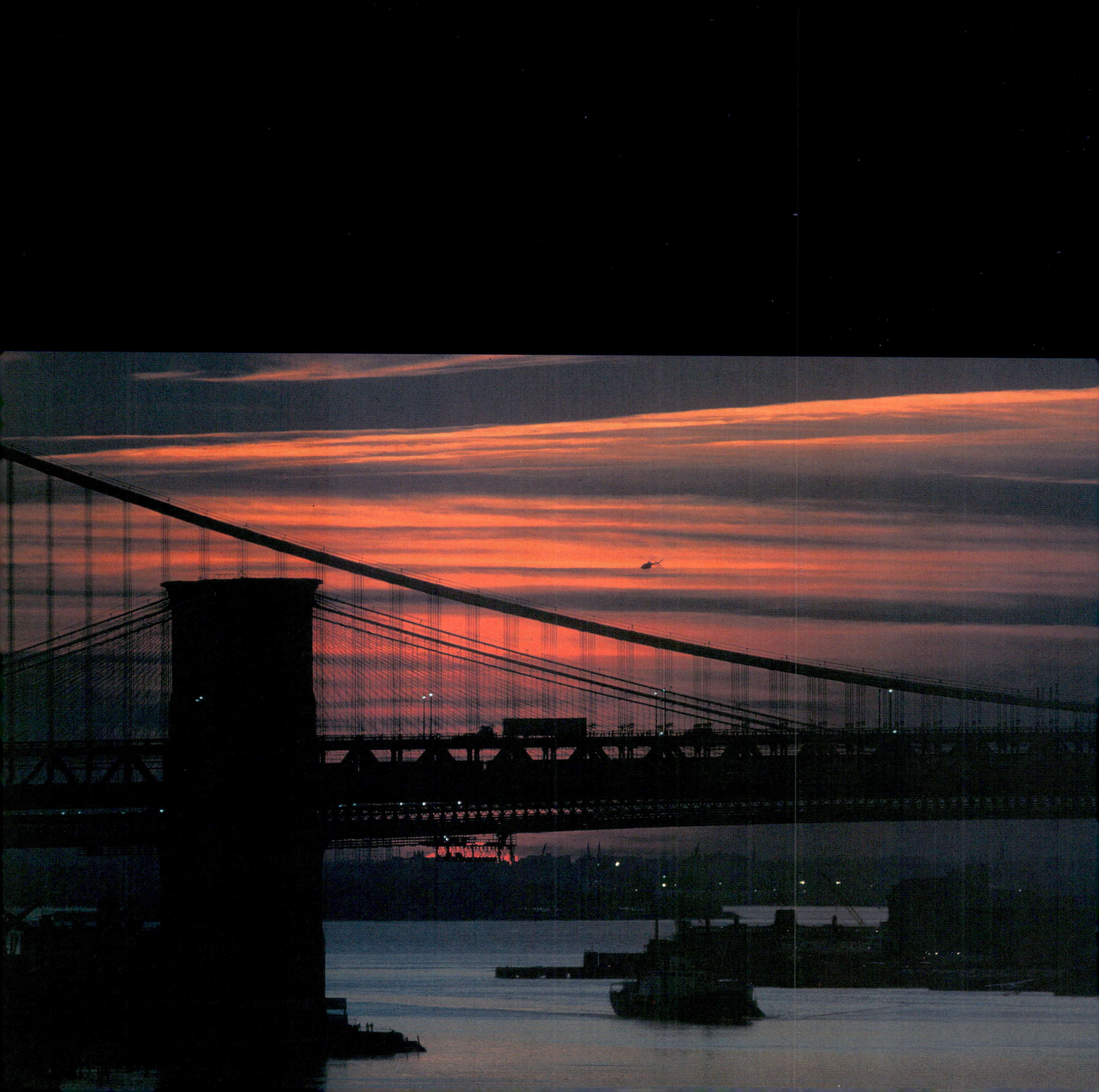

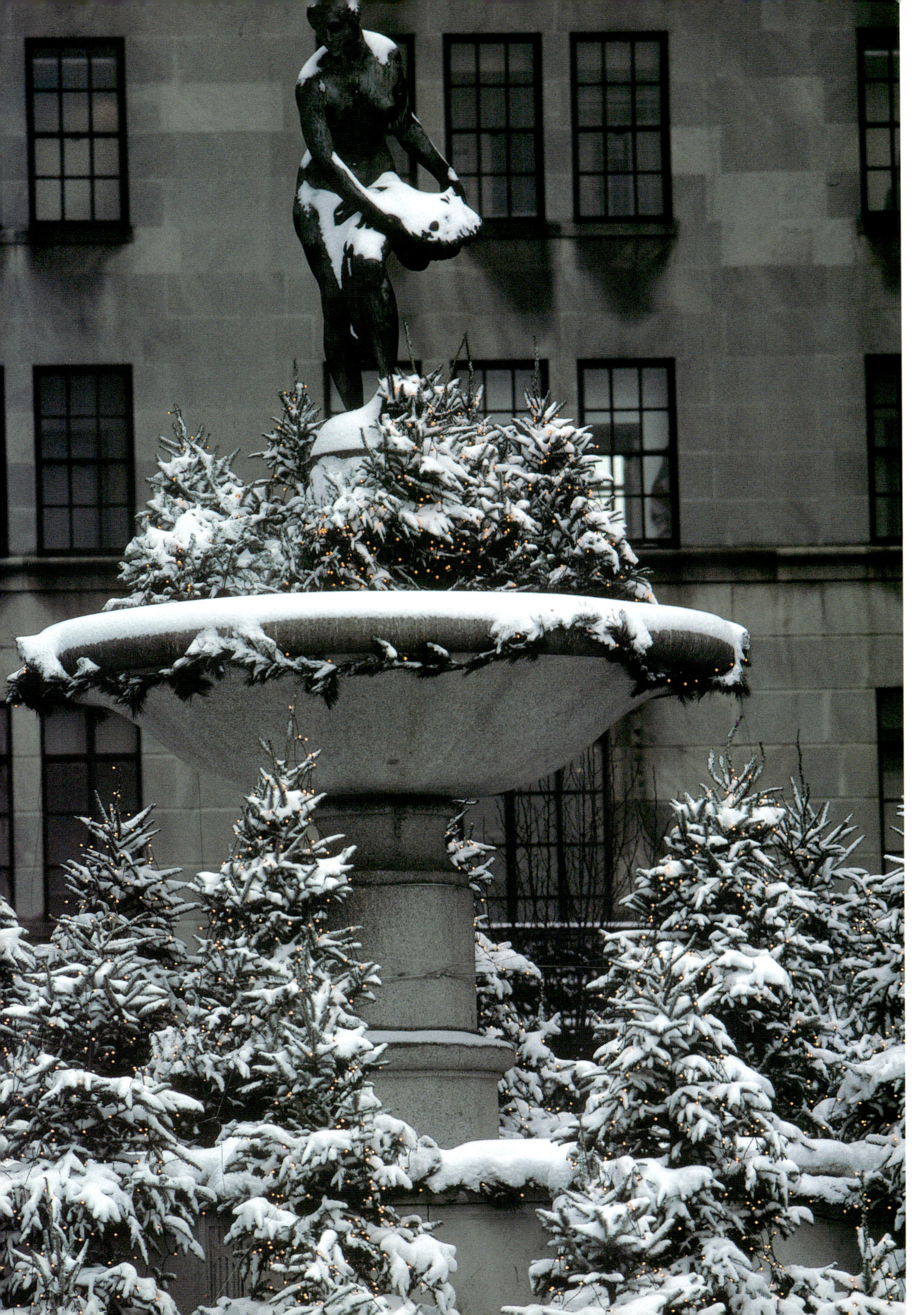

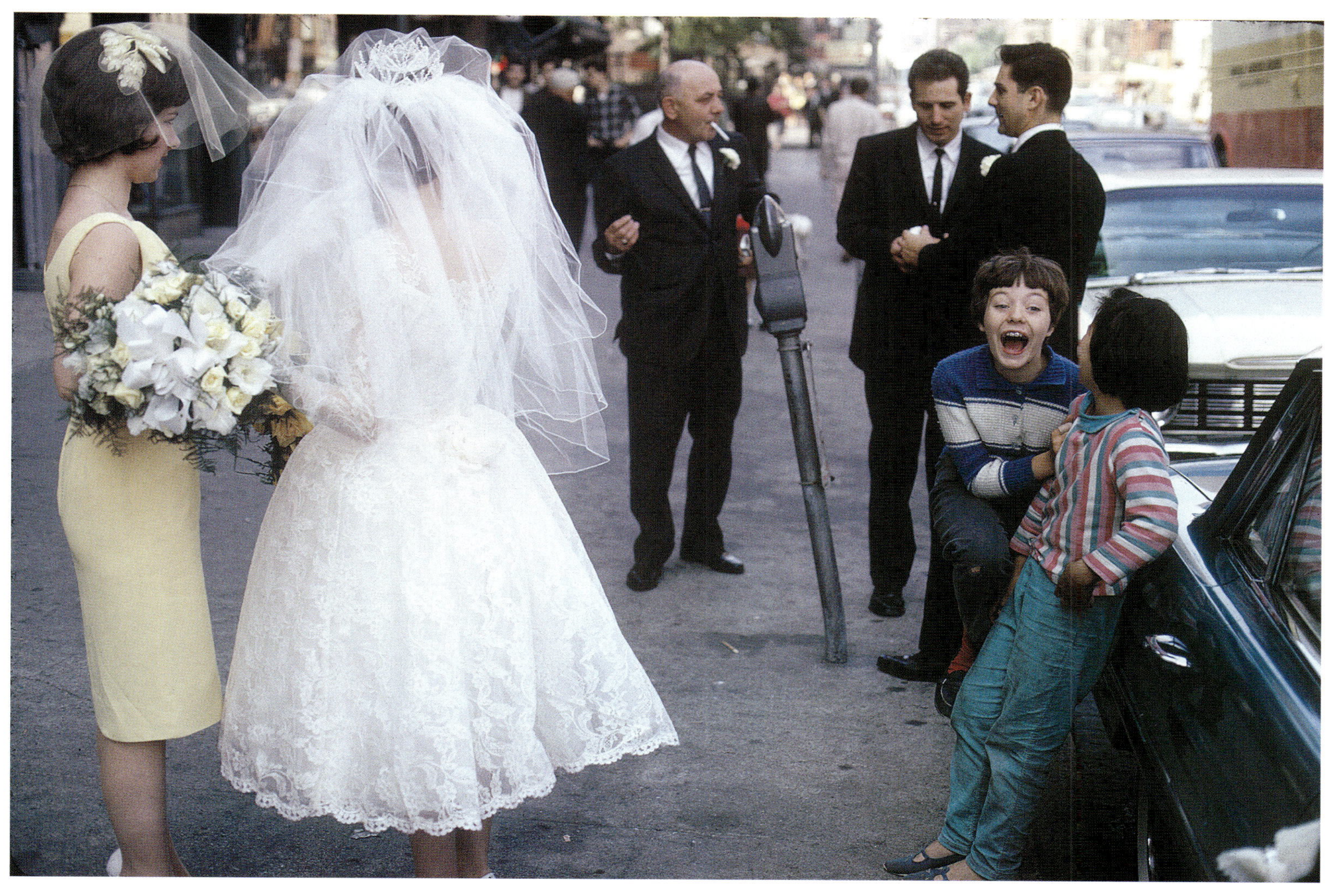

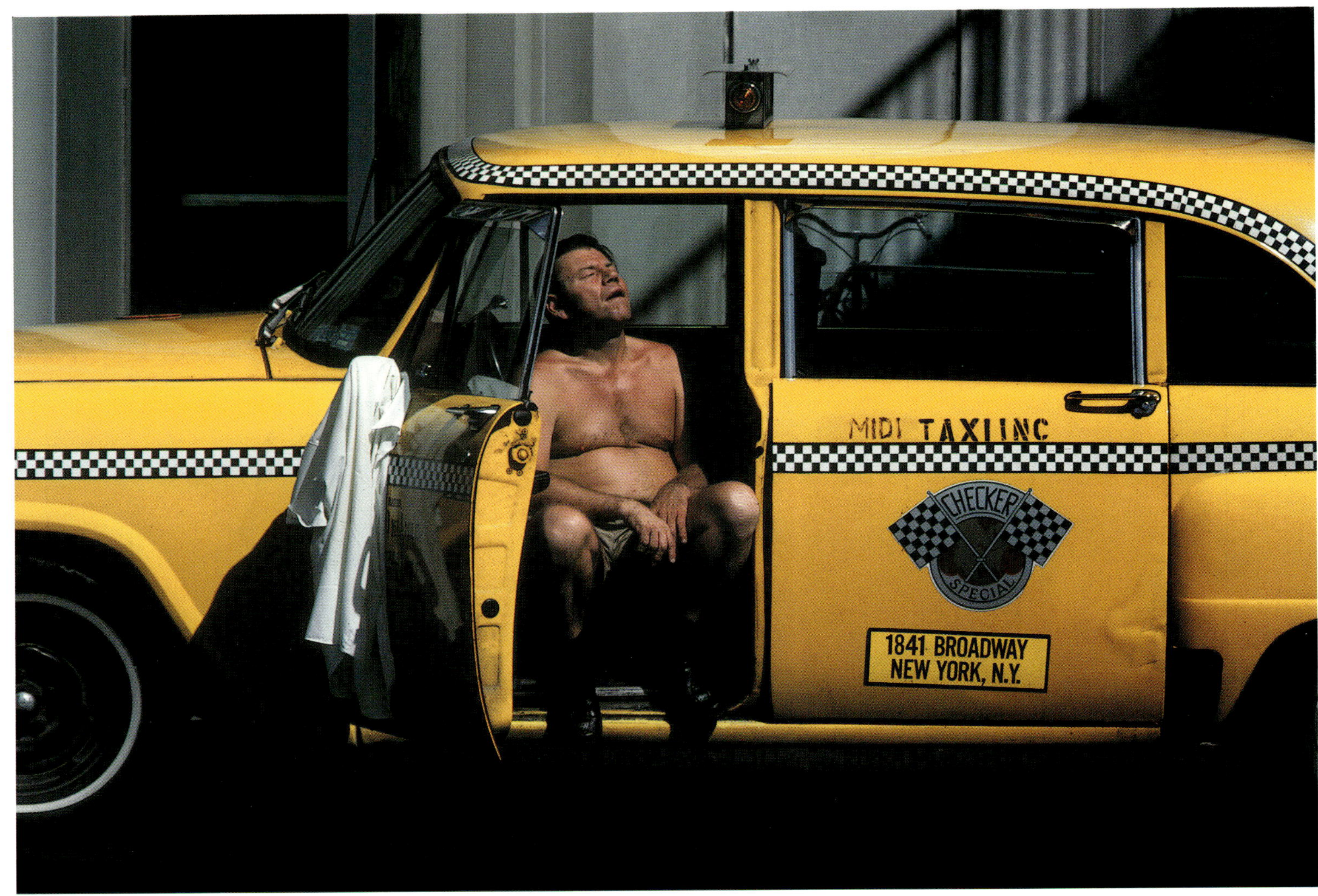

Coping with the heat. I love the individuality of New Yorkers.

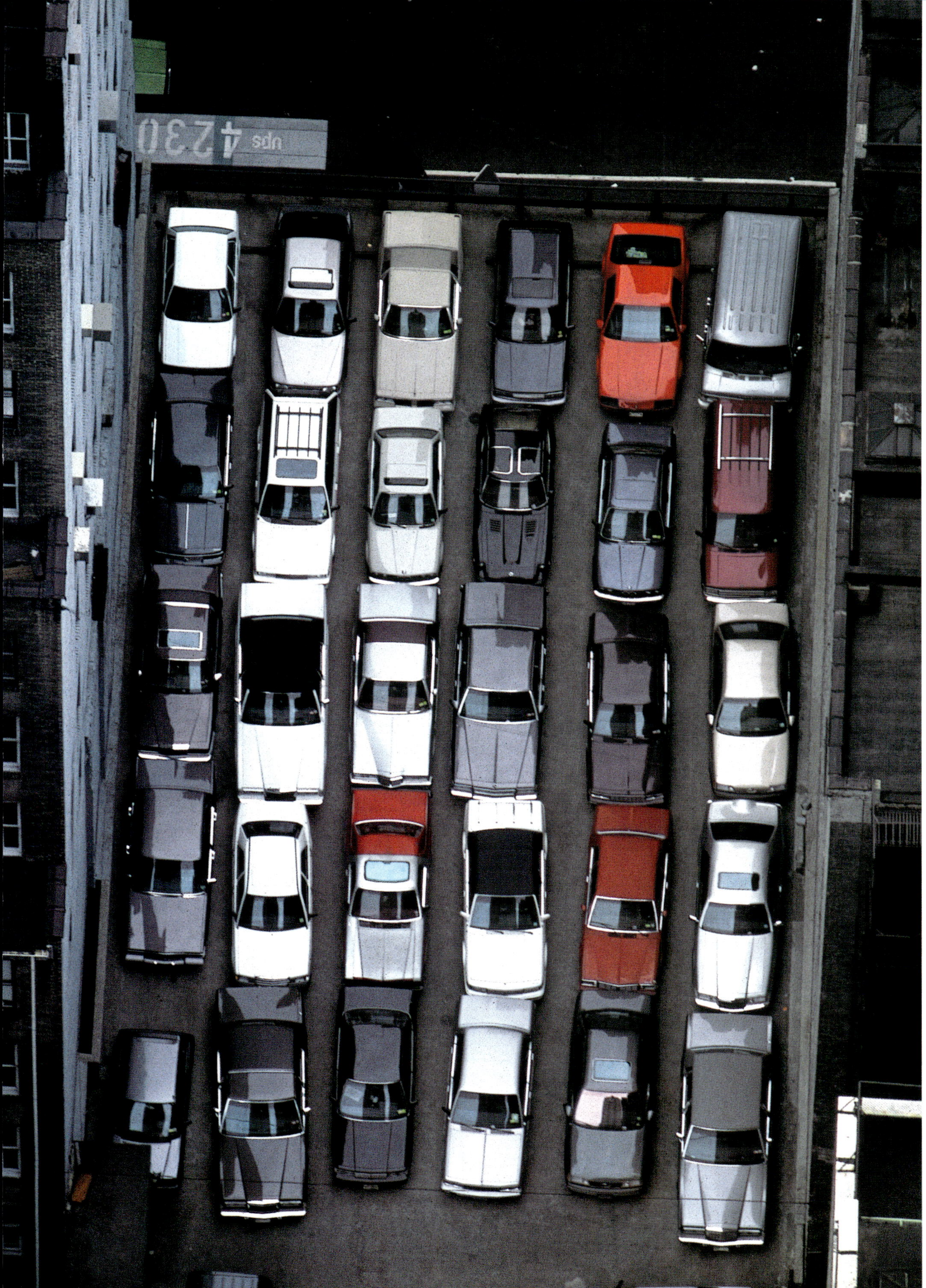
ups 4230

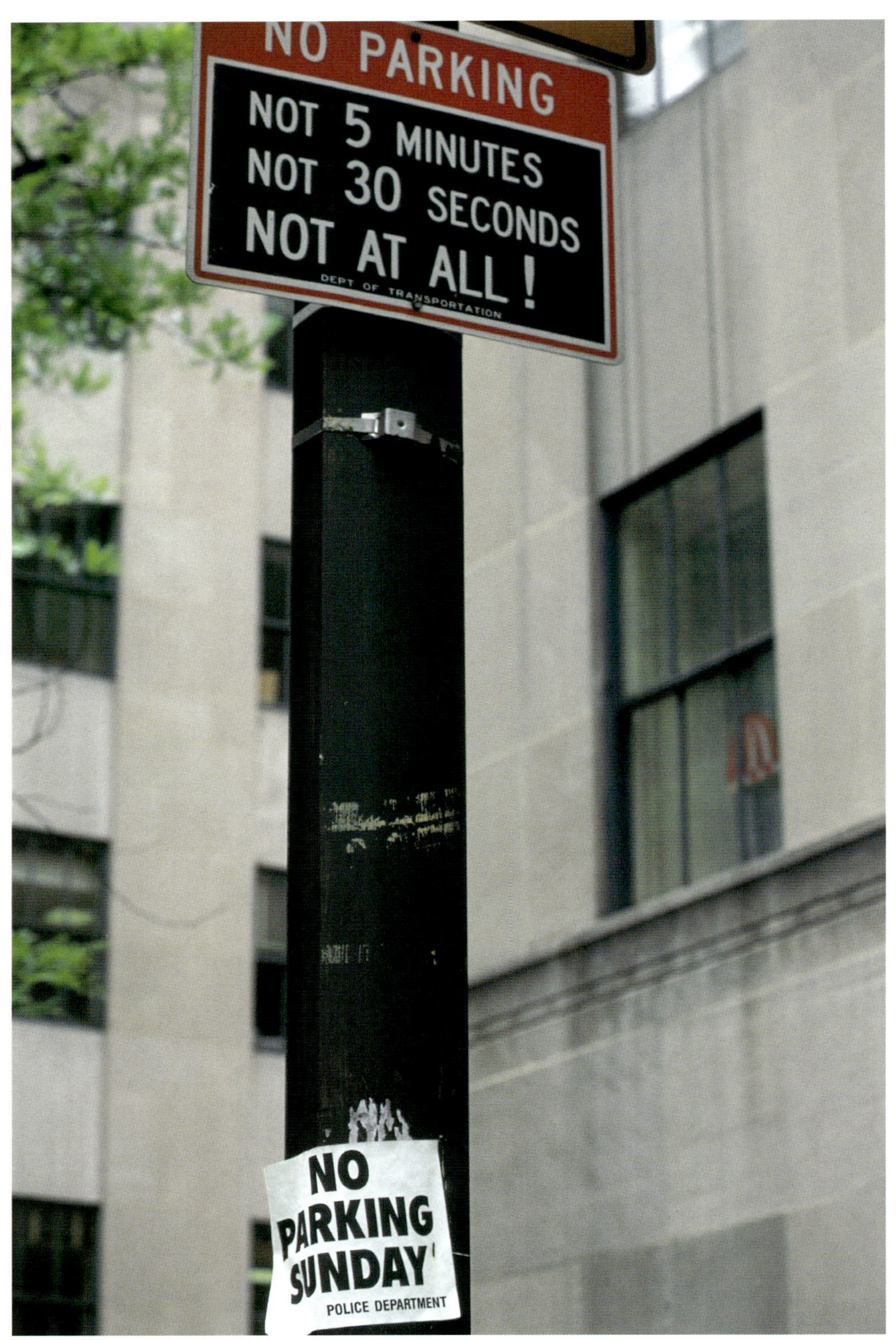
NO PARKING
NOT 5 MINUTES
NOT 30 SECONDS
NOT AT ALL!
DEPT OF TRANSPORTATION
NO
PARKING
SUNDAY
POLICE DEPARTMENT

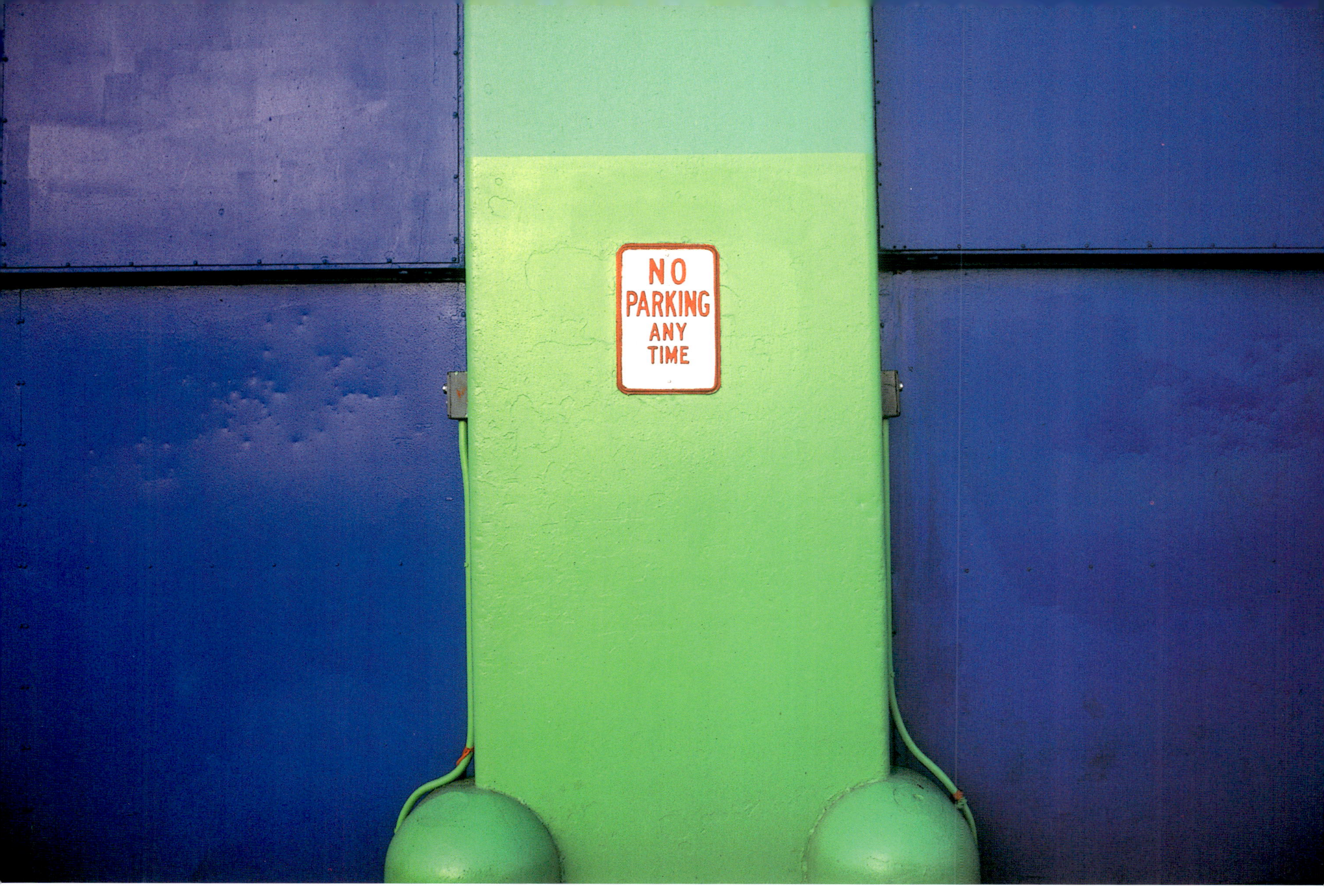
NO
PARKING
ANY
TIME

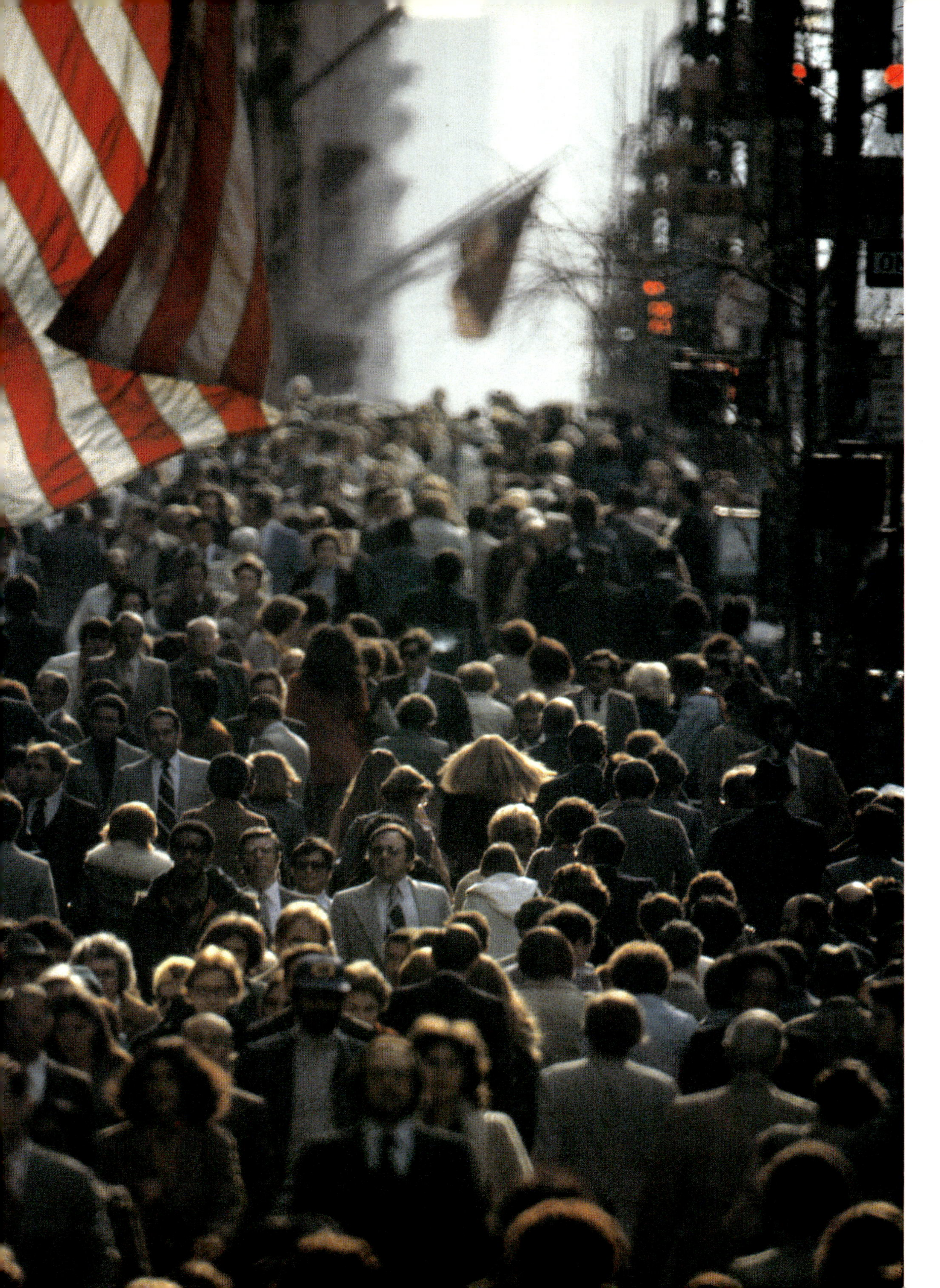

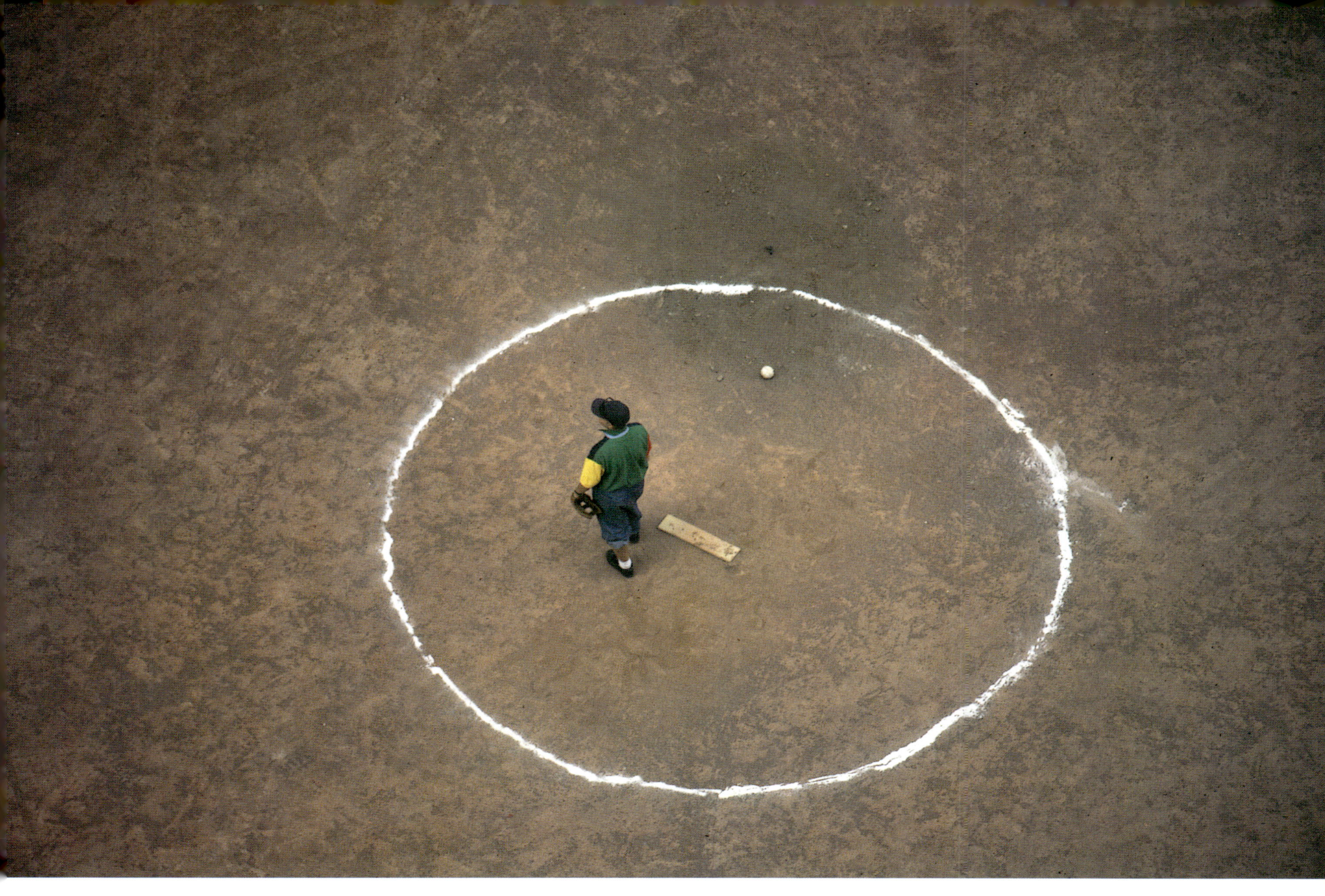

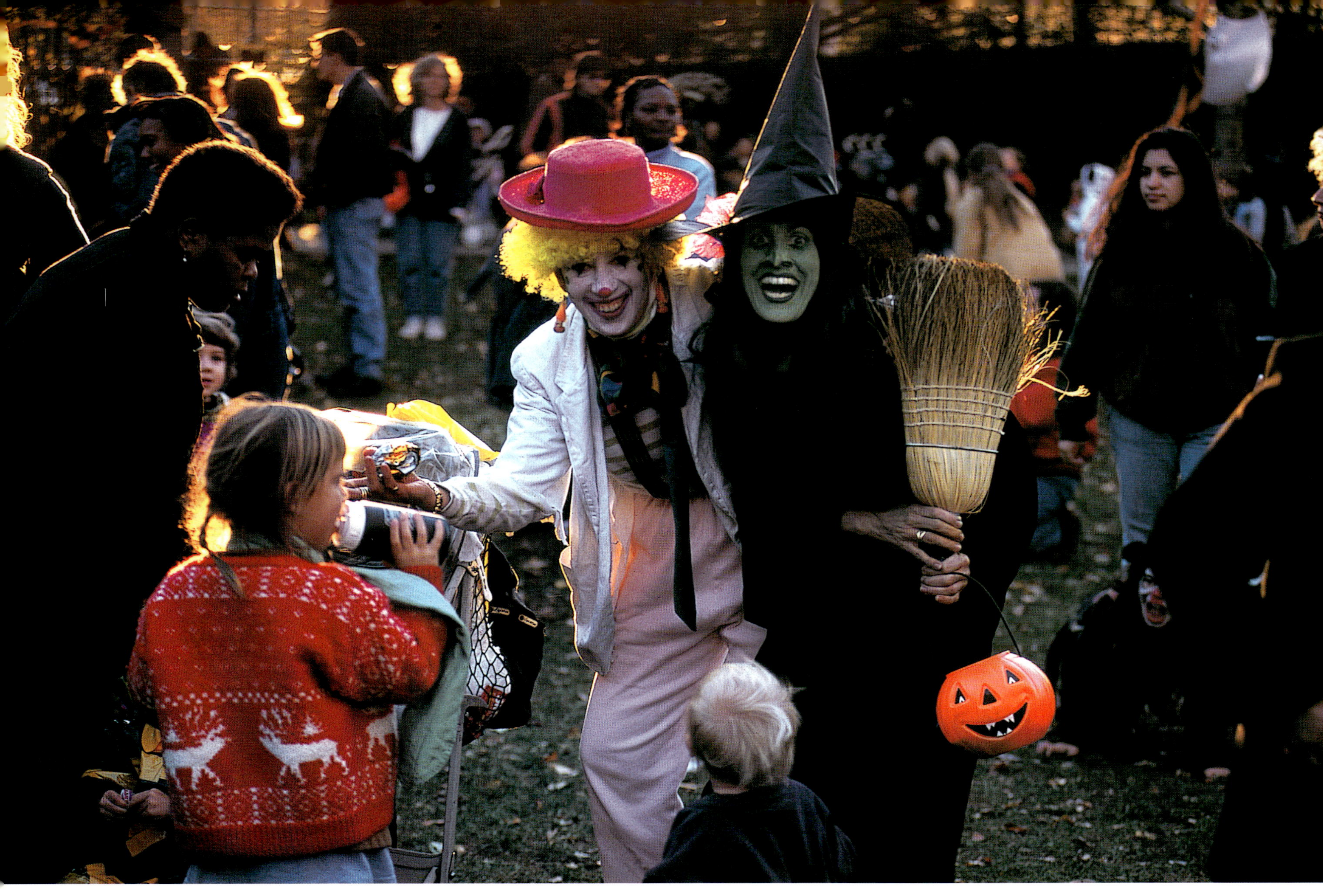

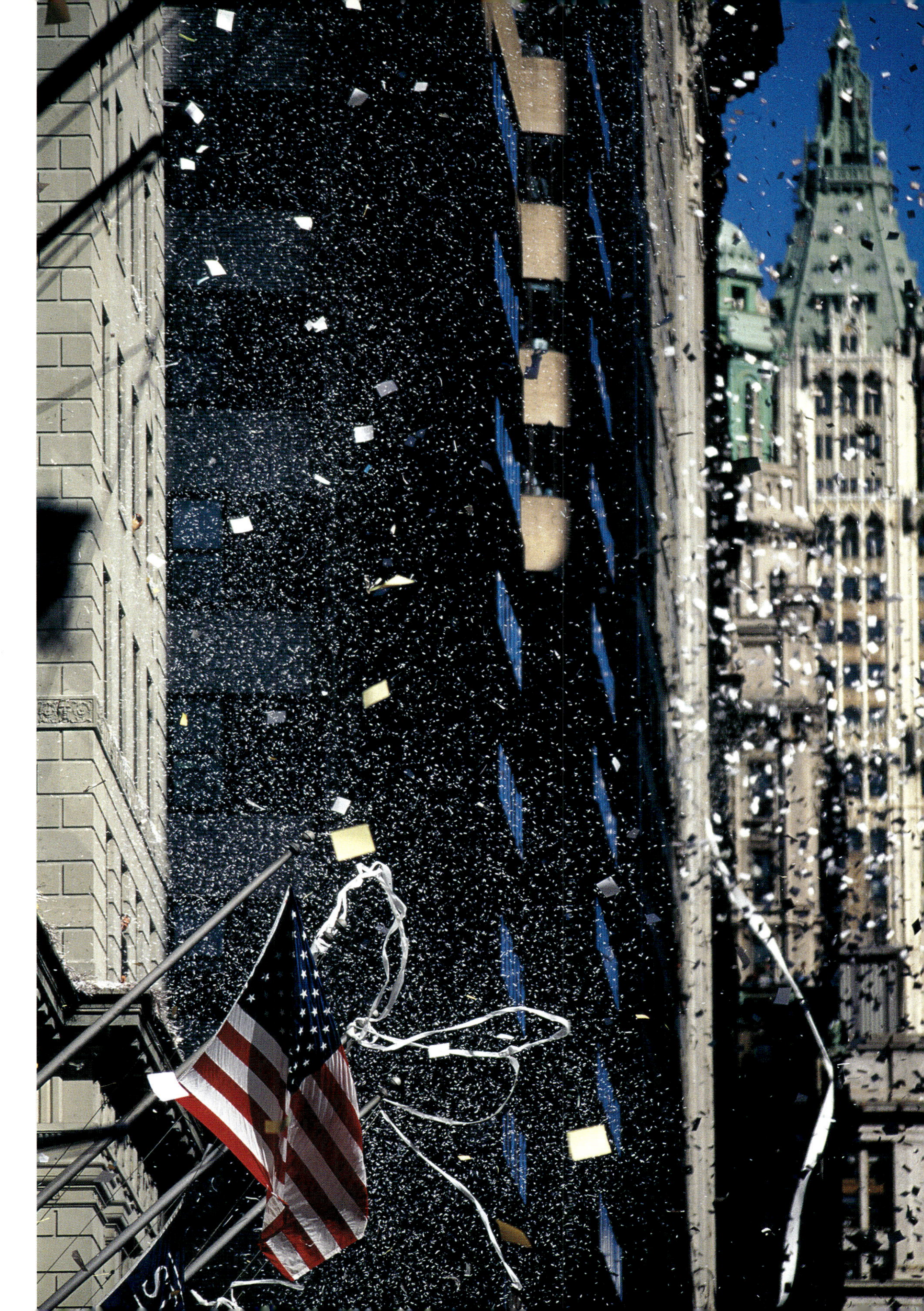

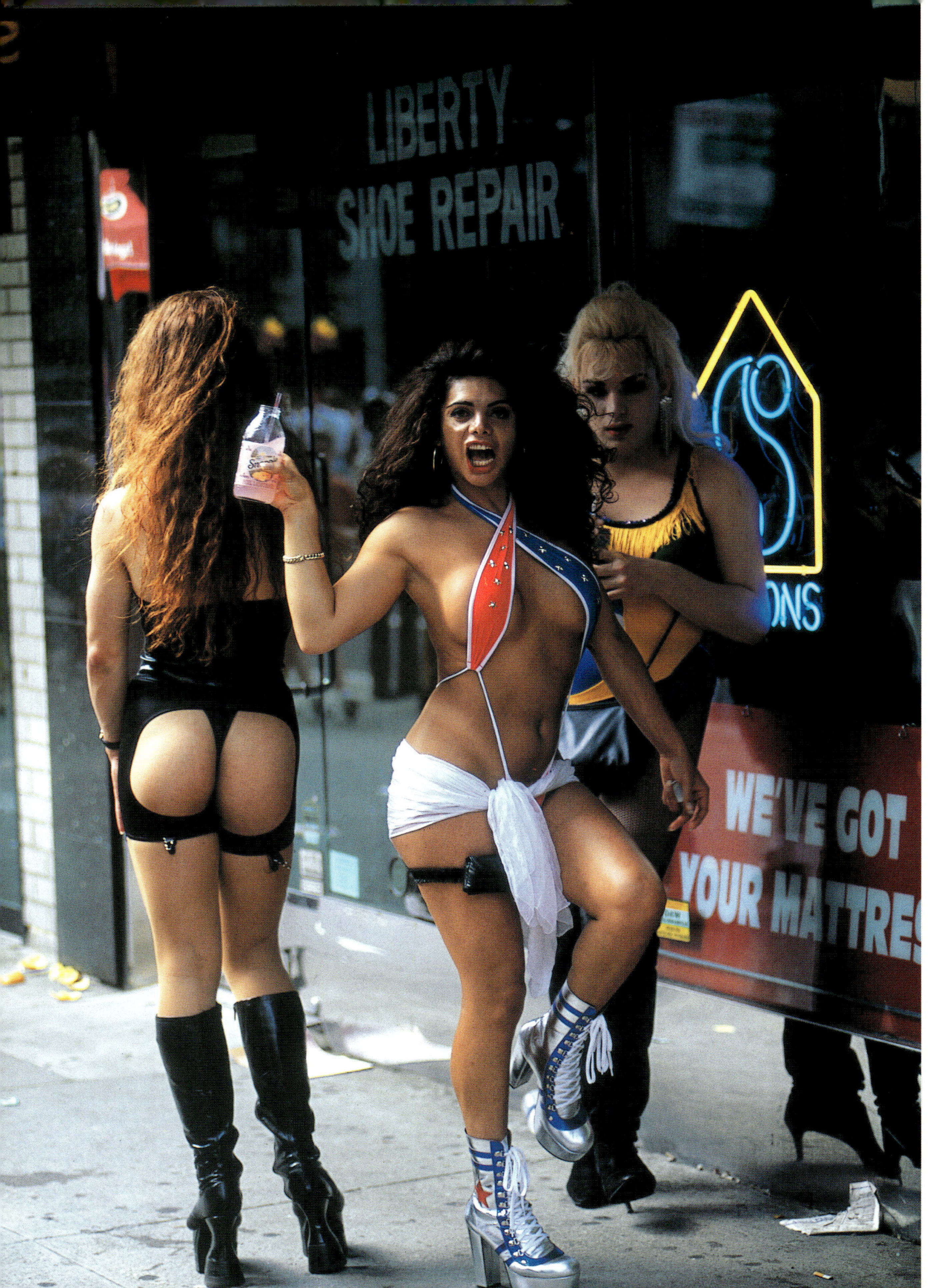
LIBERTY
SHOE REPAIR
WE'VE GOT
YOUR MATTRES

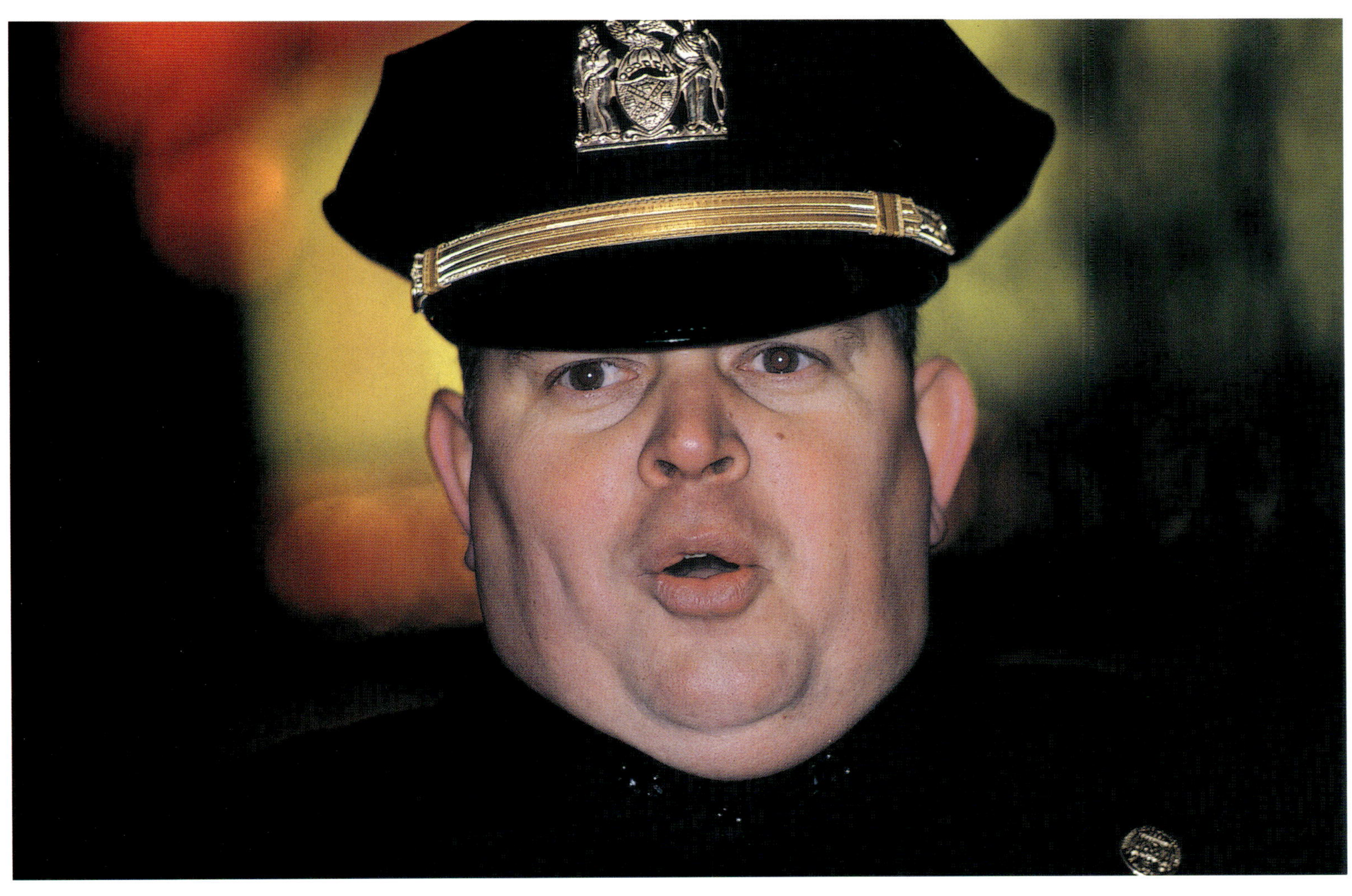

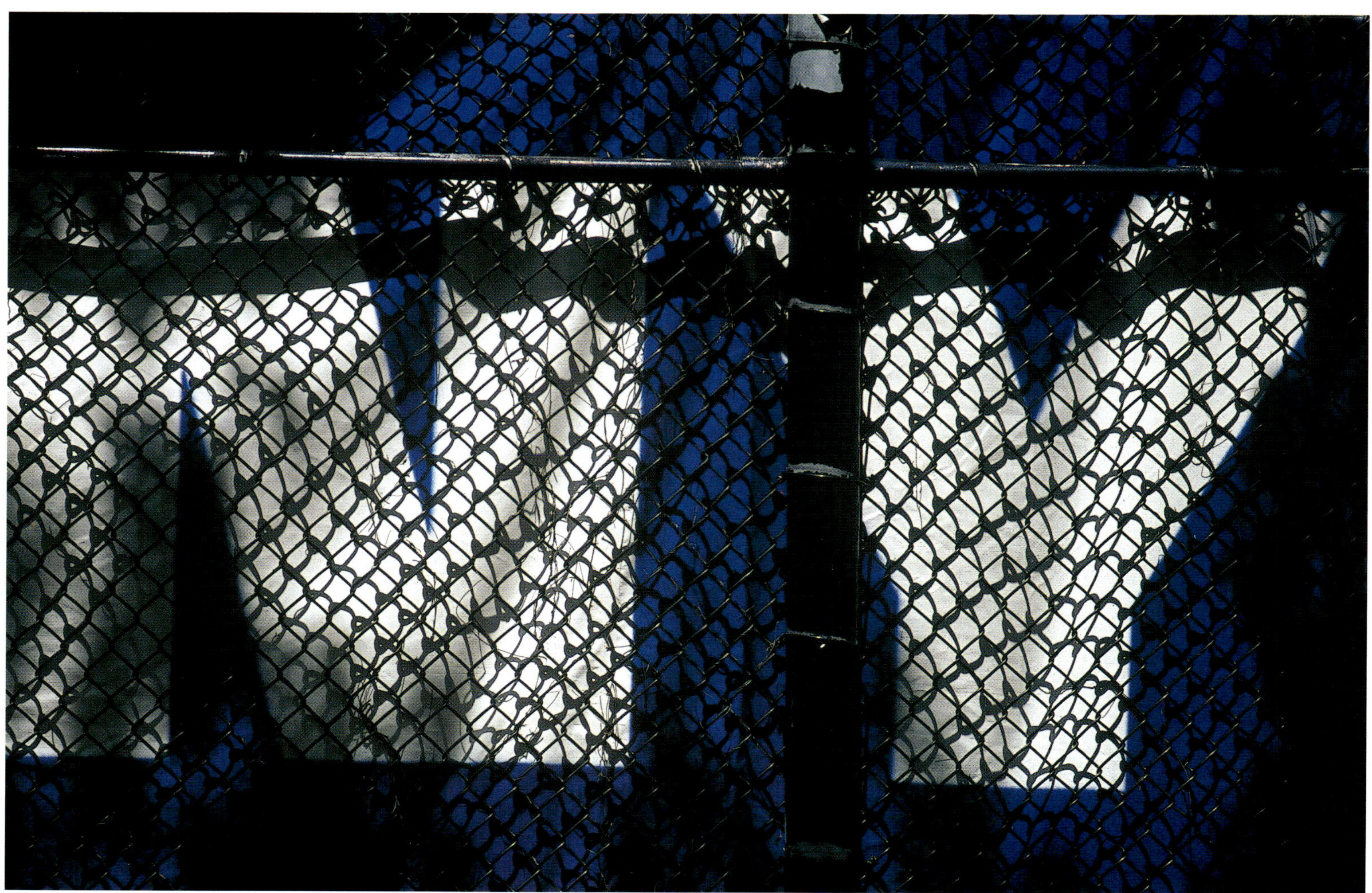

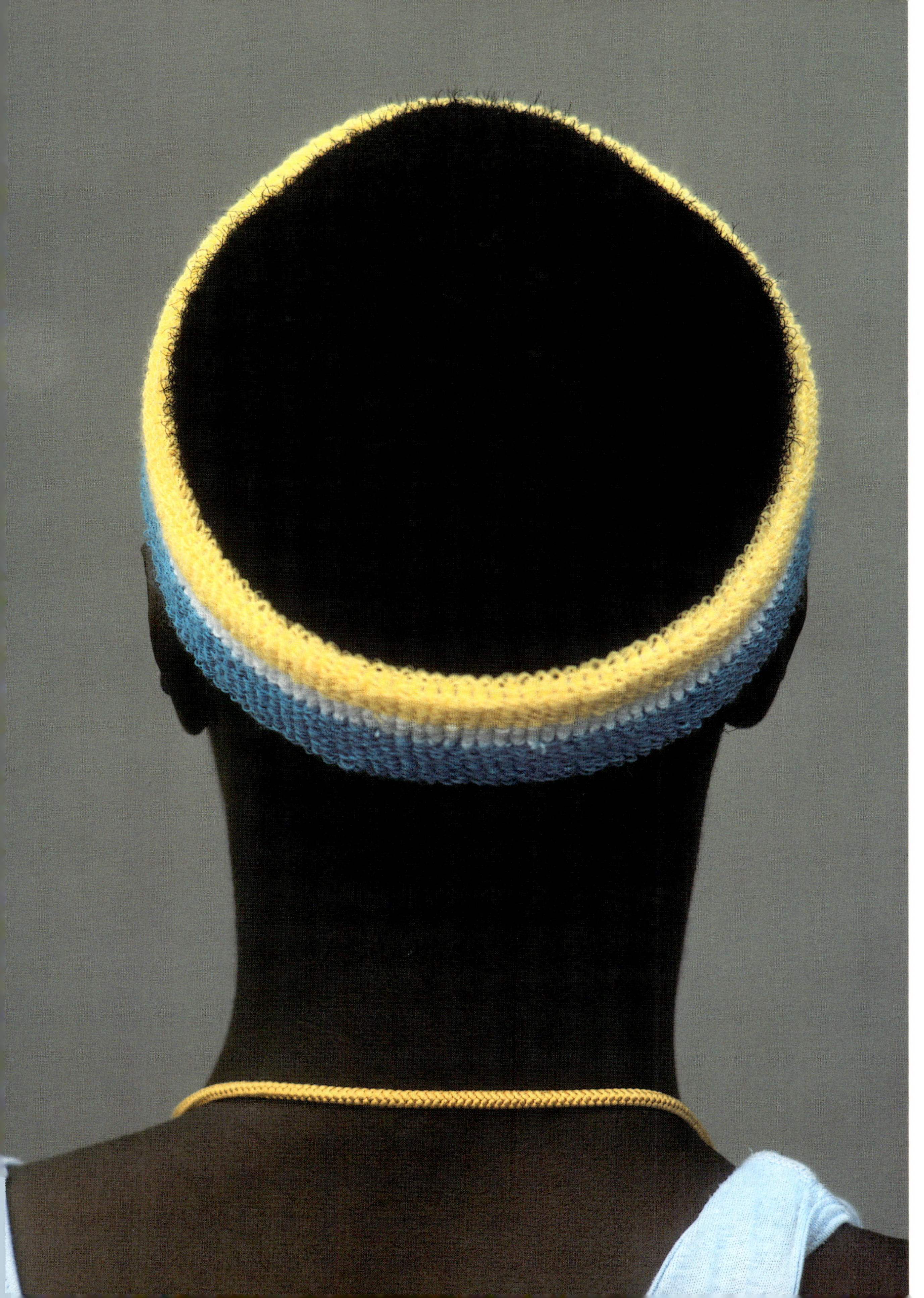

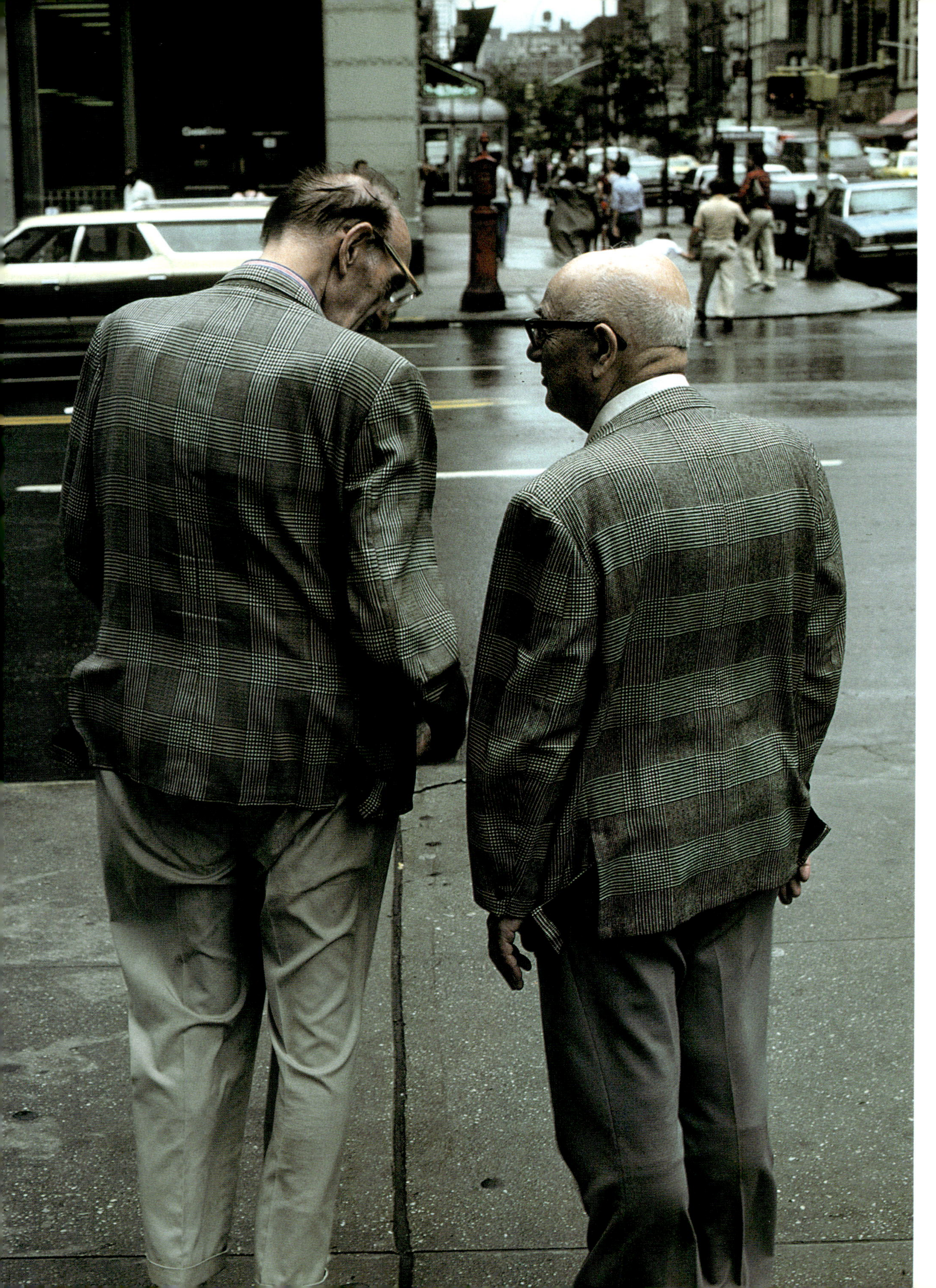

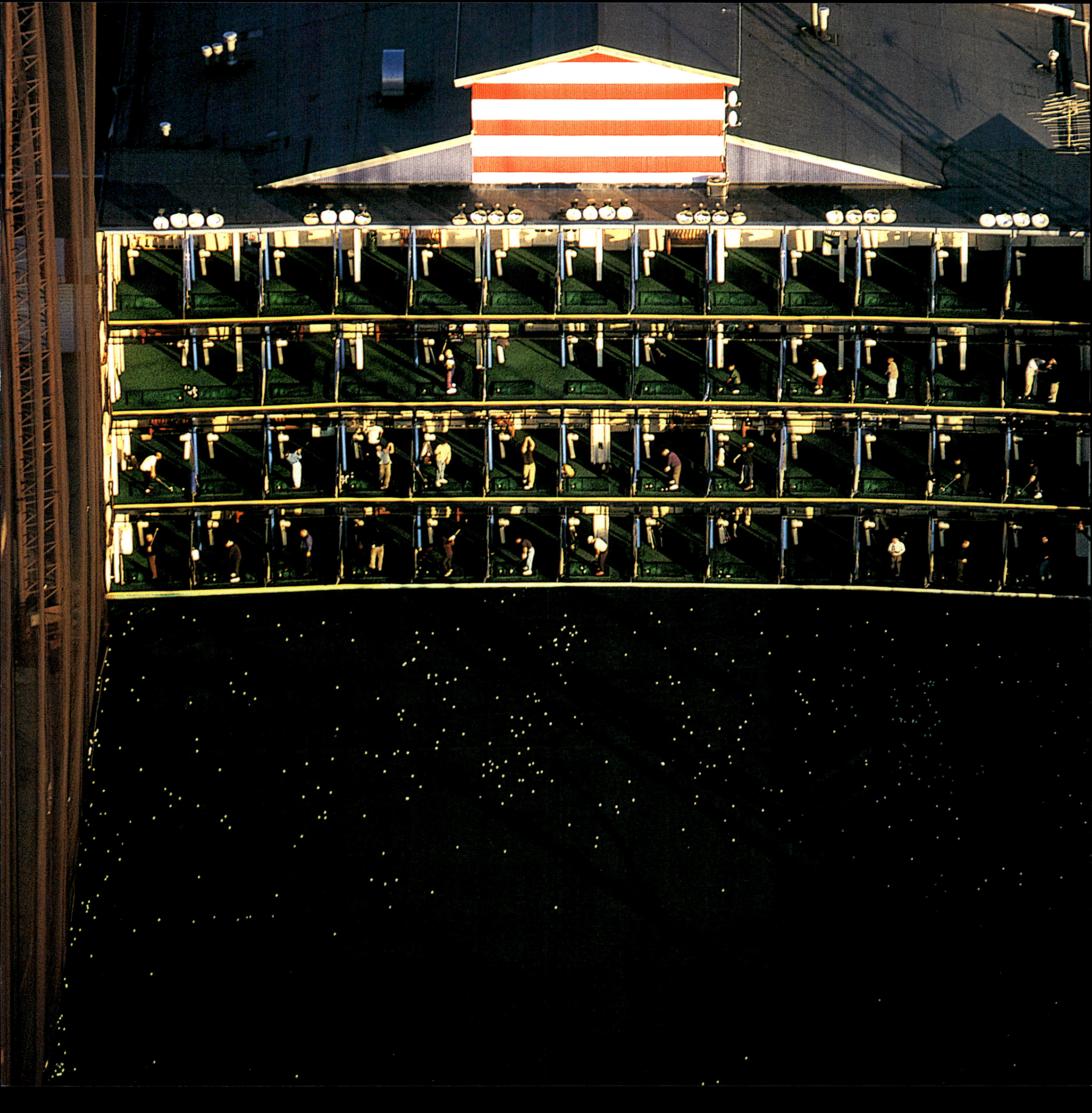

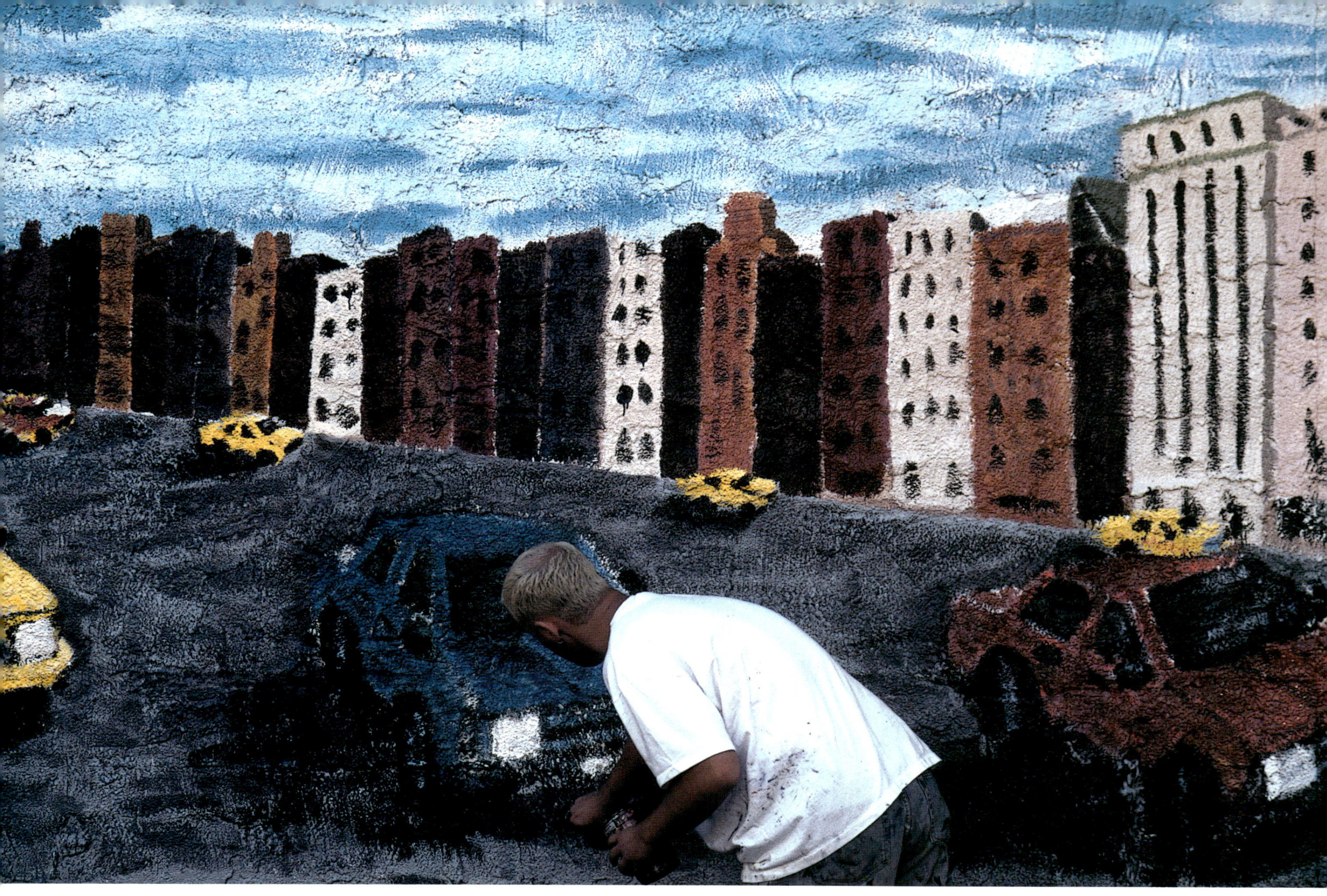

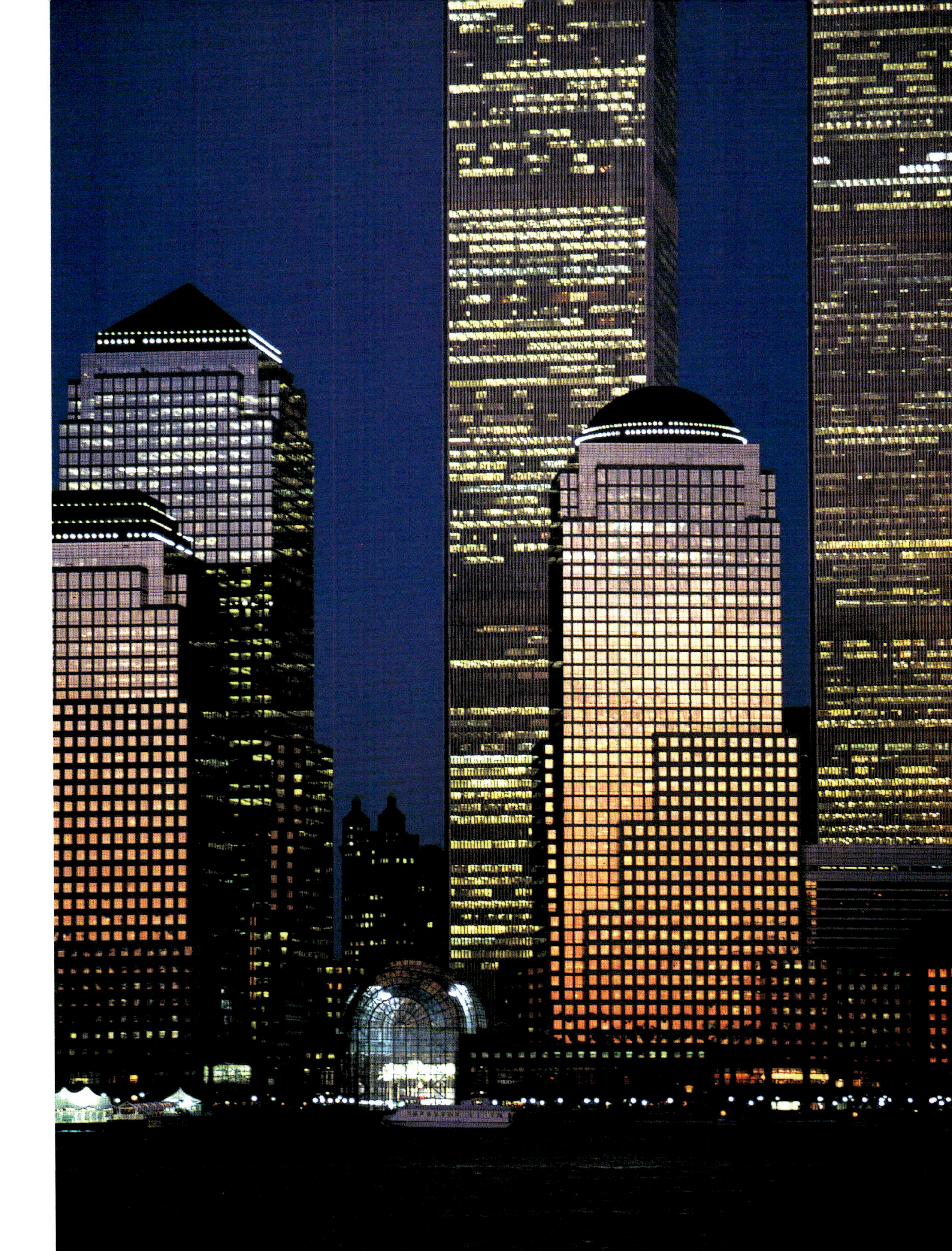

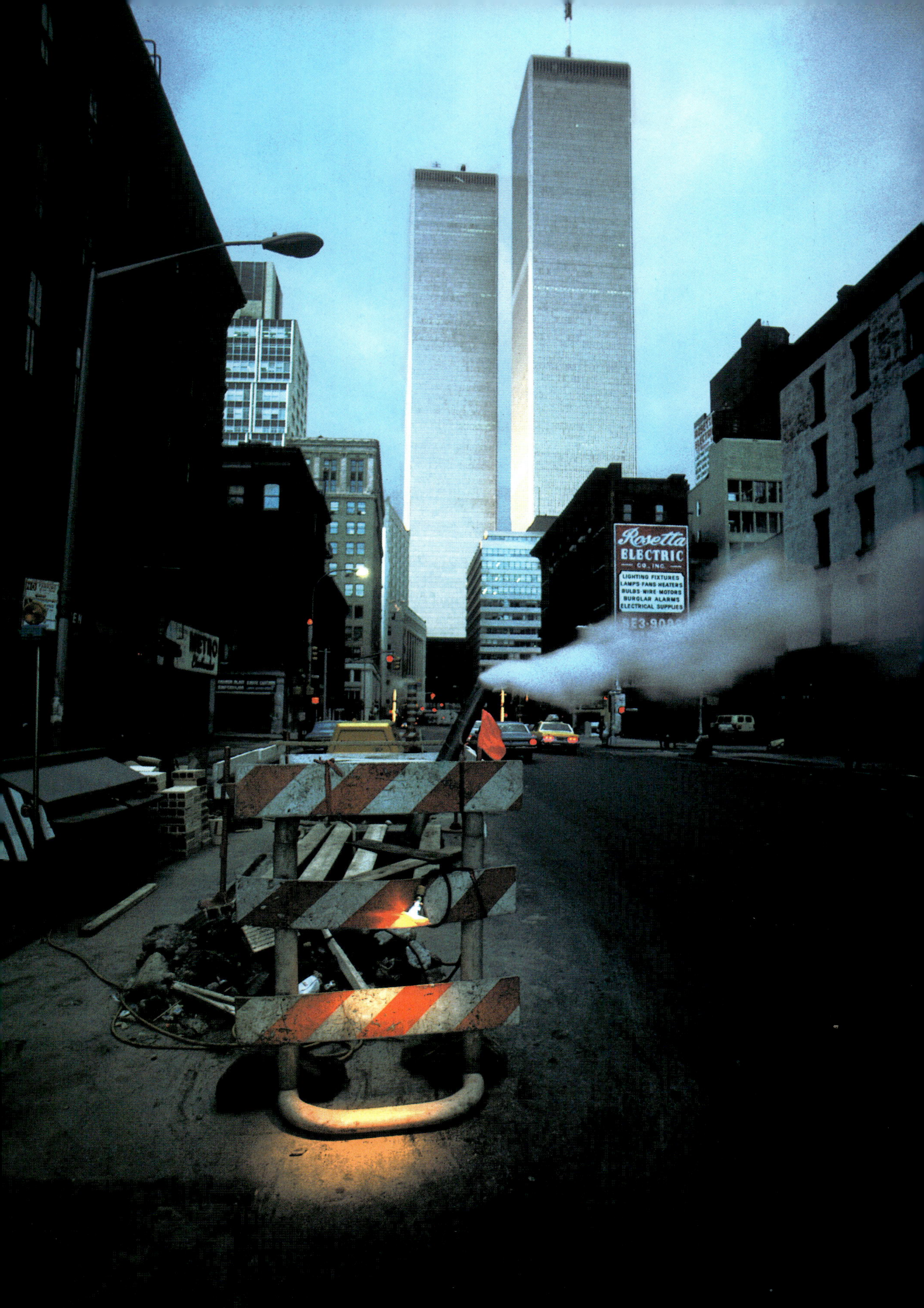
Rosetta
ELECTRIC
CO. INC.
LIGHTING FIXTURES
LAMPS FANS HEATERS
BULBS WIRE MOTORS
BURGLAR ALARMS
ELECTRICAL SUPPLIES
METRO

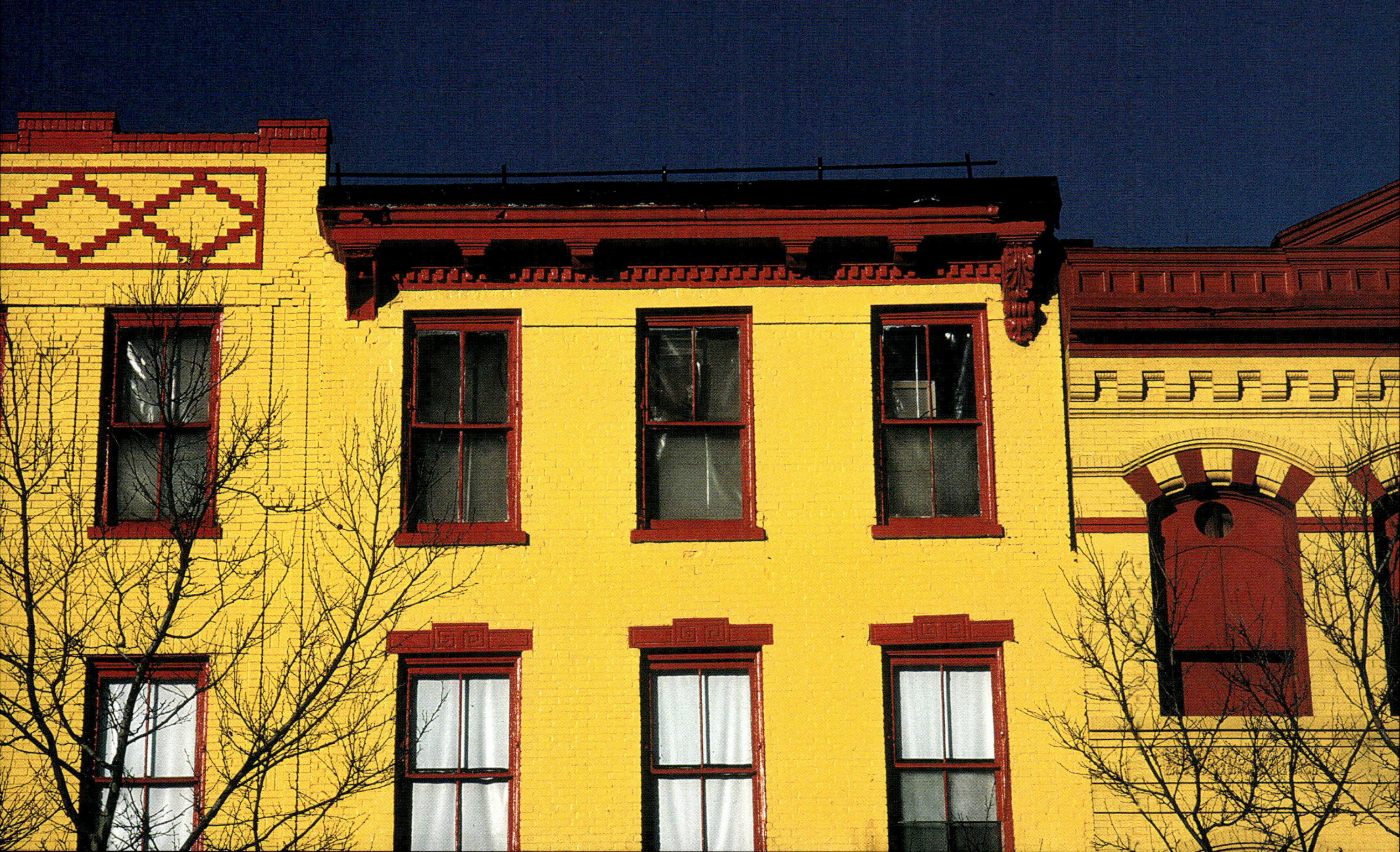

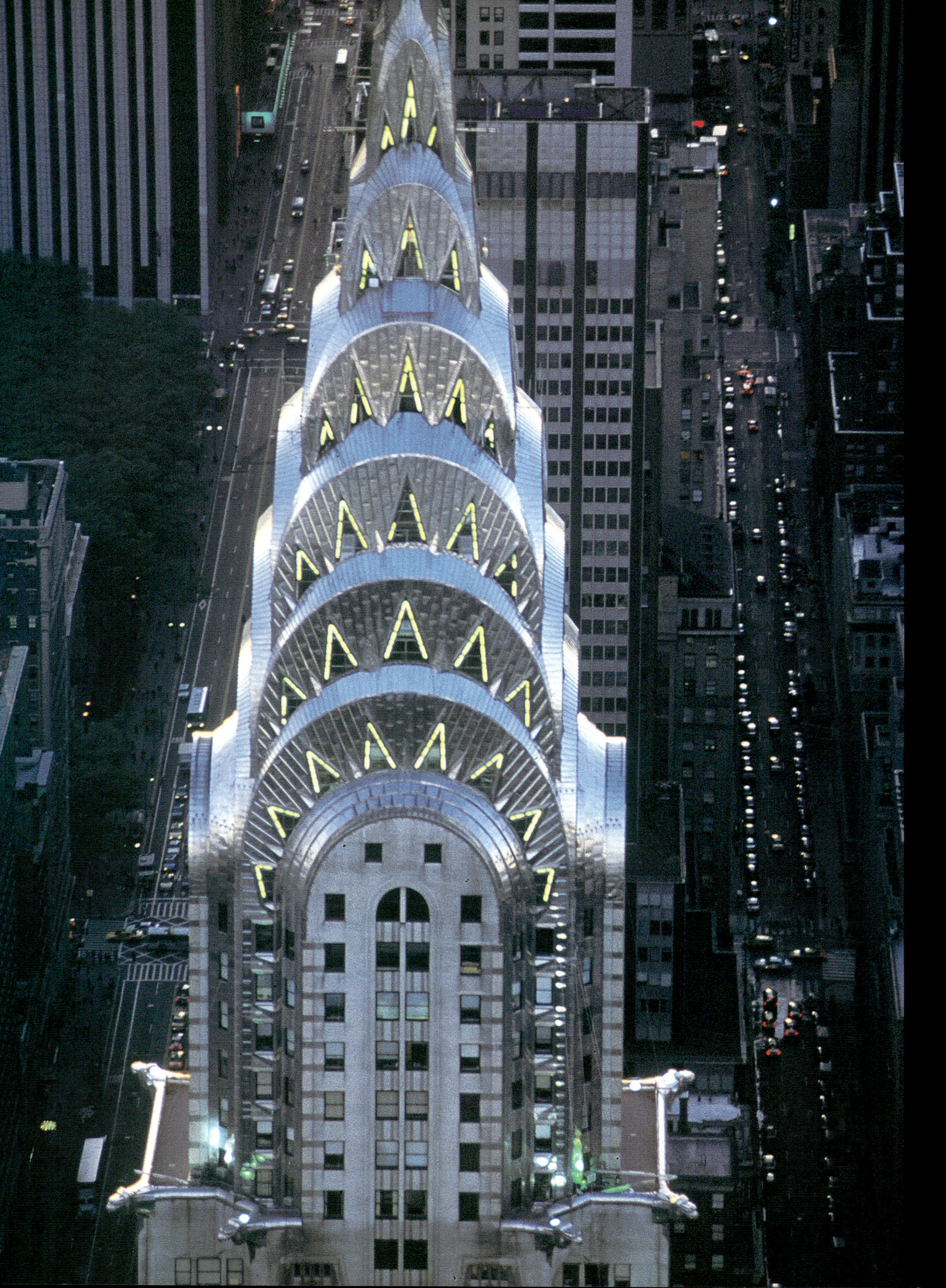

Chrysler Building

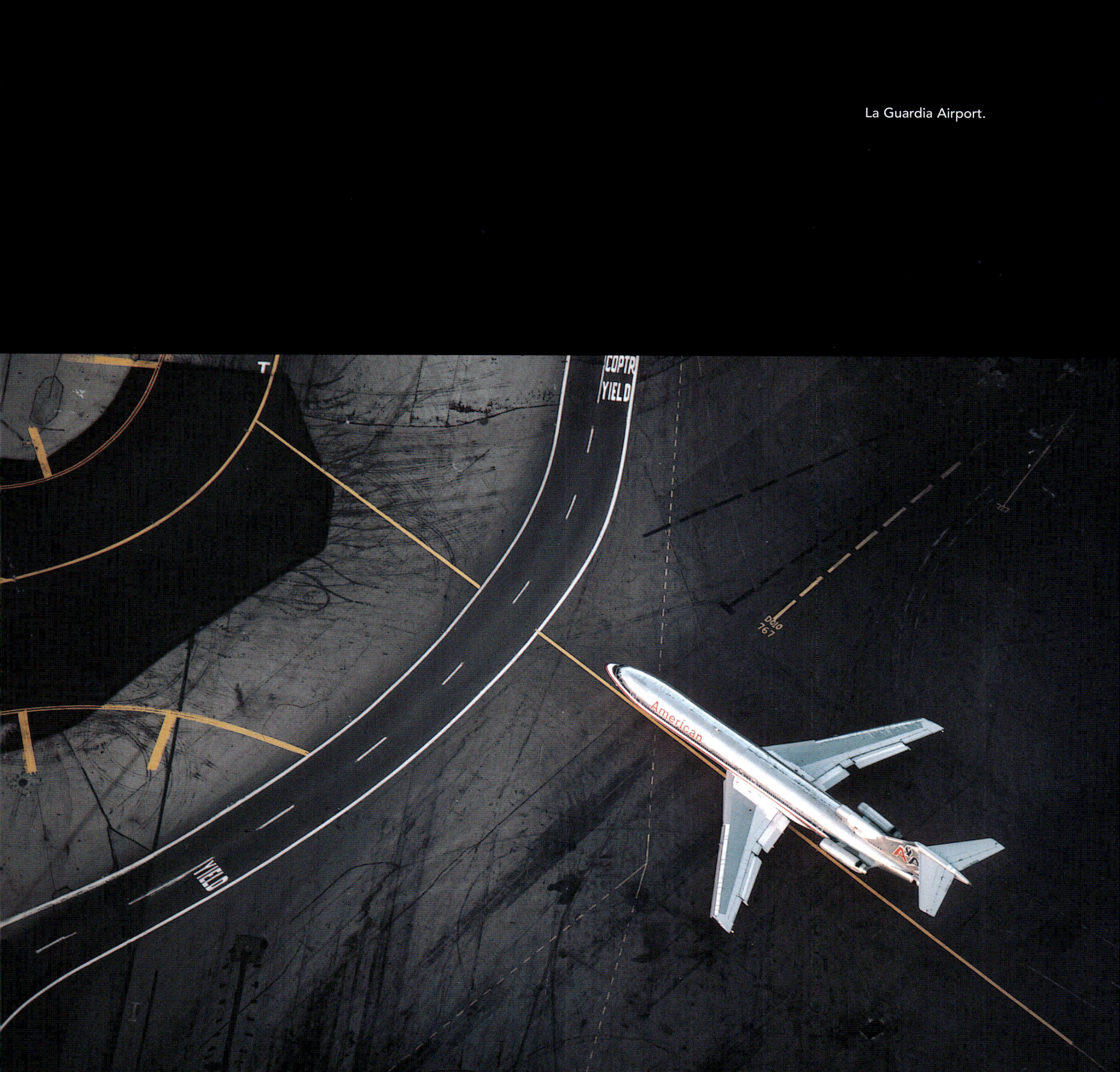

La Guardia Airport.

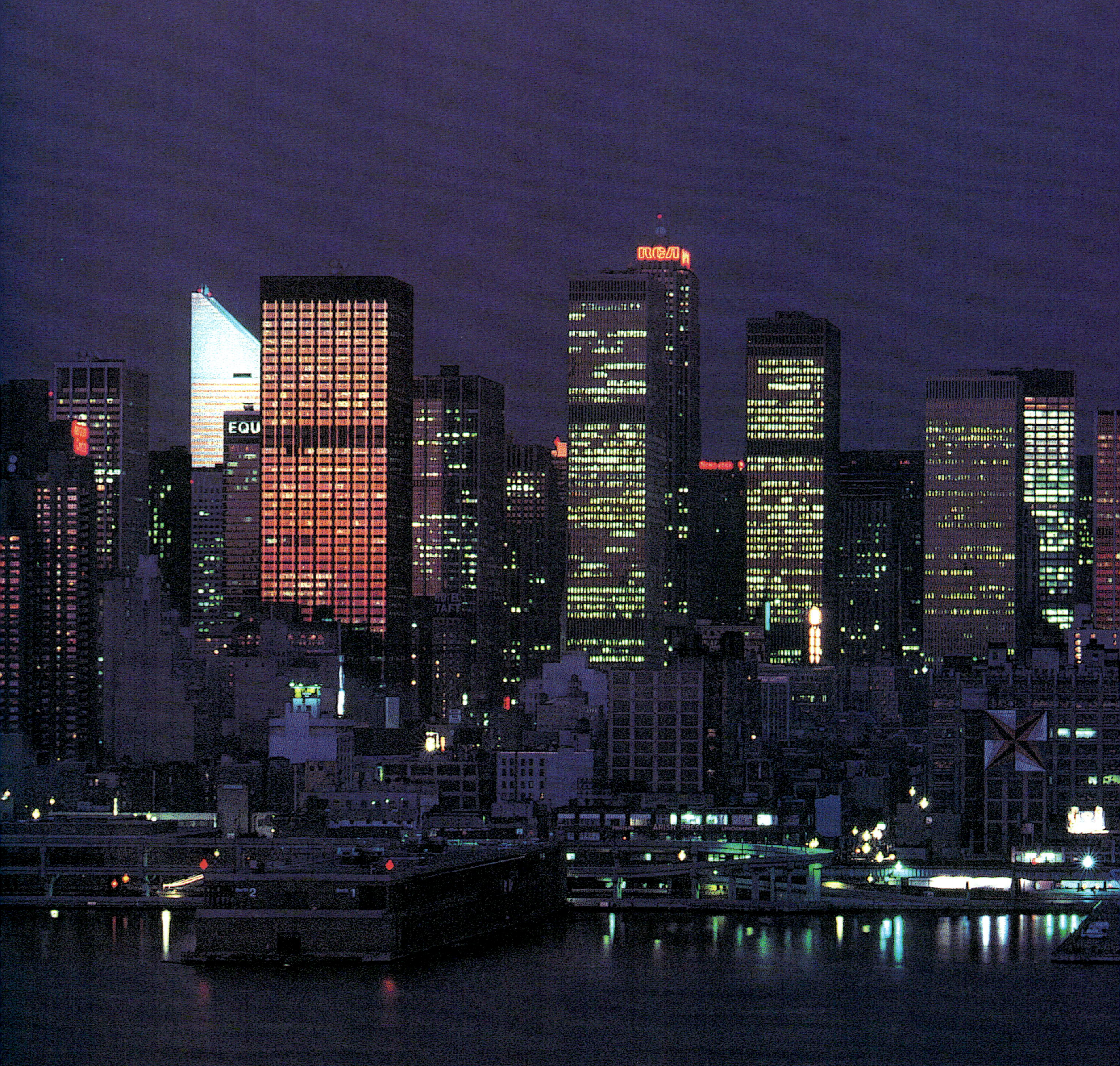
RCA
EQU

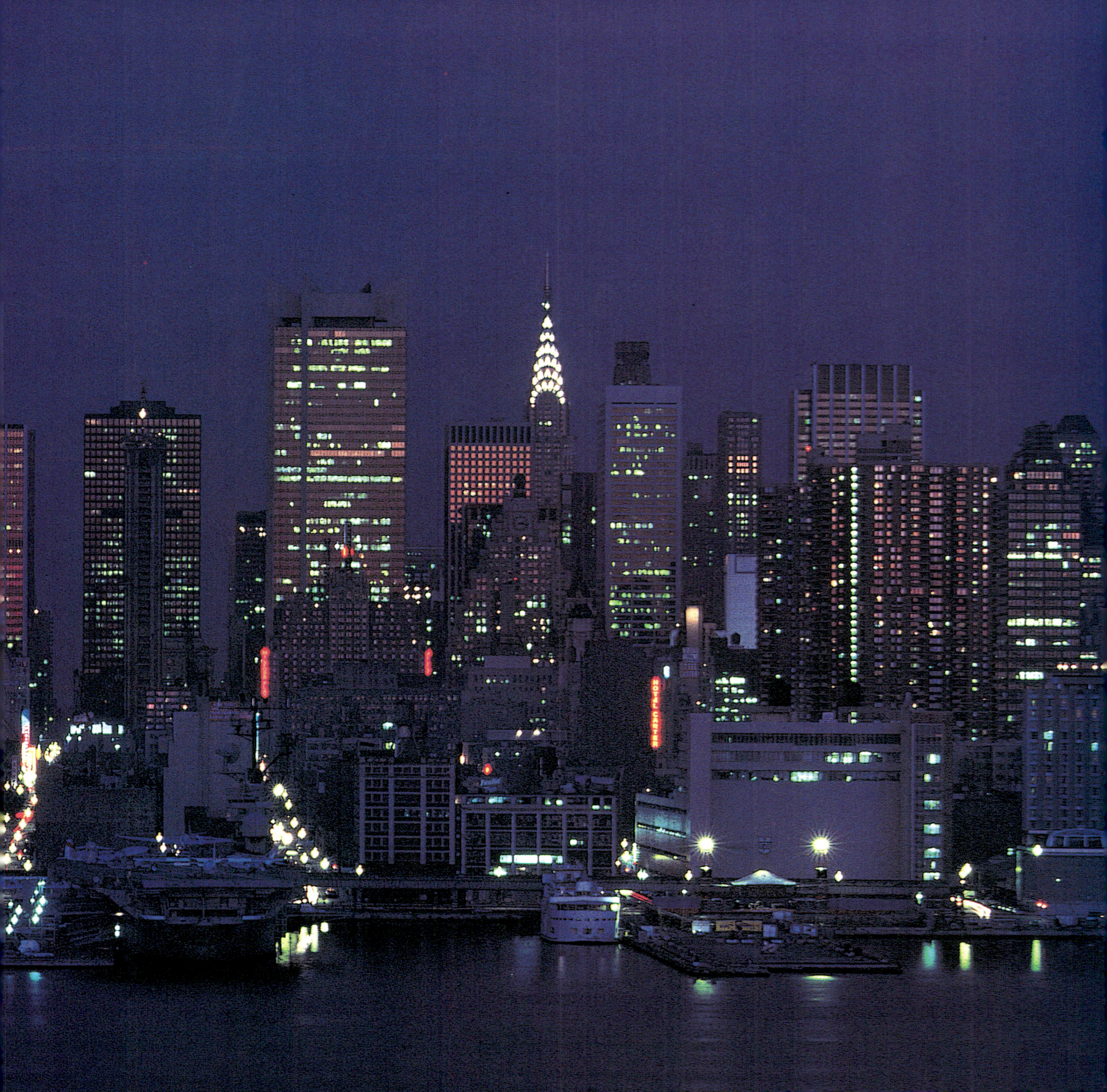
HOTEL CARTER

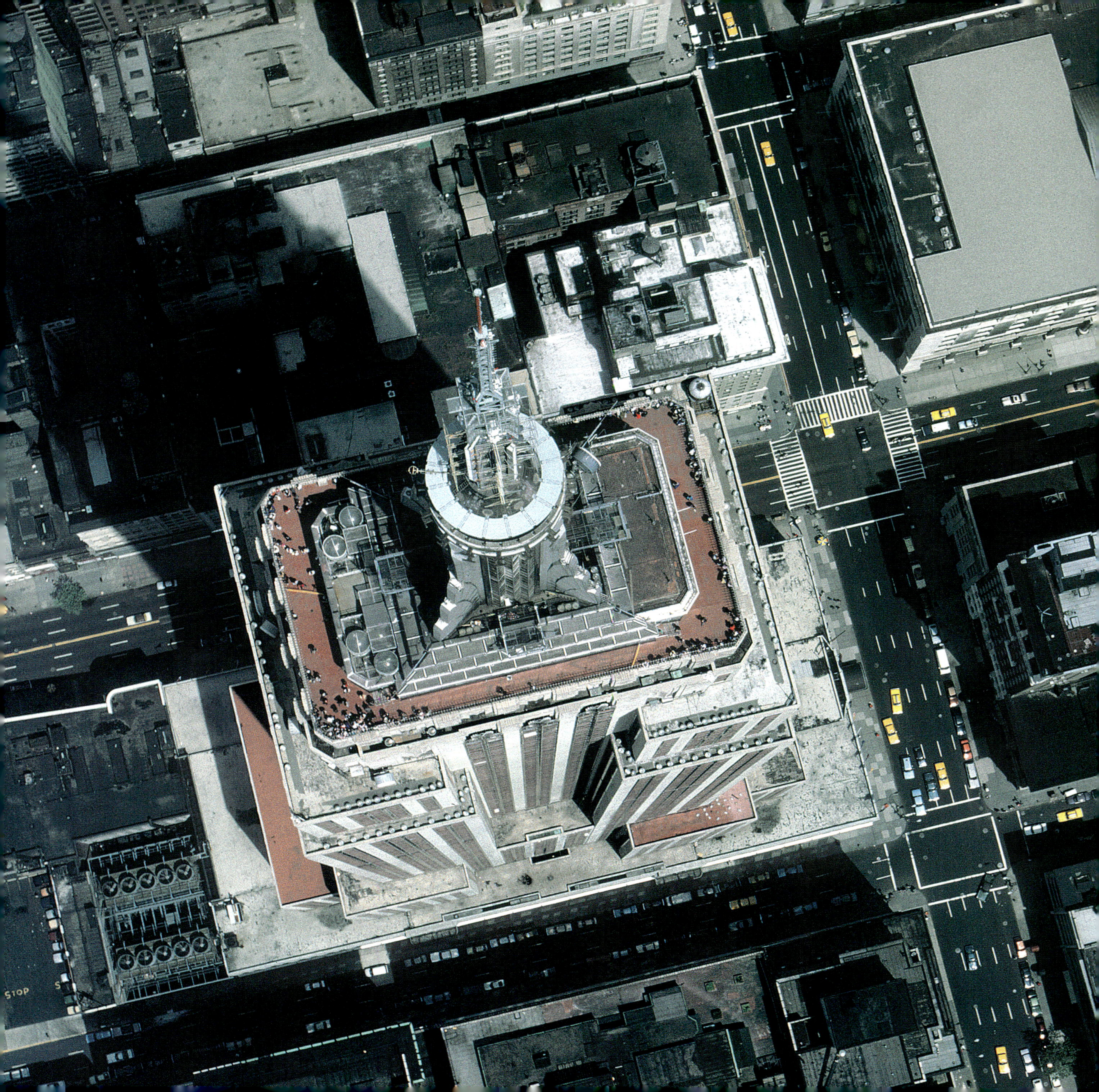
STOP

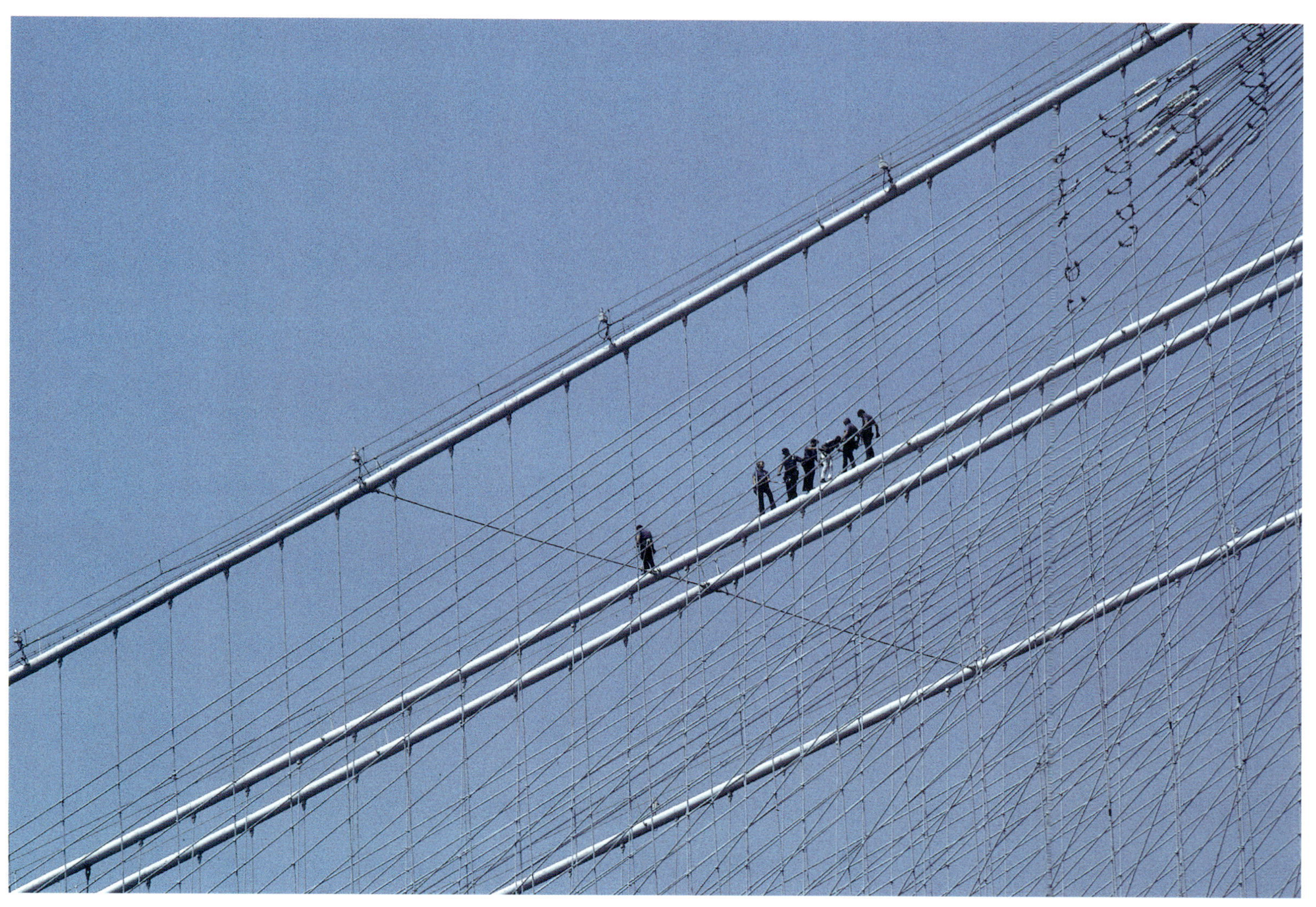

After thwarting an attempted suicide,
police officers walk him down to safety.

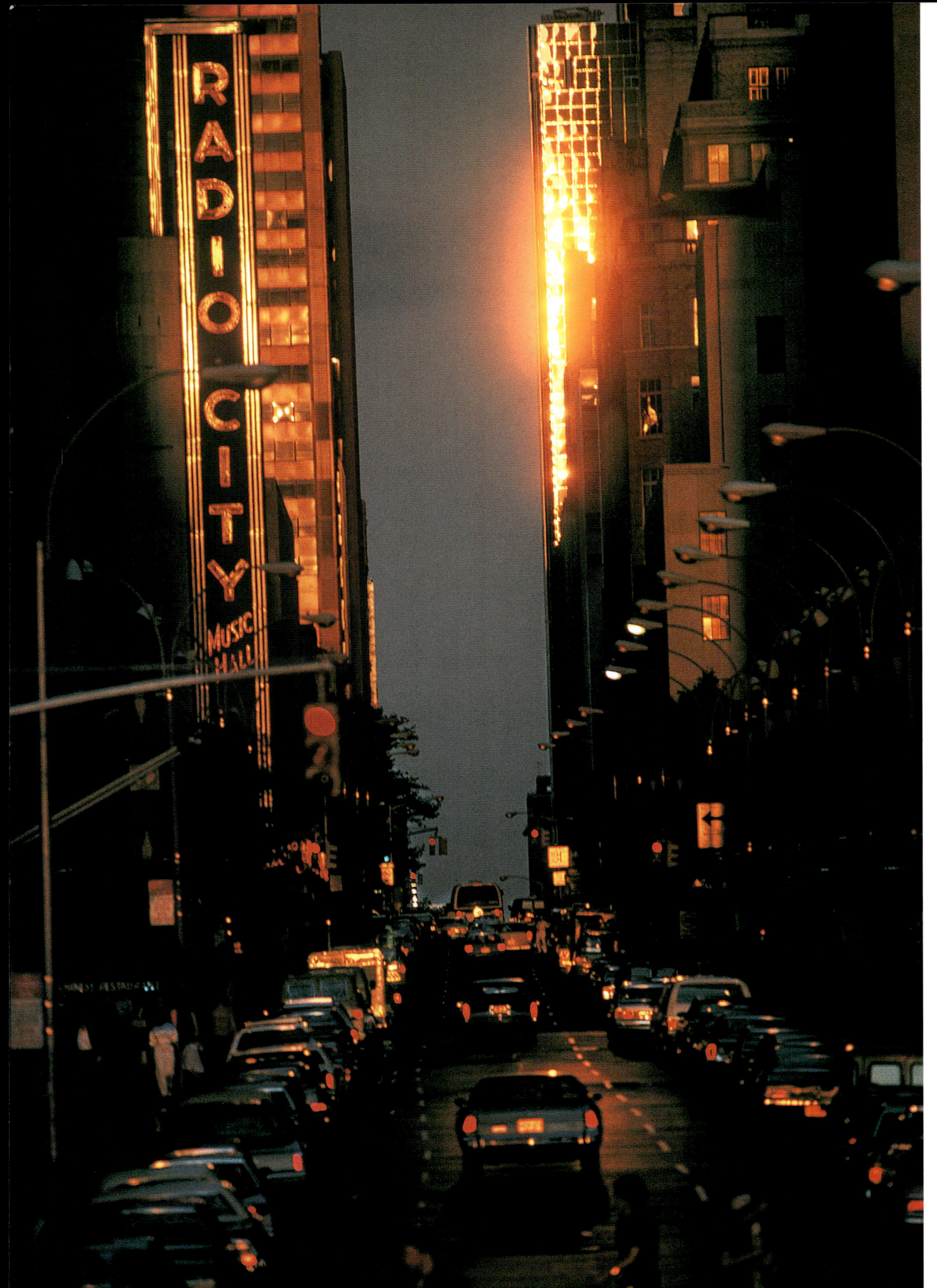
RADIO CITY
MUSIC HALL

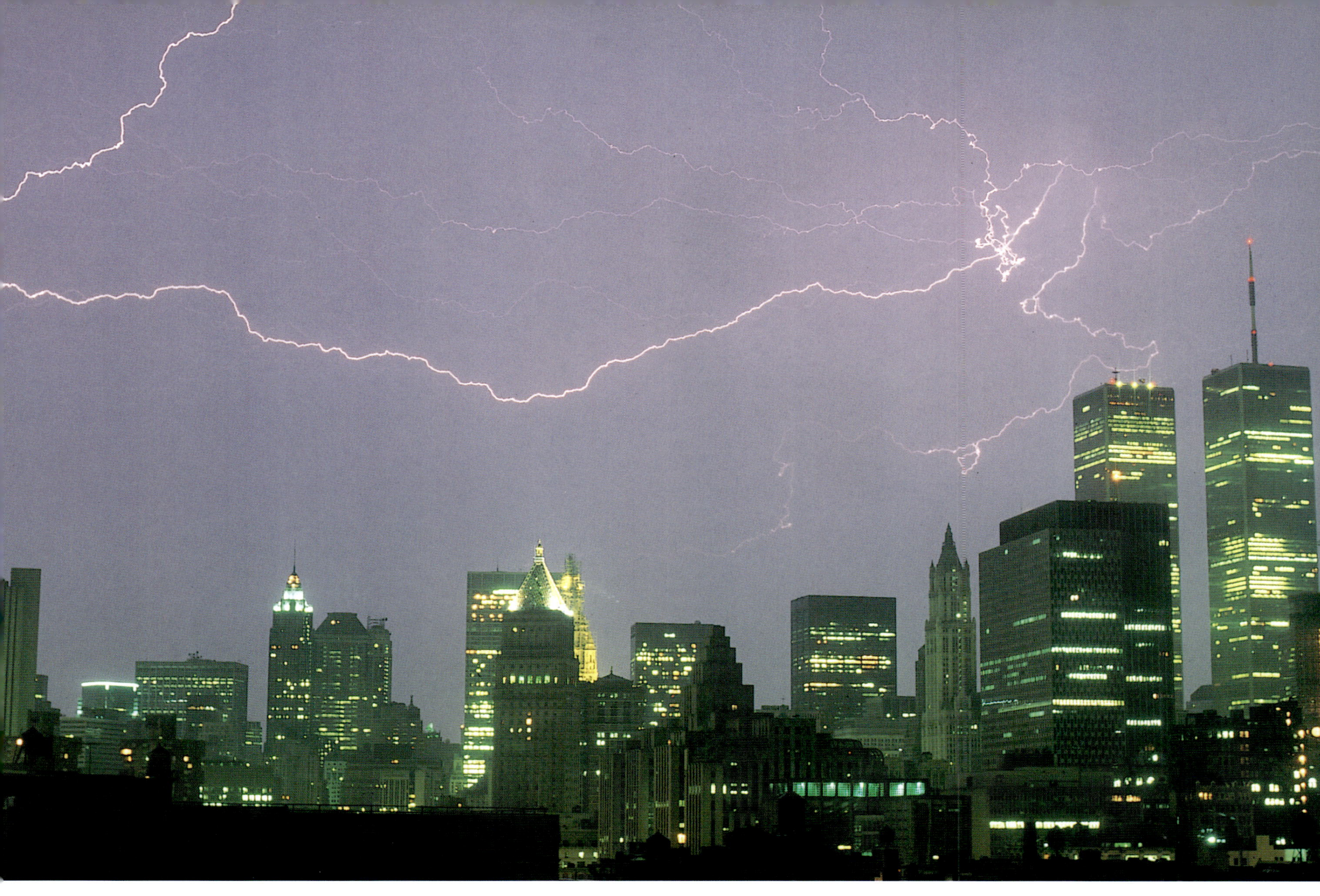

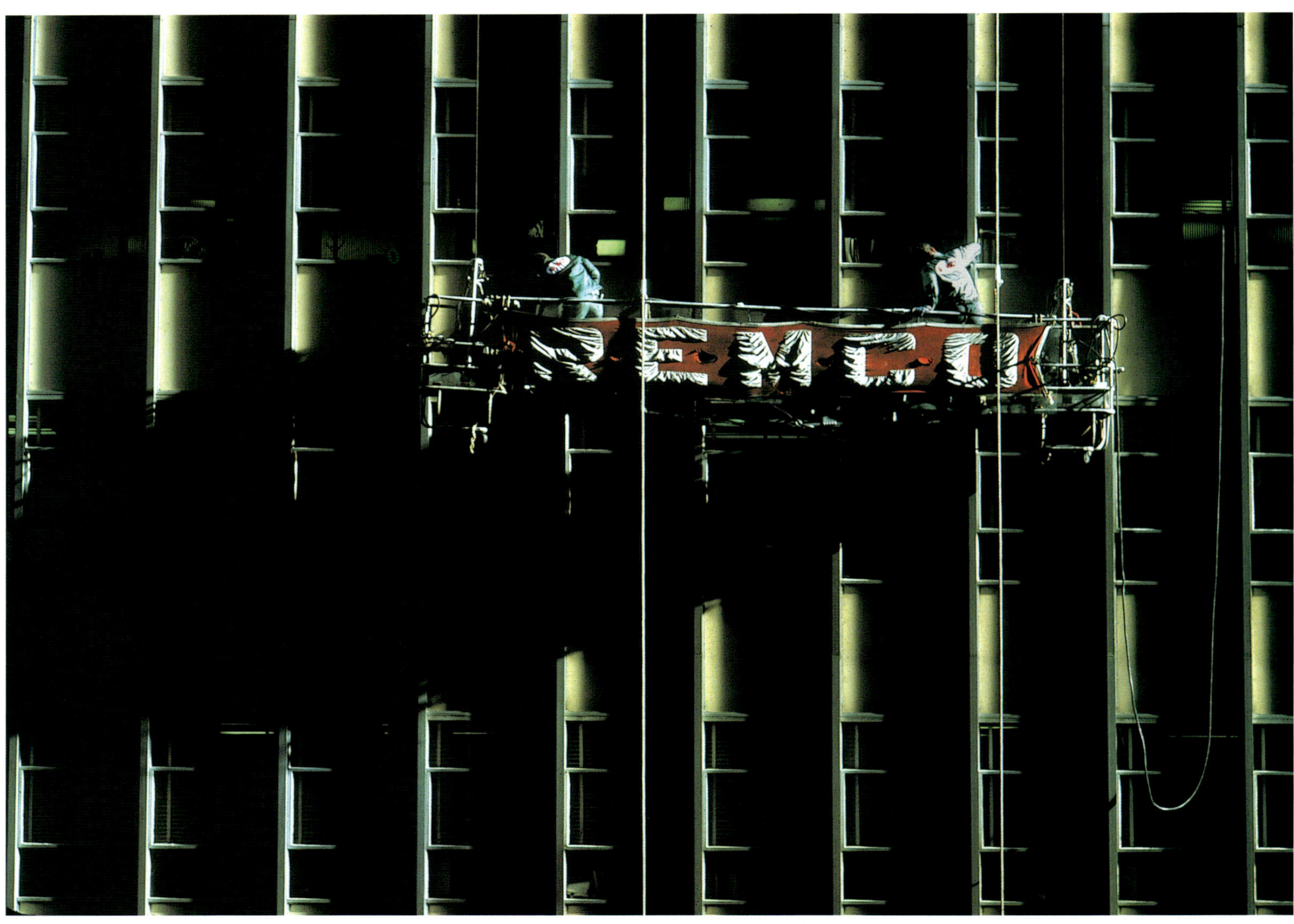
REMCO

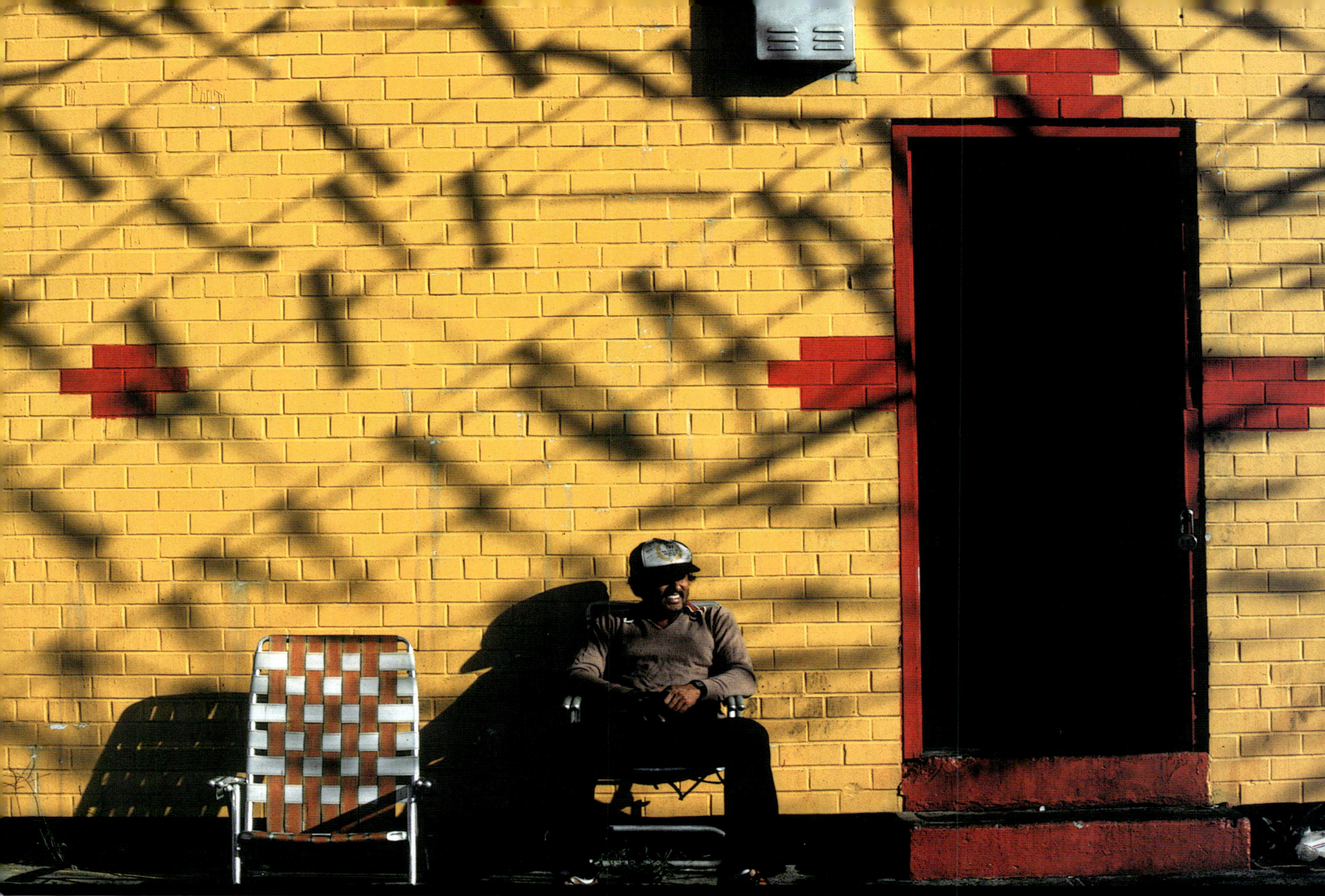

When I shot this, the guy in the chair walked over to me, looked at the wall, and asked, “What are you shooting?”

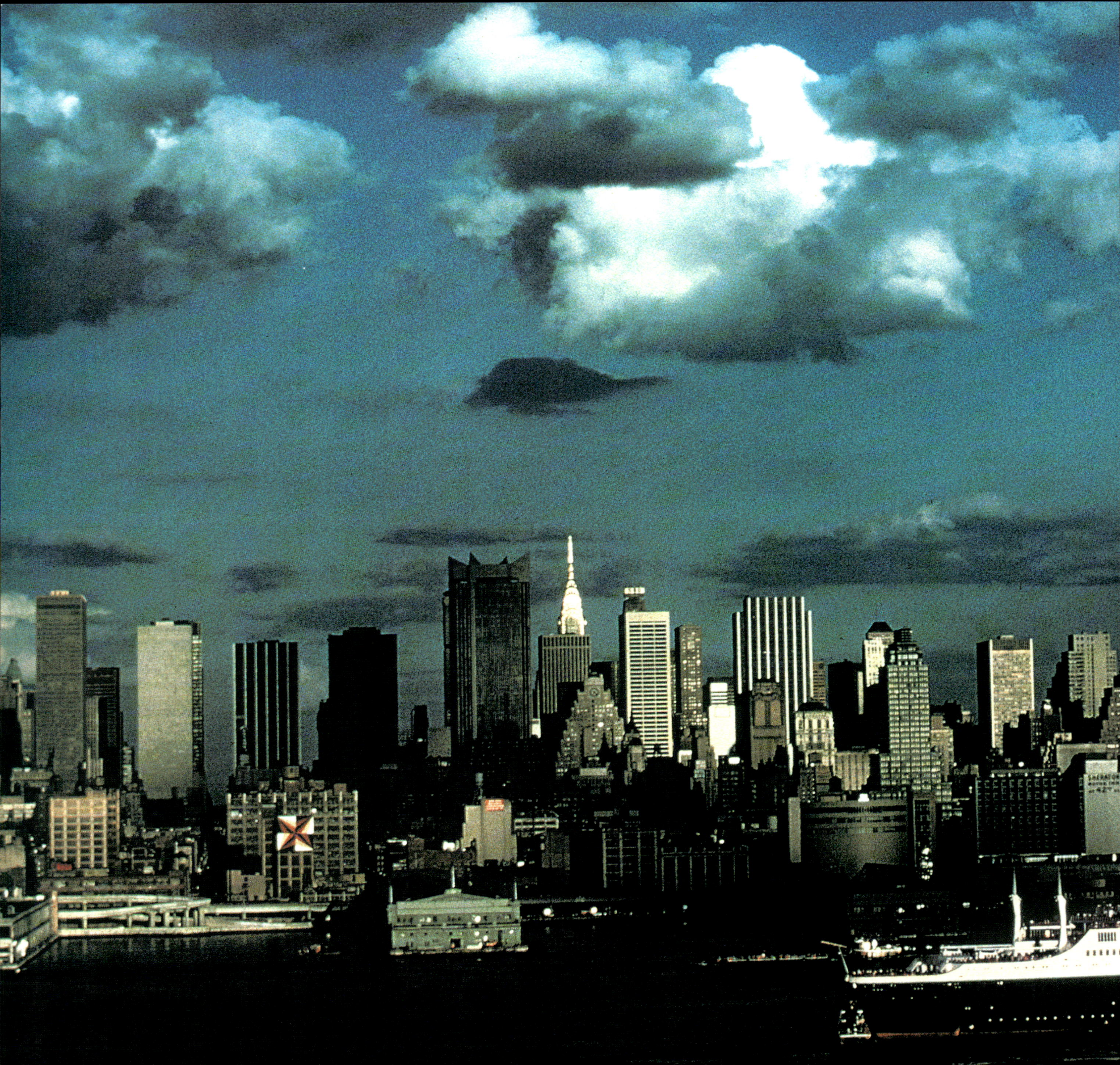

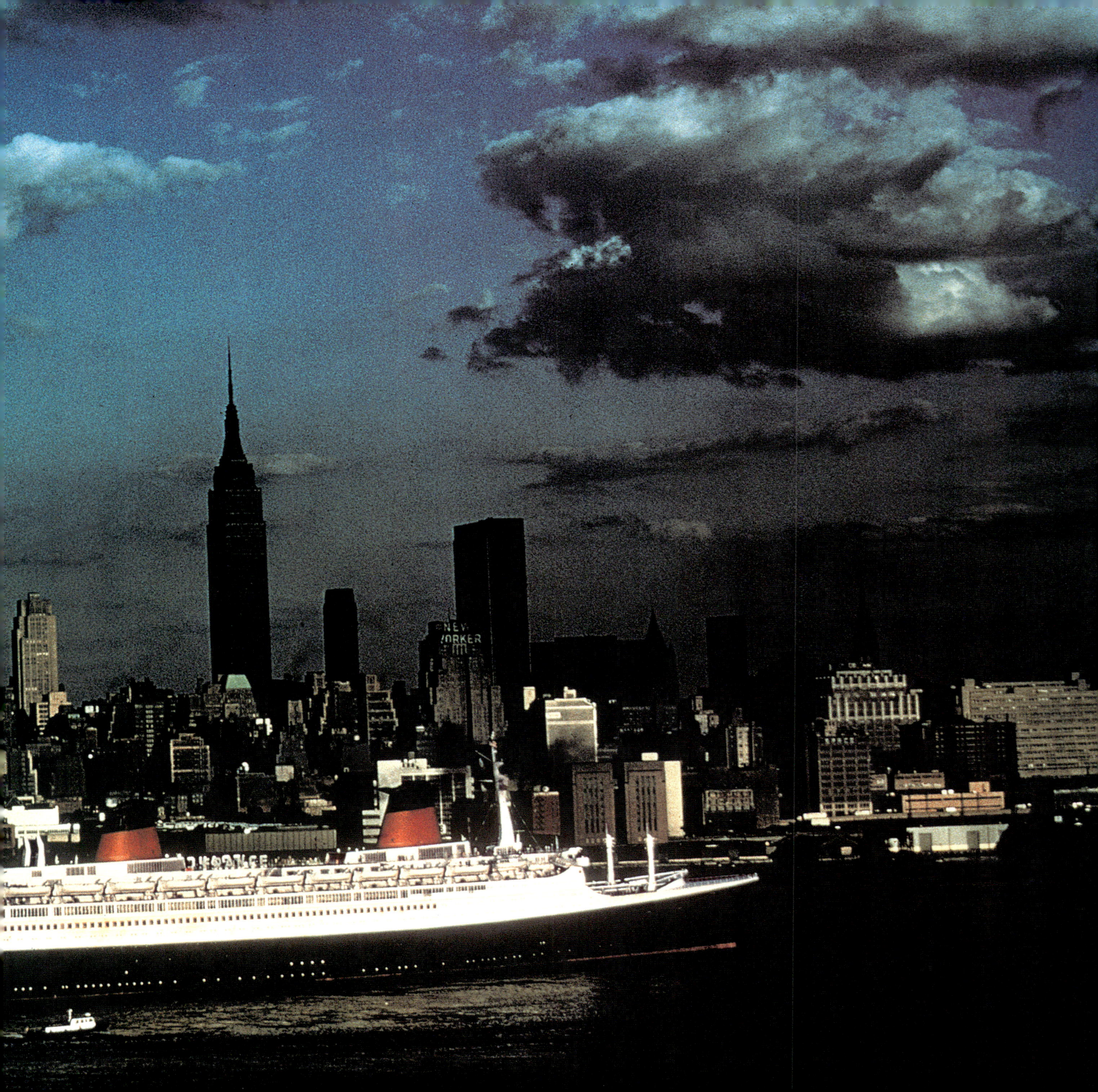
NEW YORKER

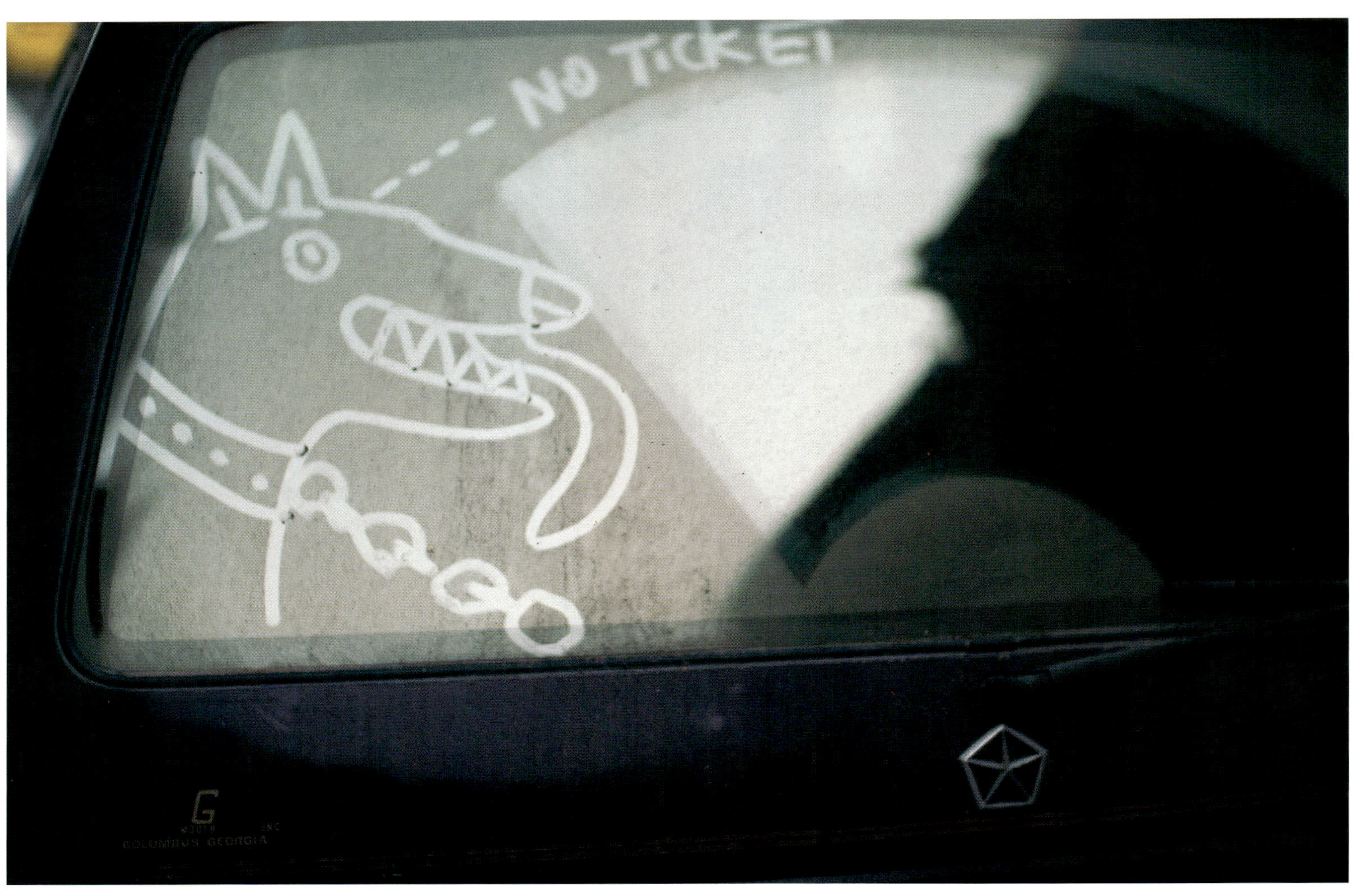
NO TICKET
COLUMBUS GEORGIA

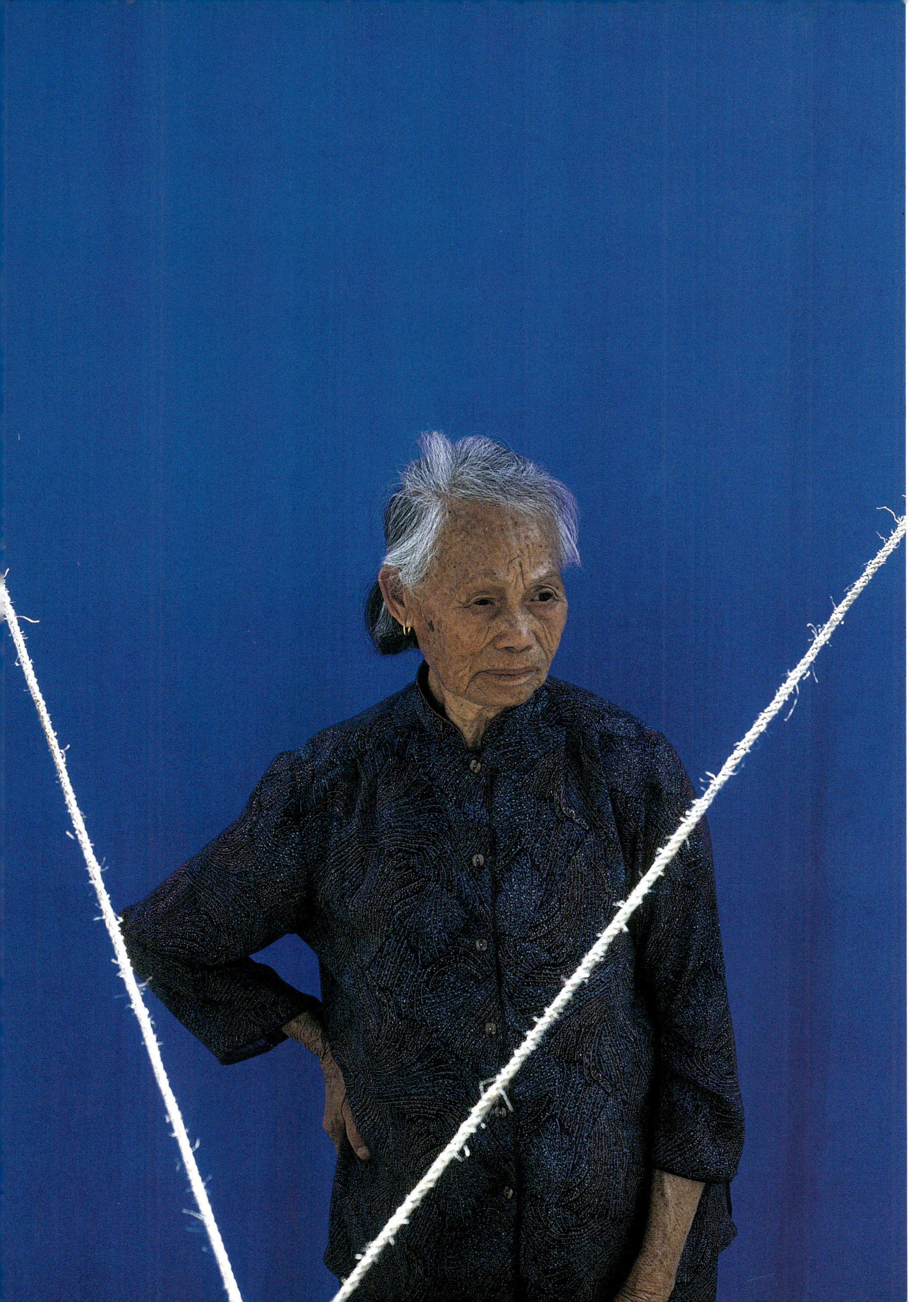

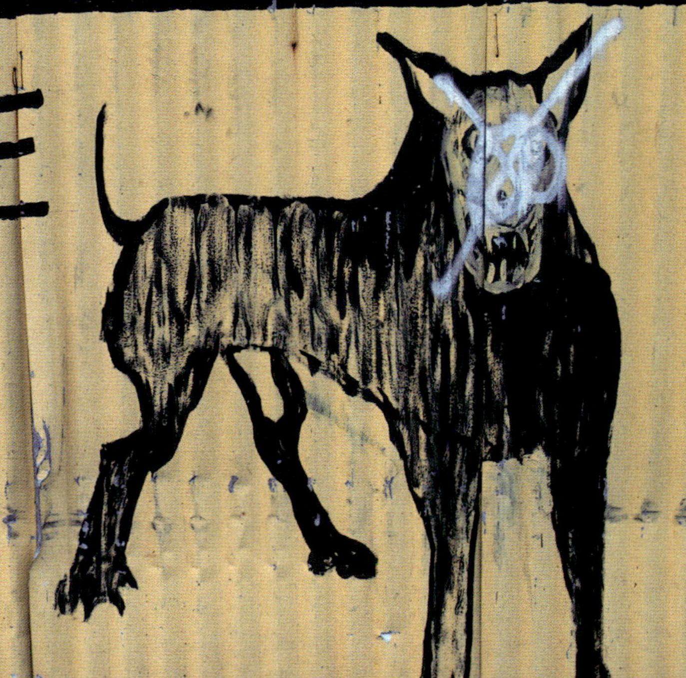
DO NOT ENTER
BEWARE

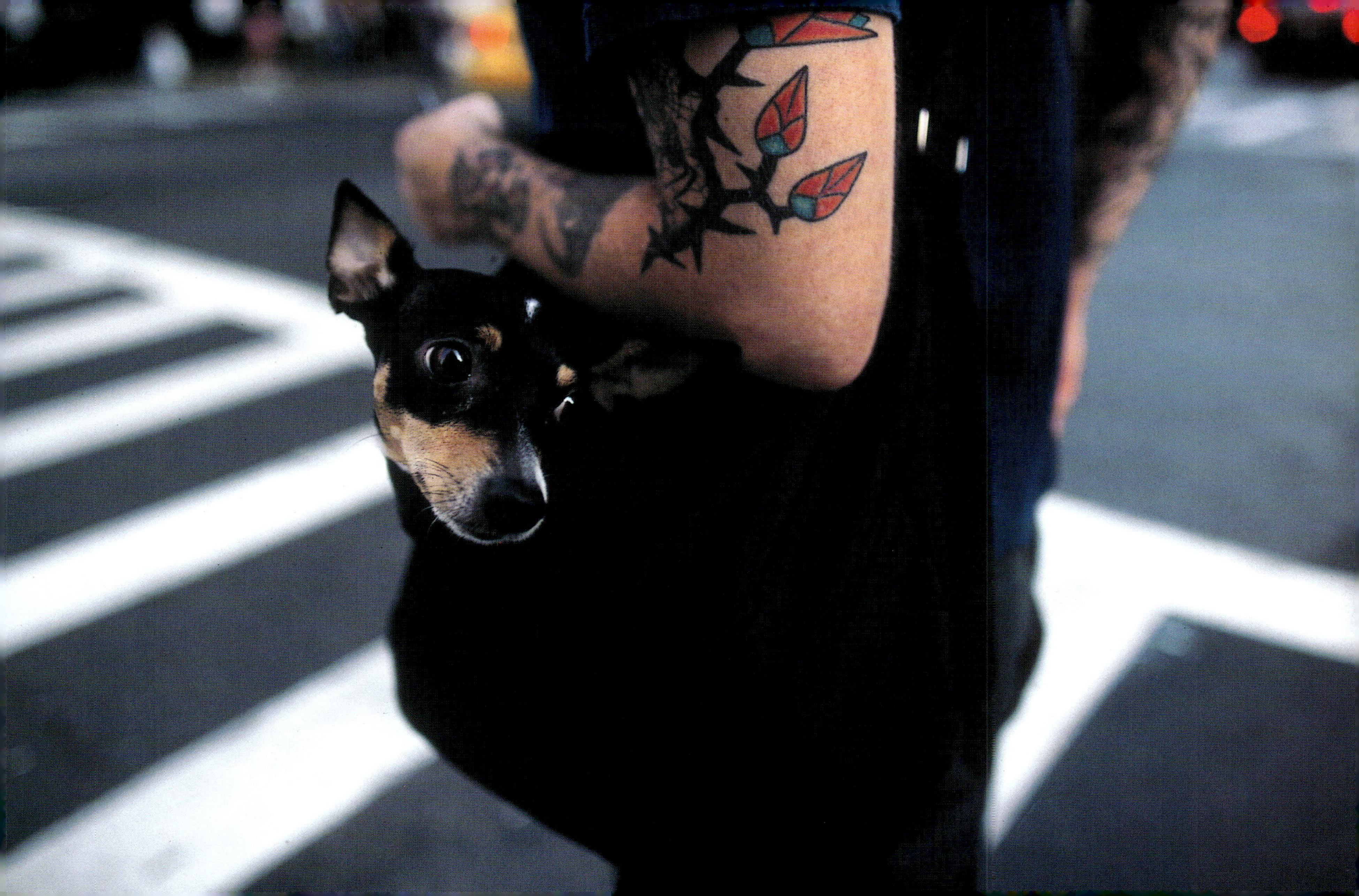

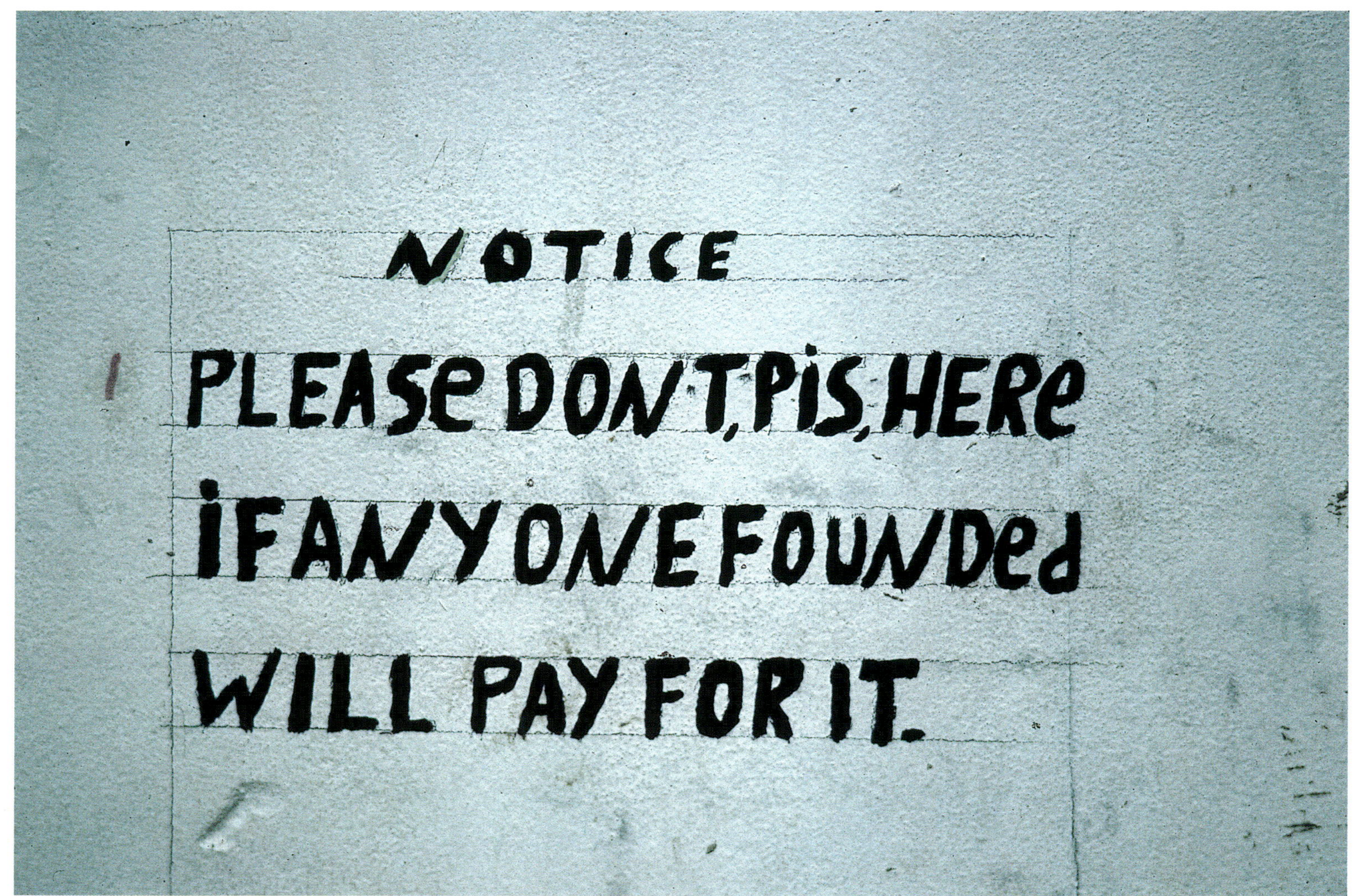
NOTICE
PLEASE DON T, PiS, HERE
iF ANYONE FOUNDed
WILL PAY FOR IT.

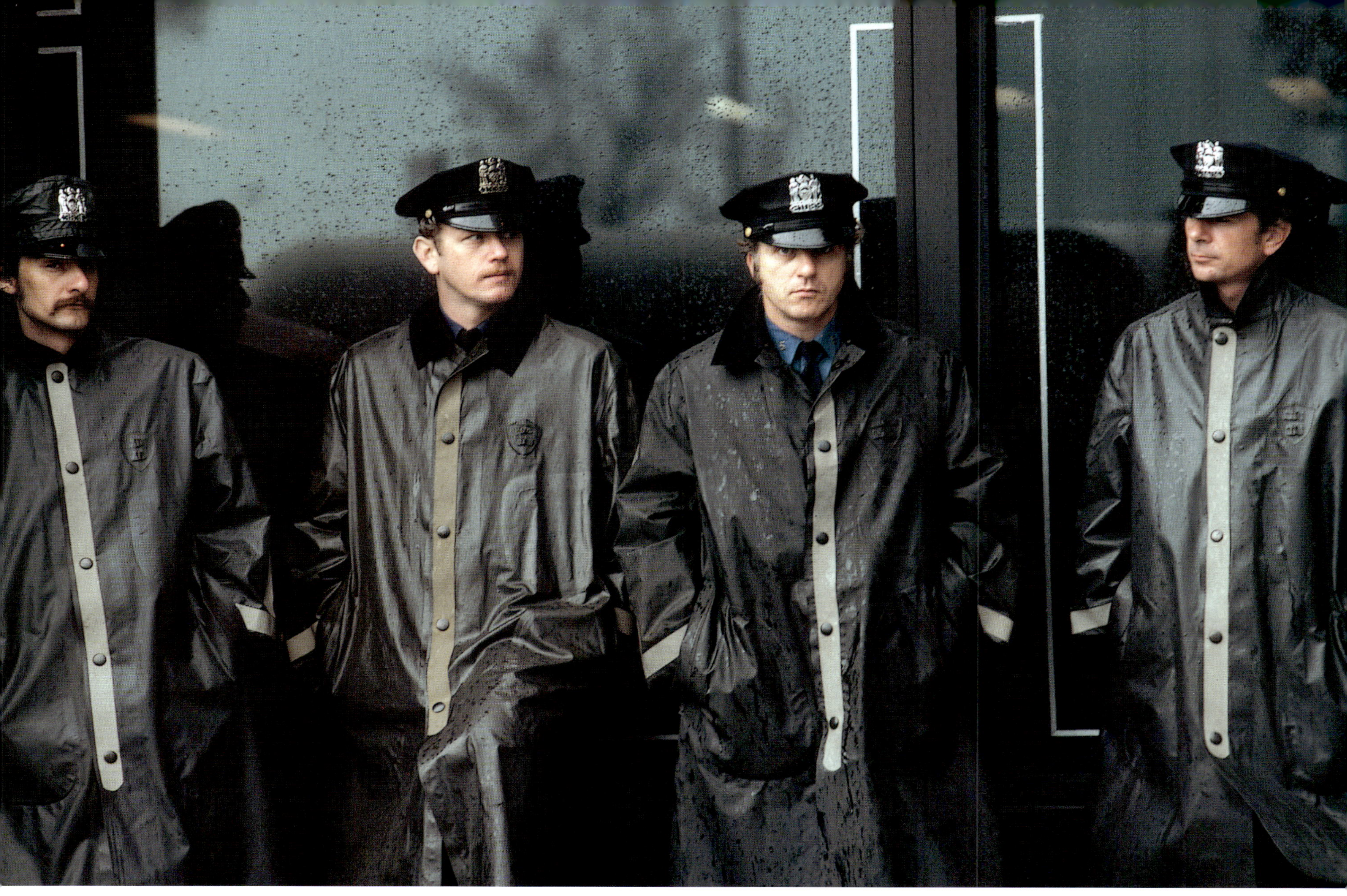

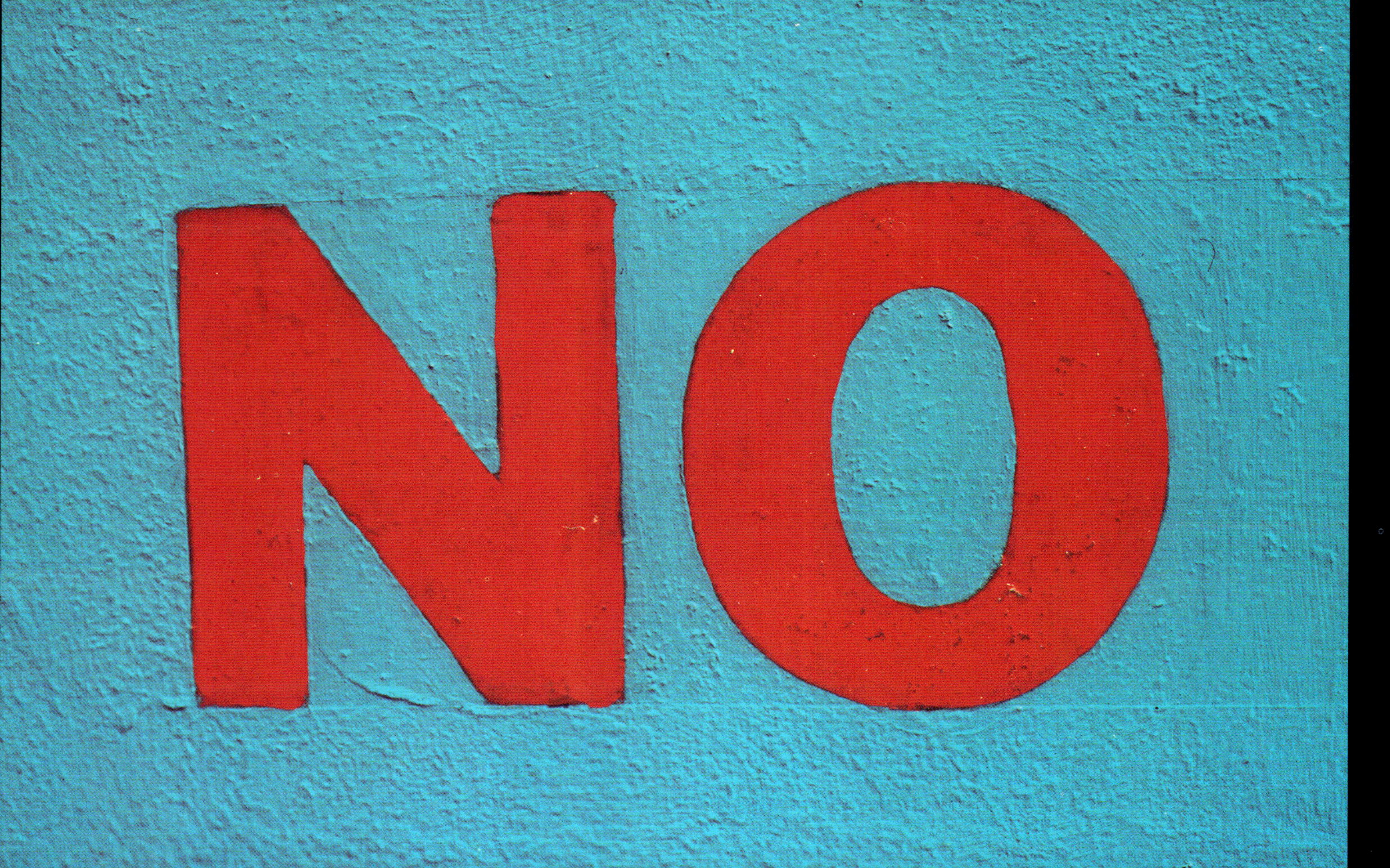
NO

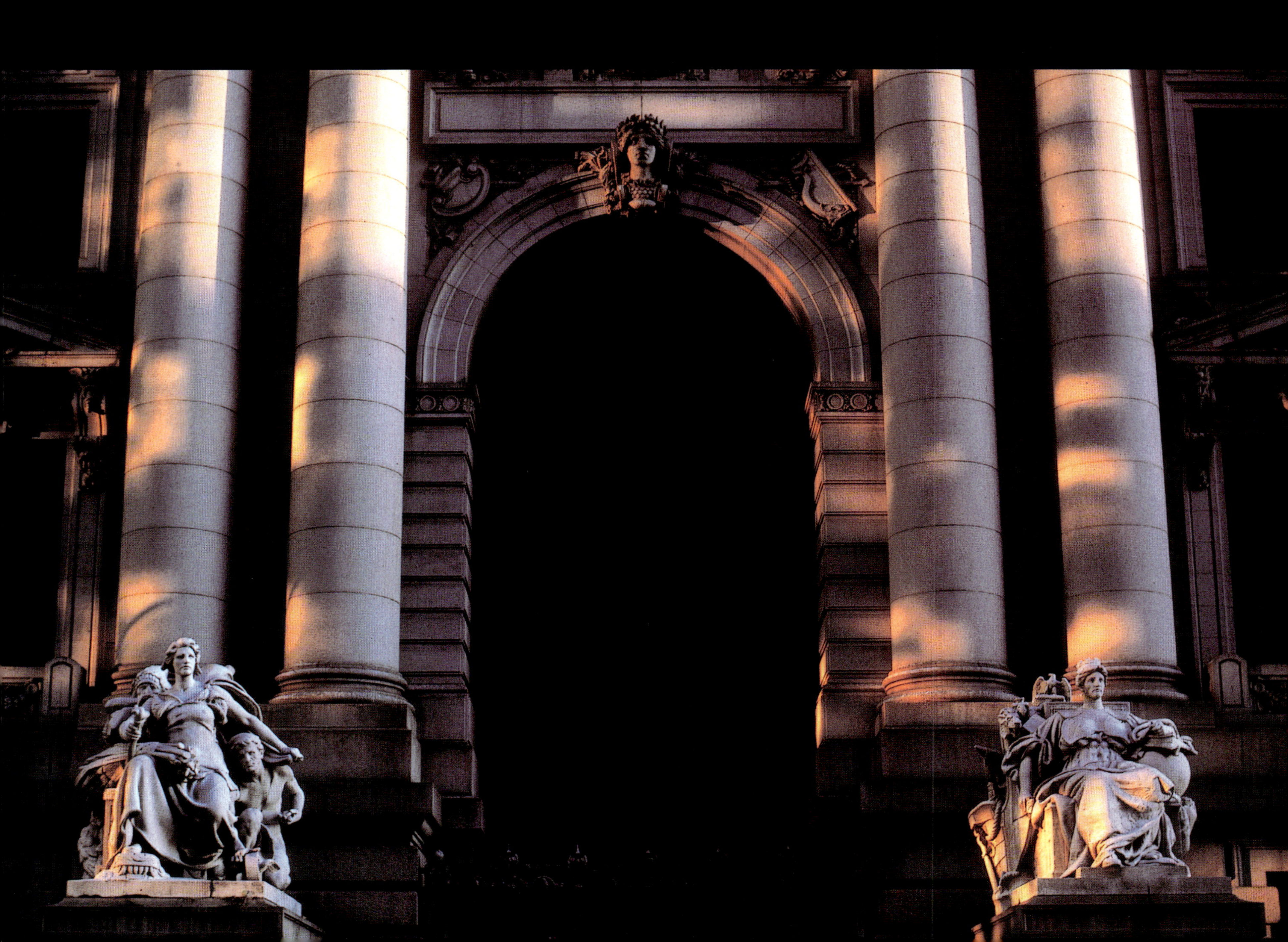

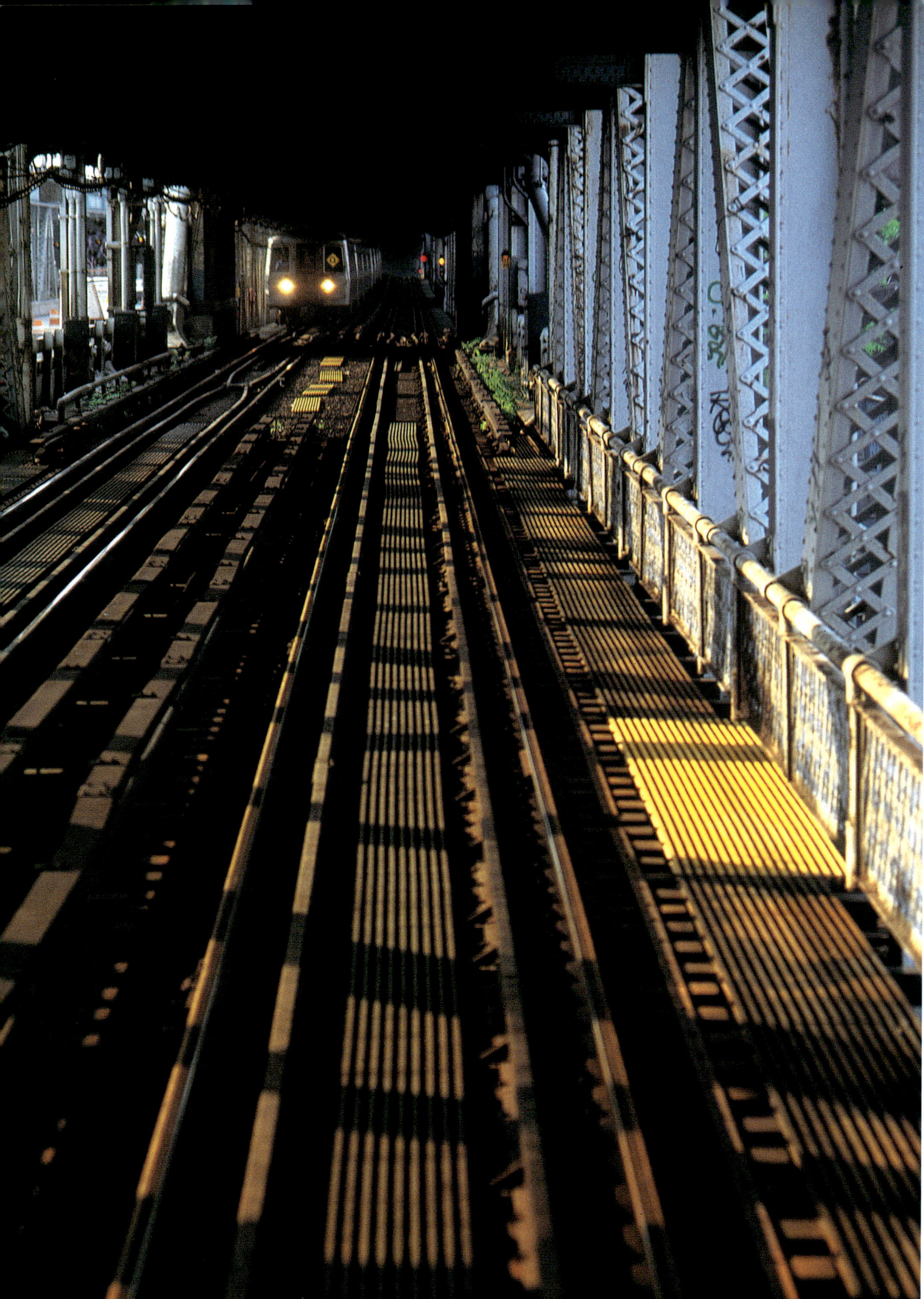

Subway over the Manhattan Bridge.

West 57th Street.

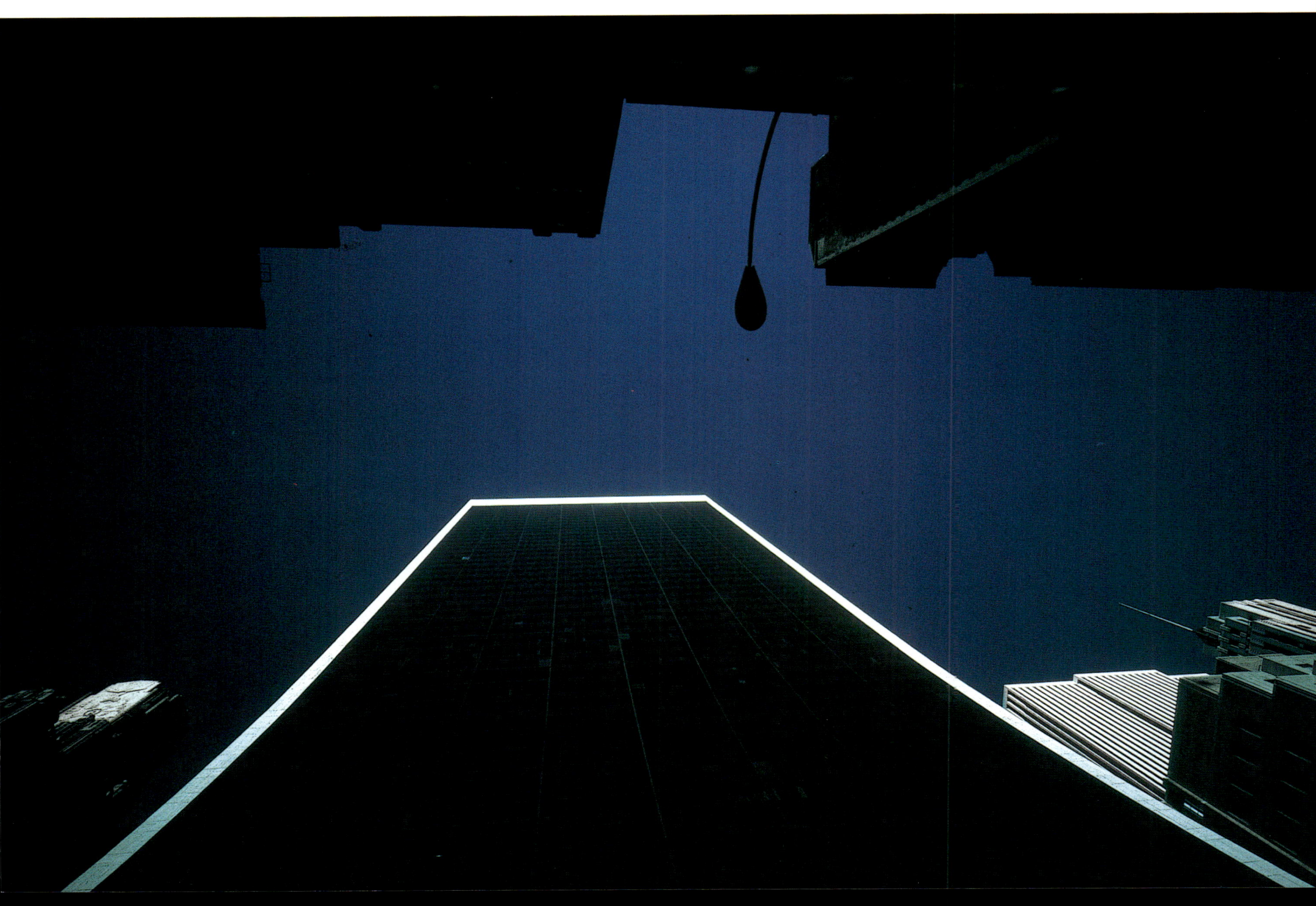

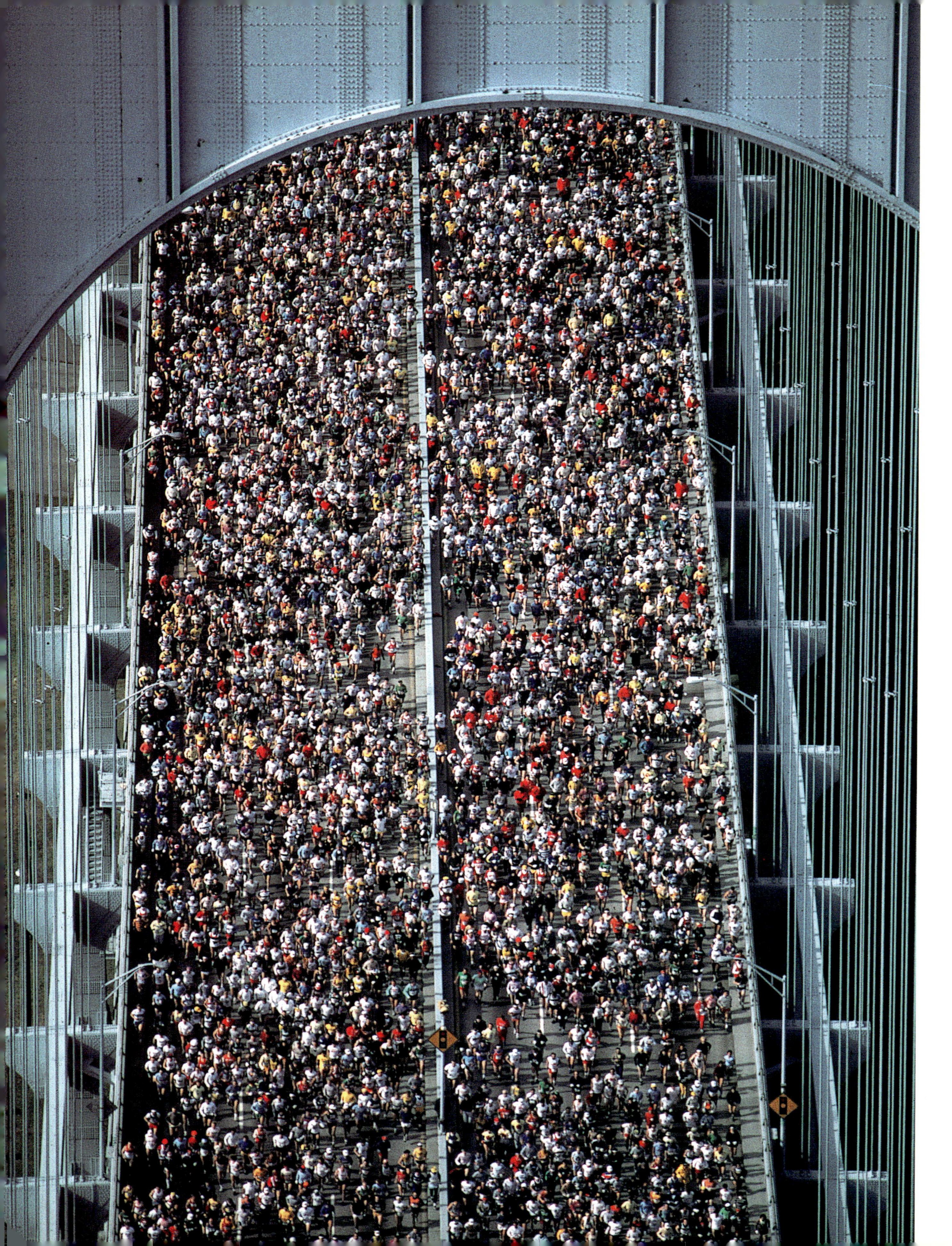

Both images are of the Verrazano Narrows Bridge.

On the left is the beginning of the NYC Marathon.

On the right, Gravesend Bay, with ships anchored.

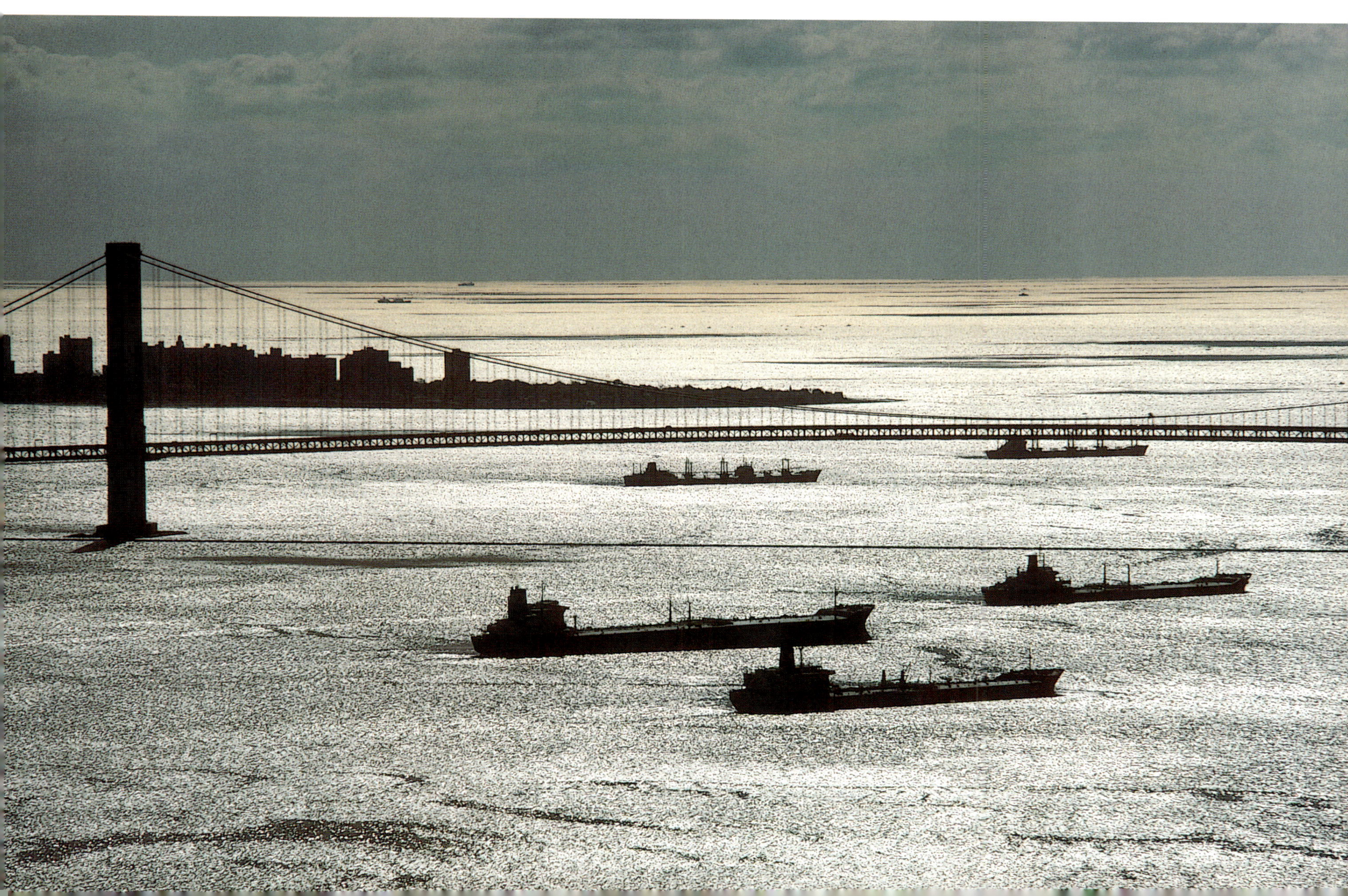

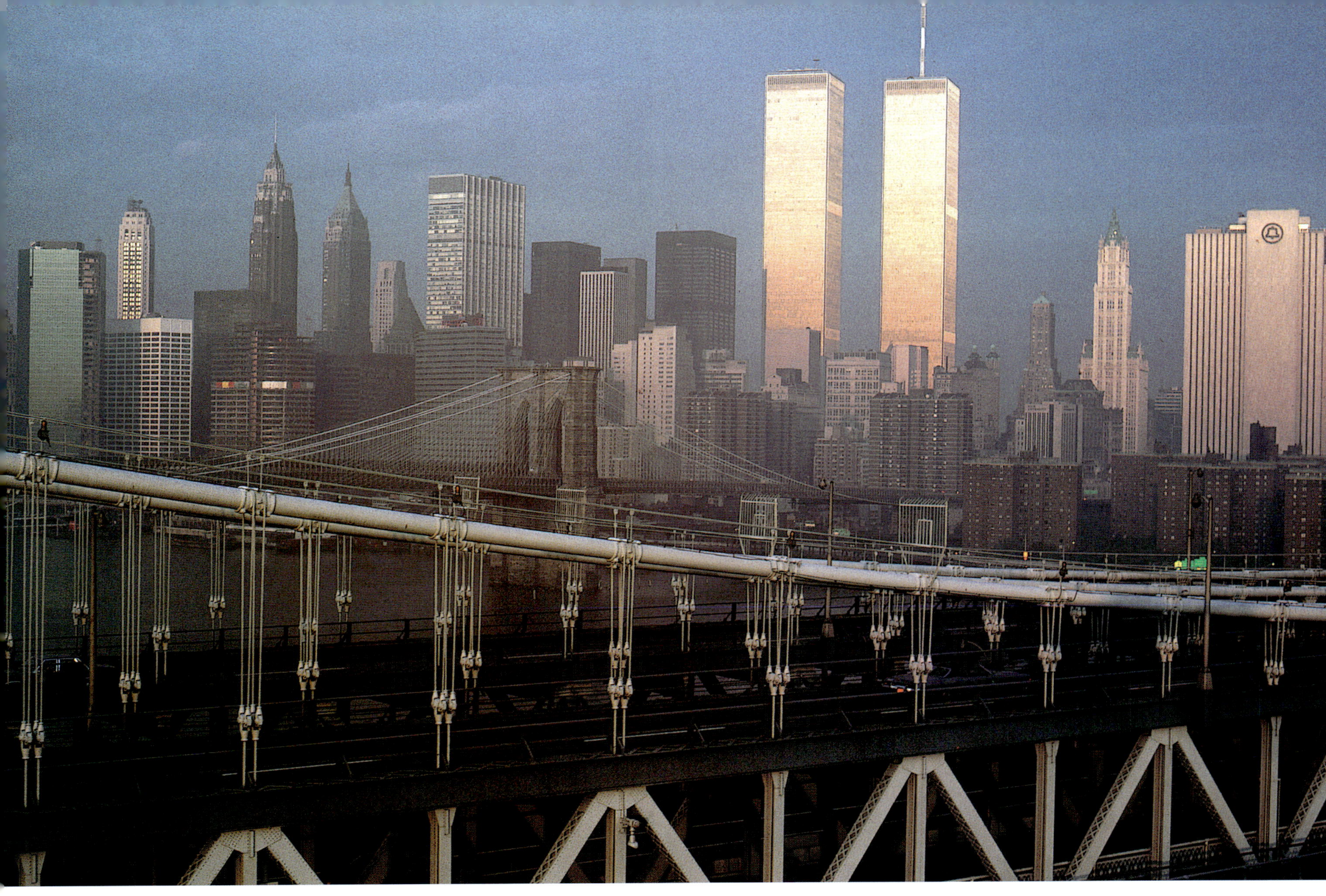

The Manhattan Bridge, with downtown New York in the background.

A compressed view of the Brooklyn Bridge.

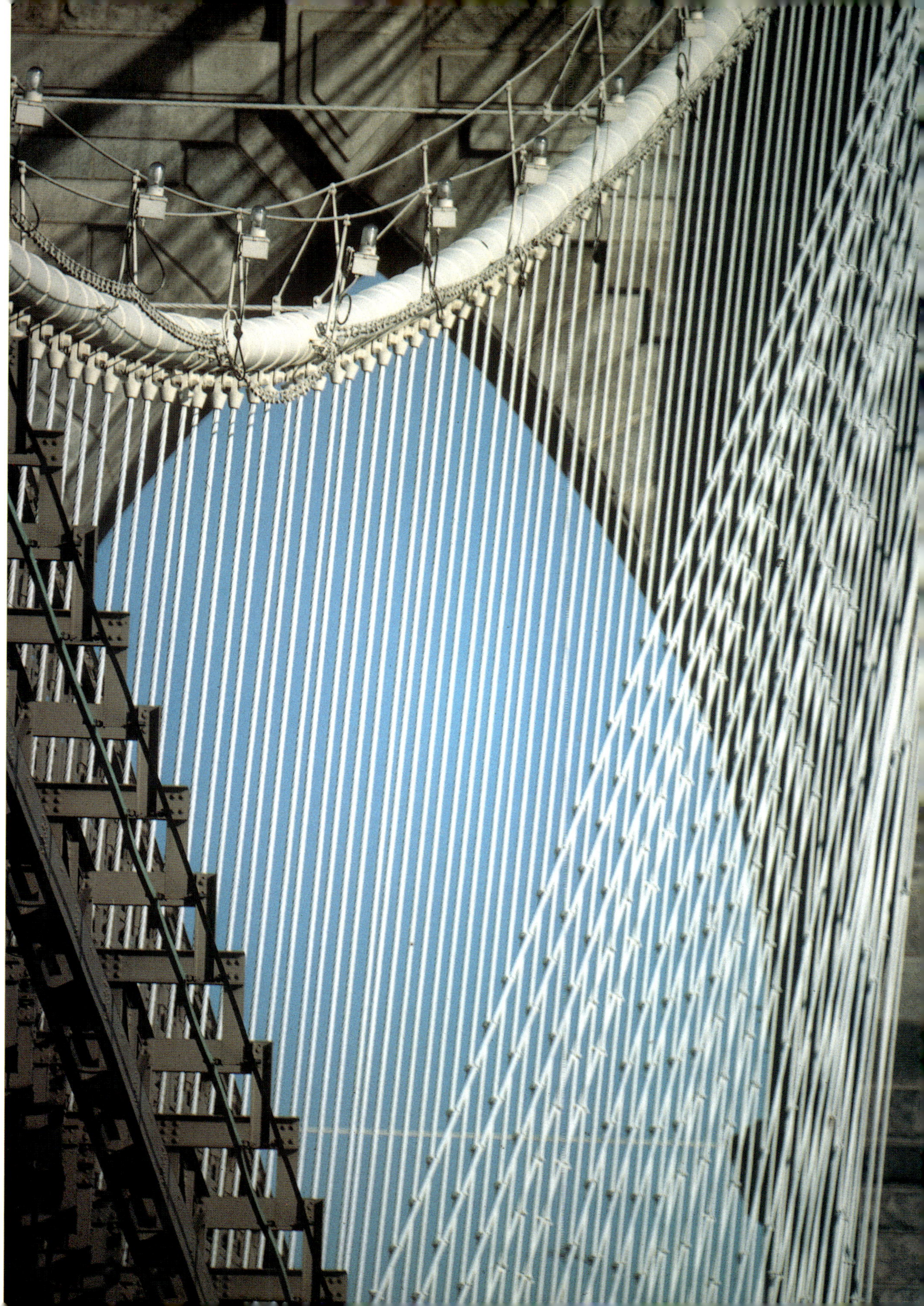

The Brooklyn Bridge during a transit strike.

Thousands walked to and from work.

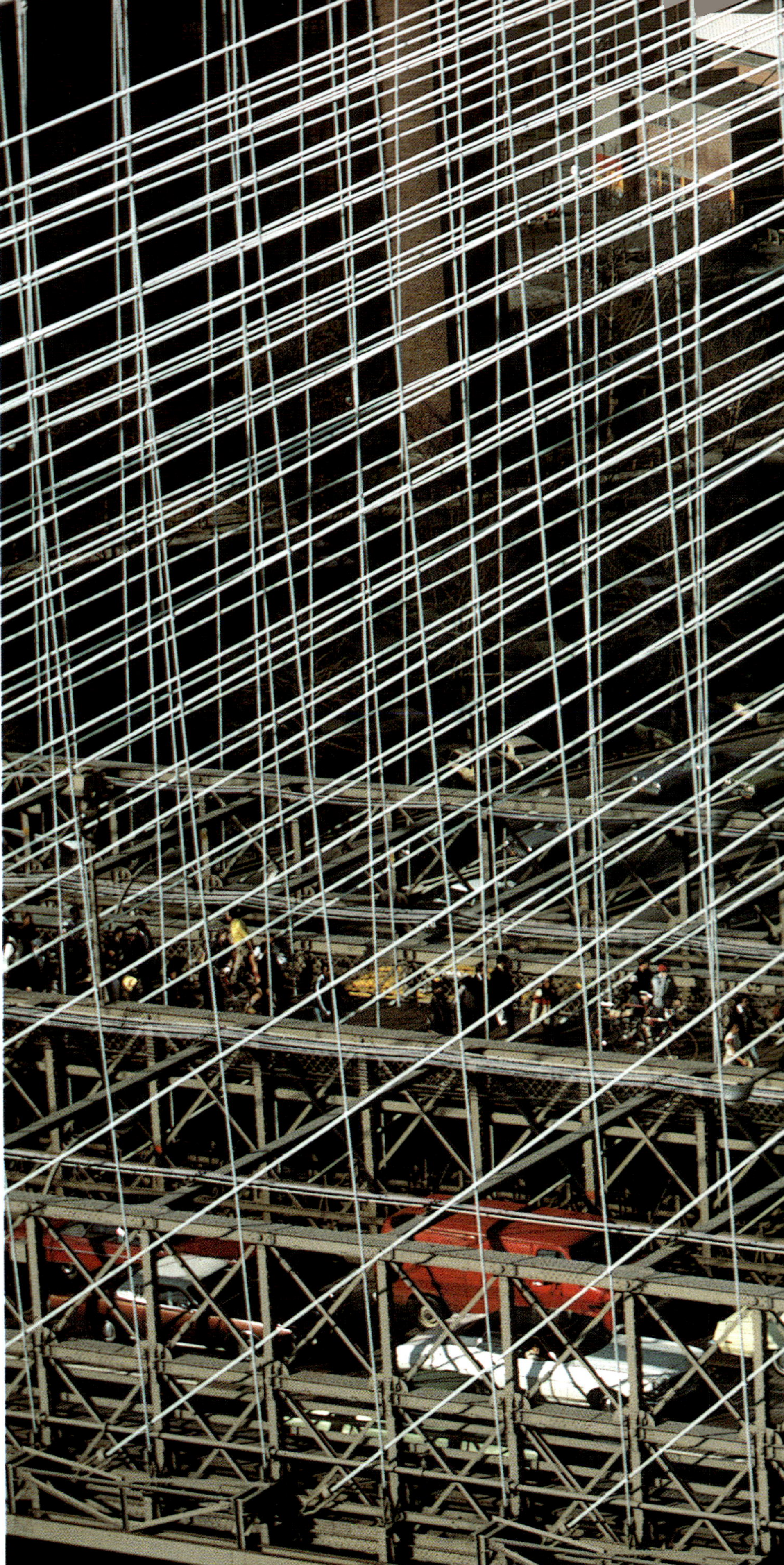

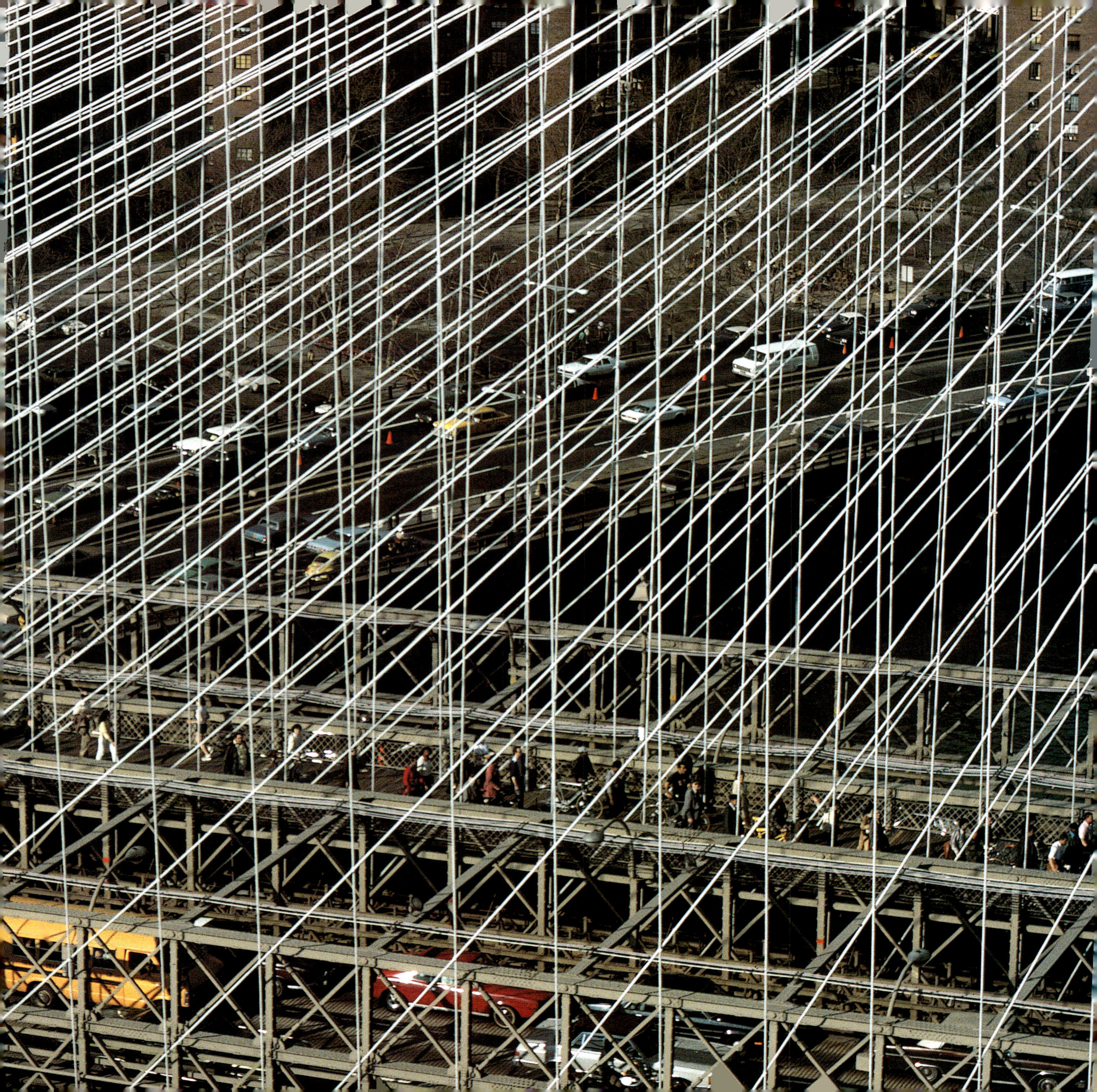

I shot a great deal of the construction of this building next door to me, which would eventually block my view.

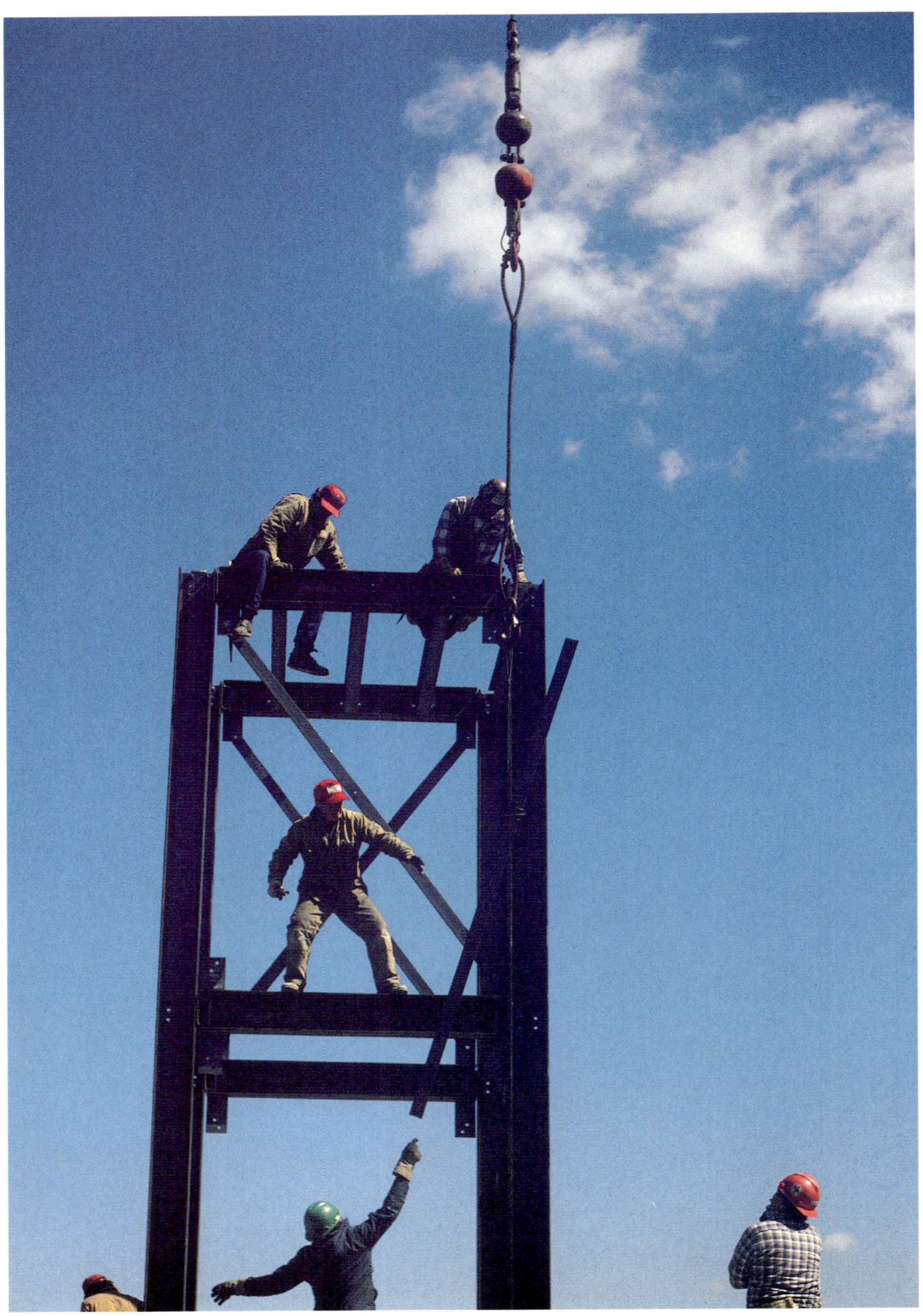

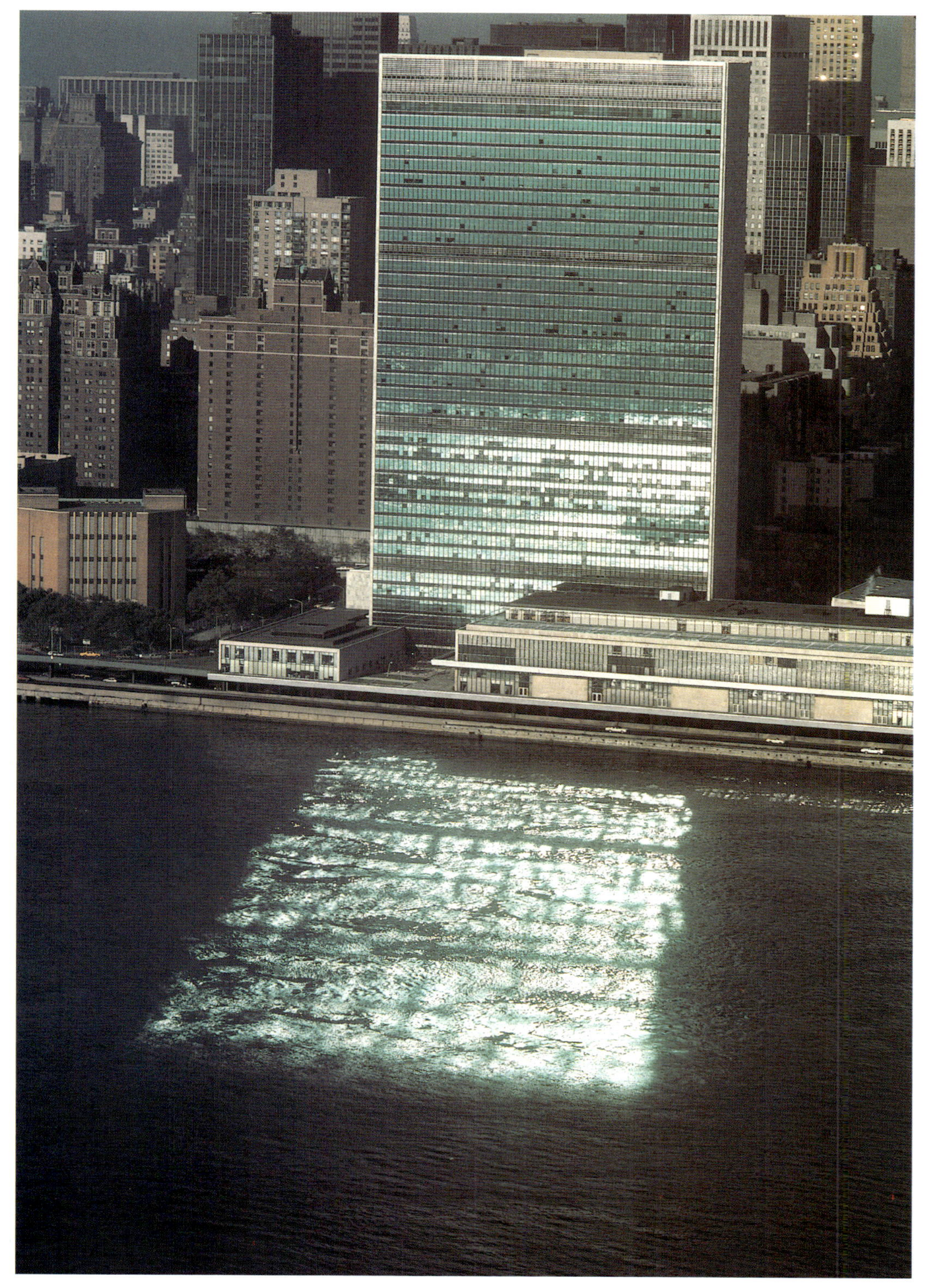

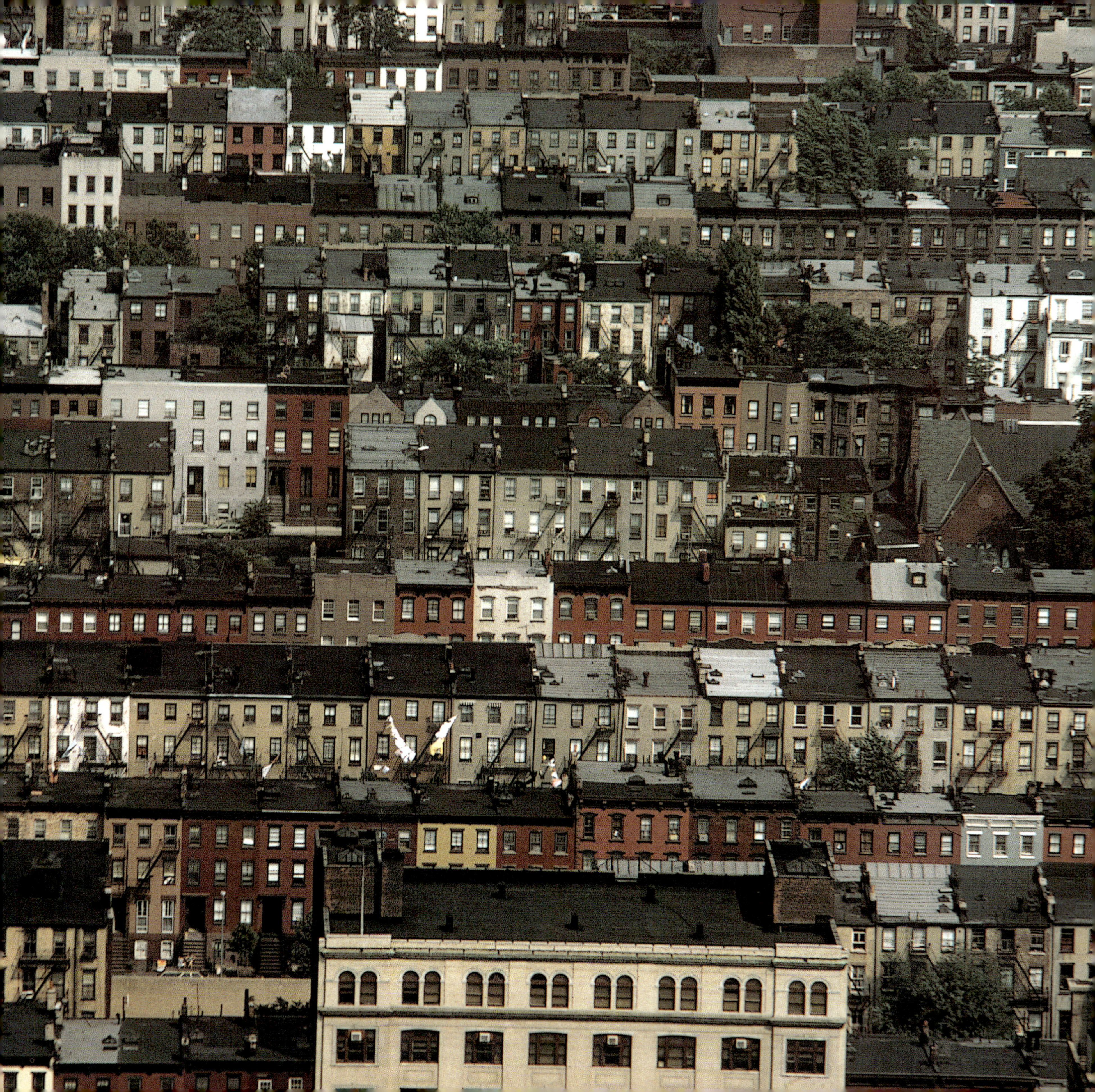

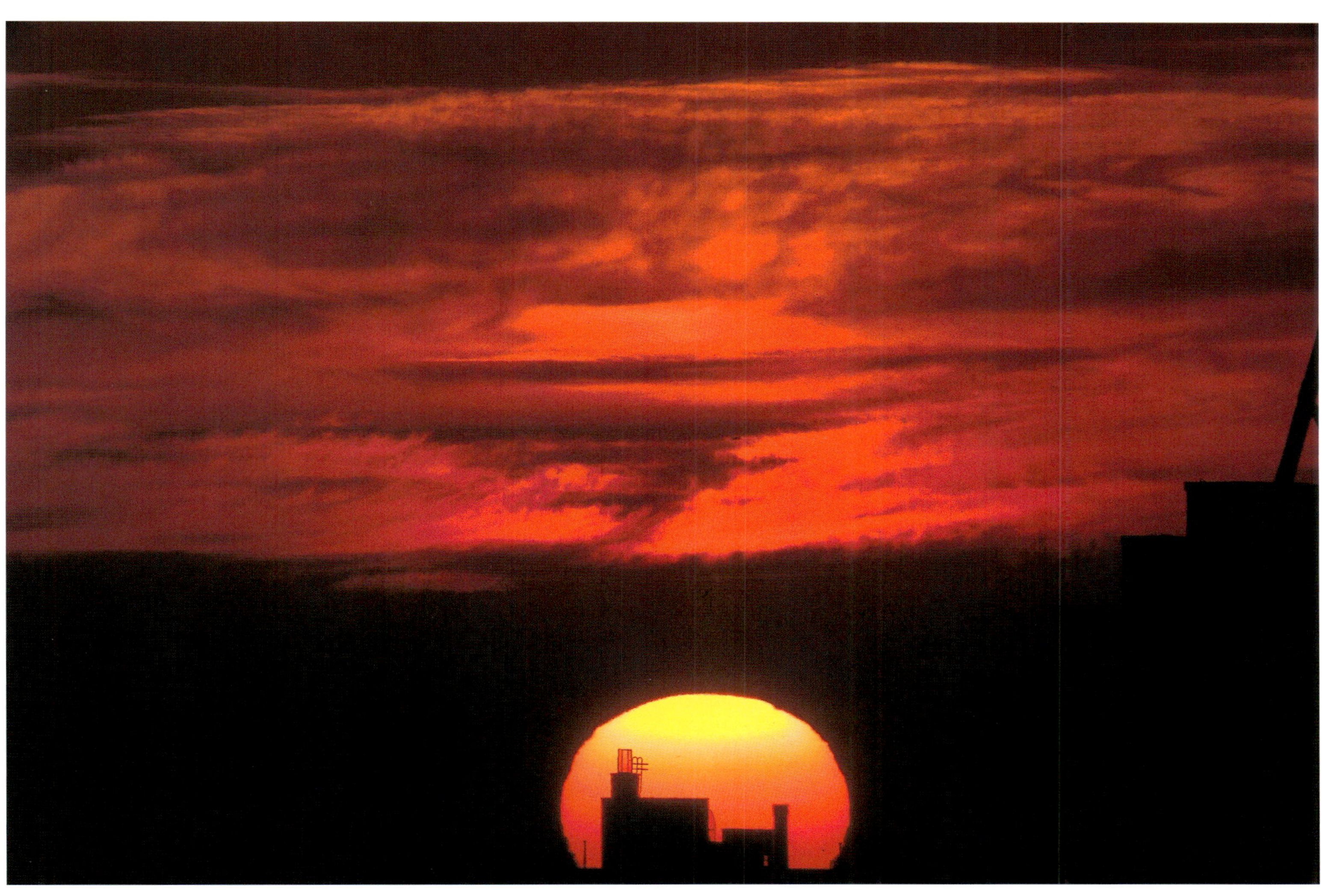

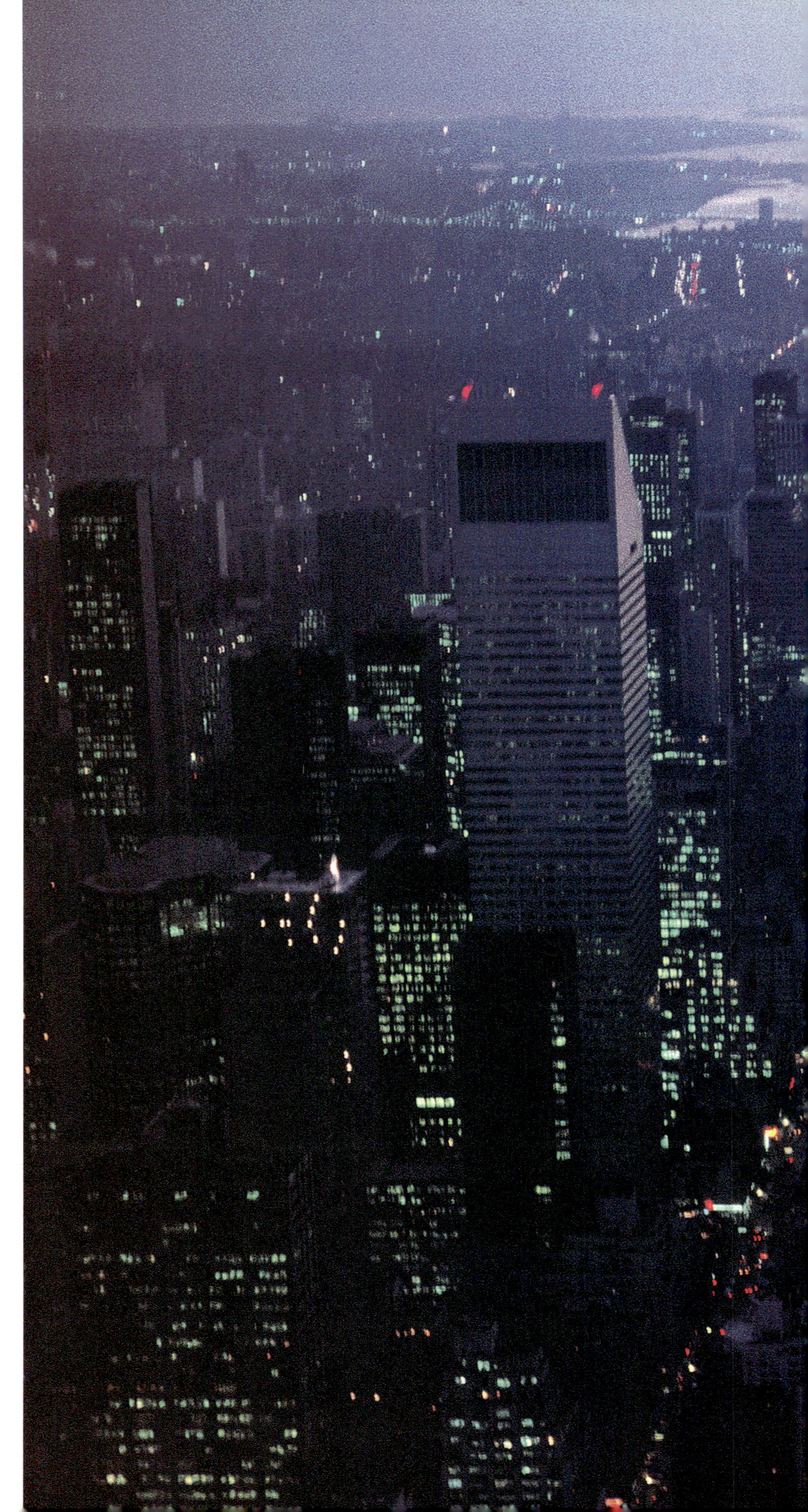

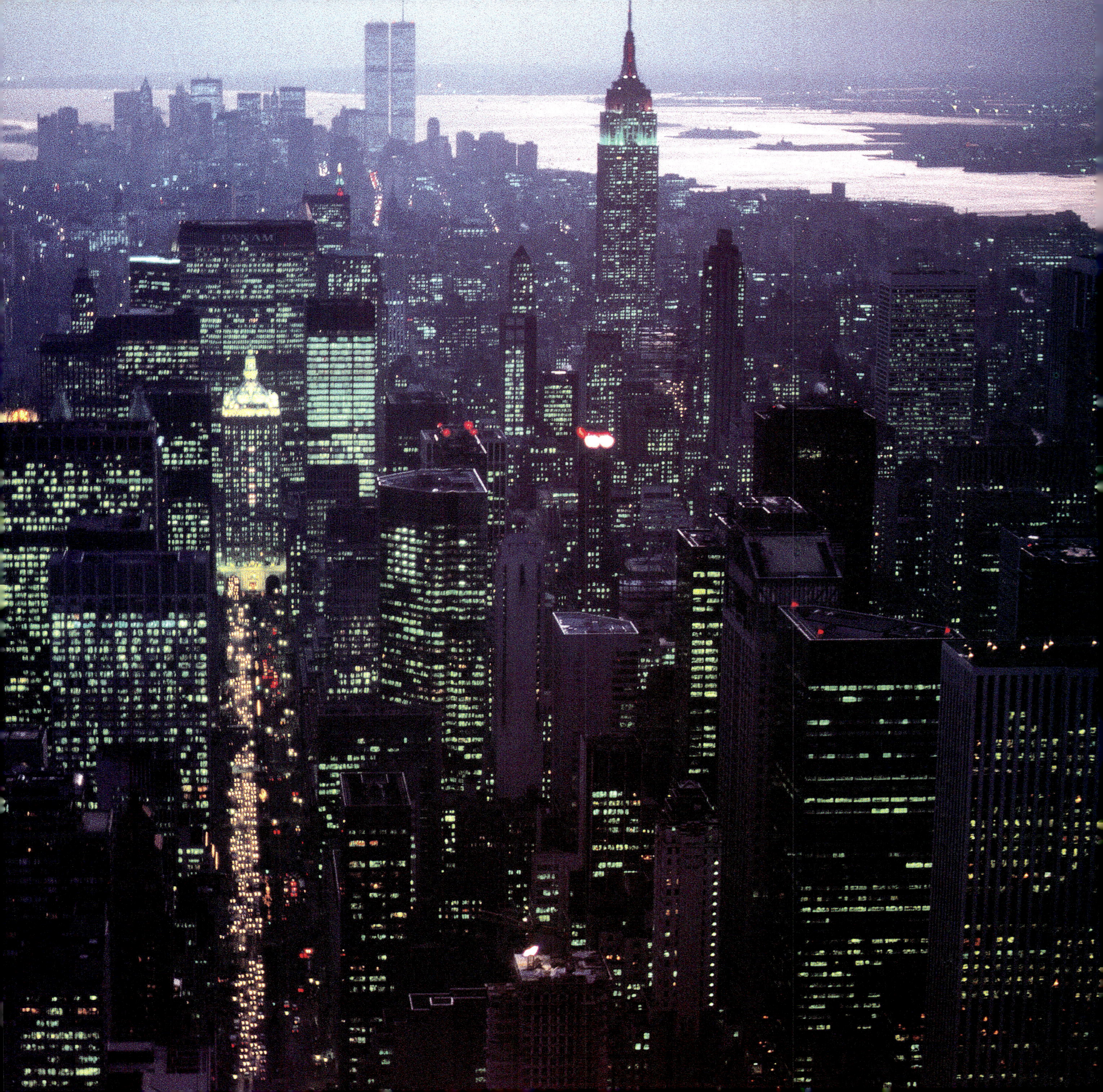

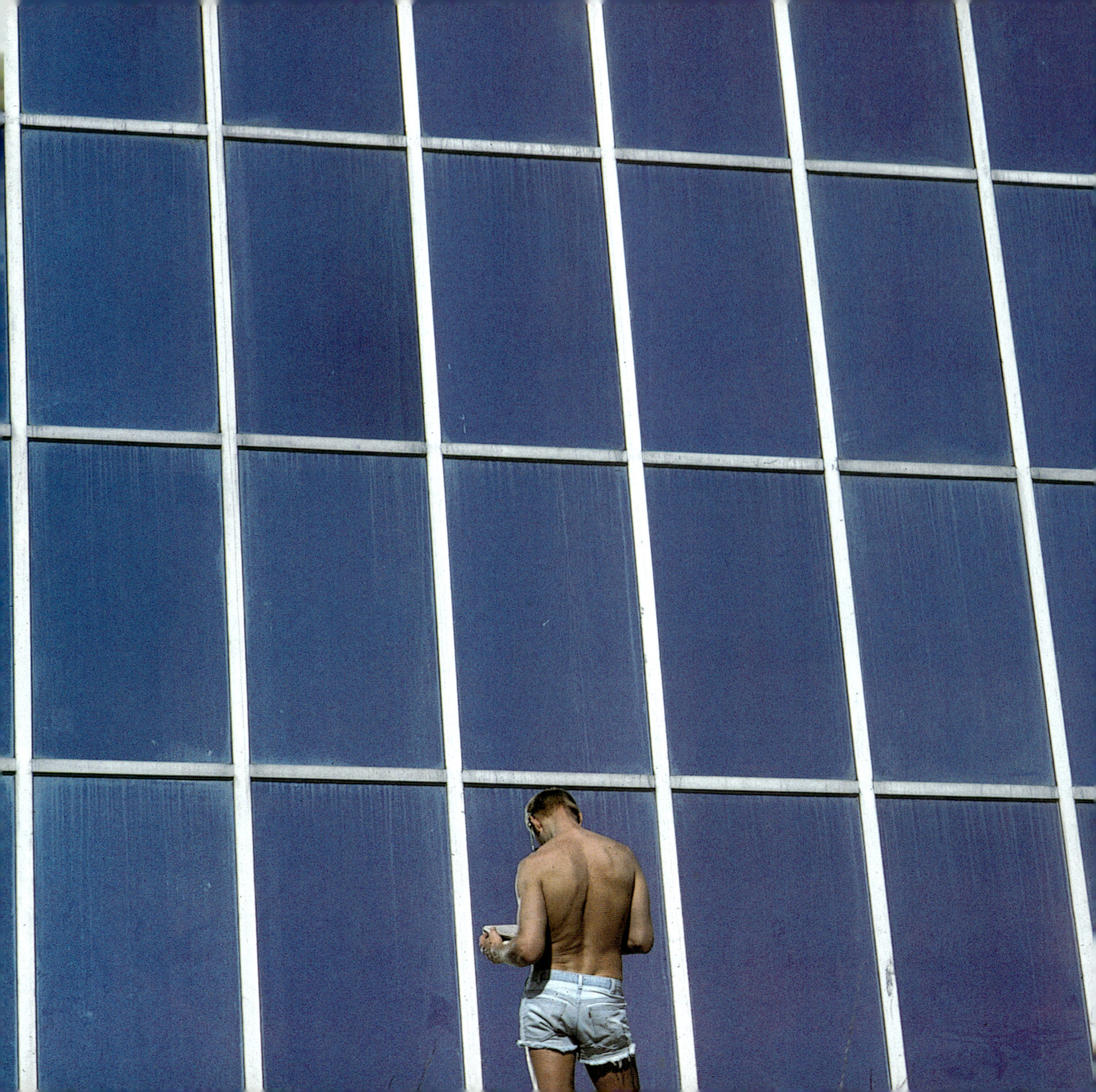

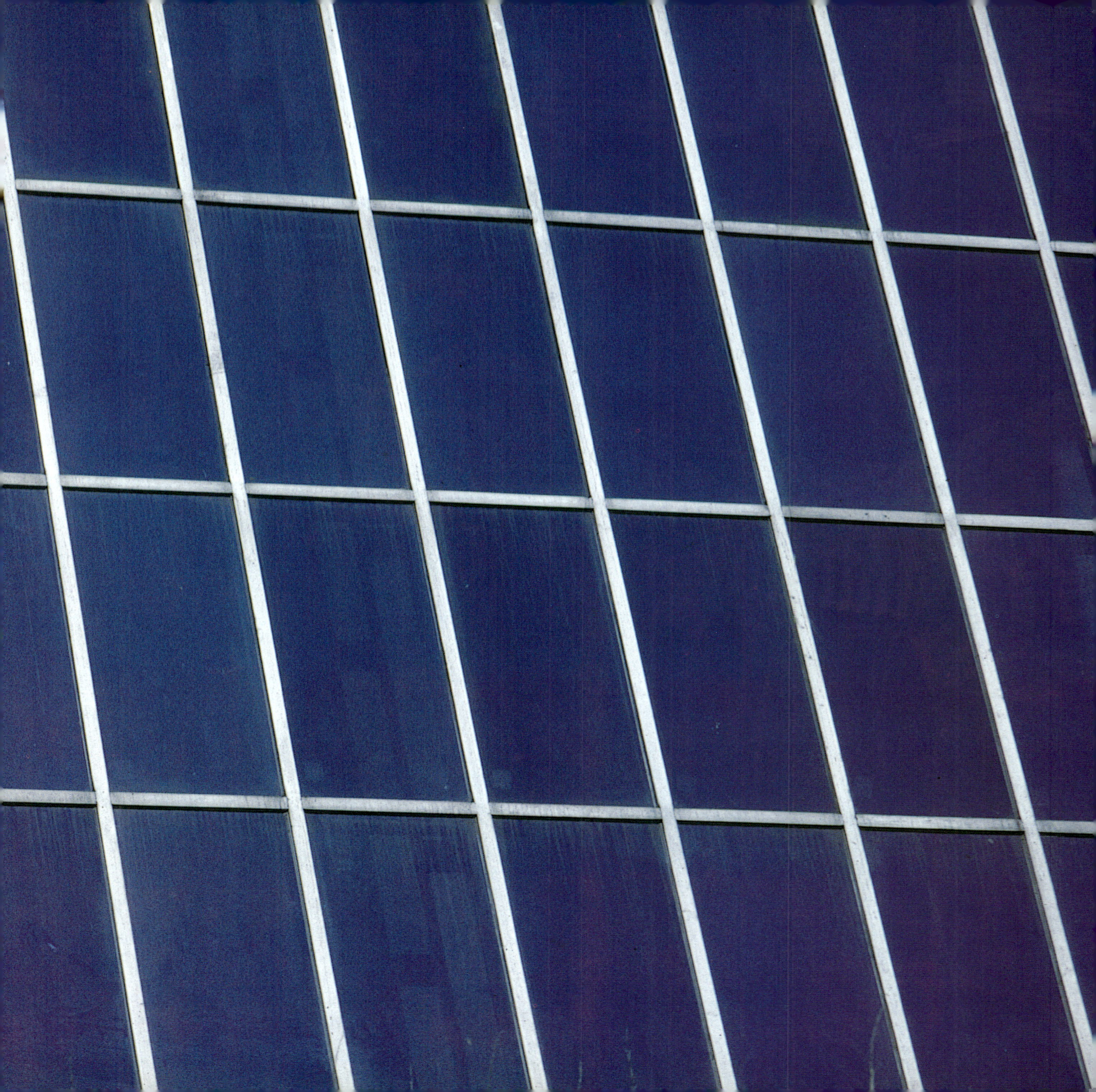

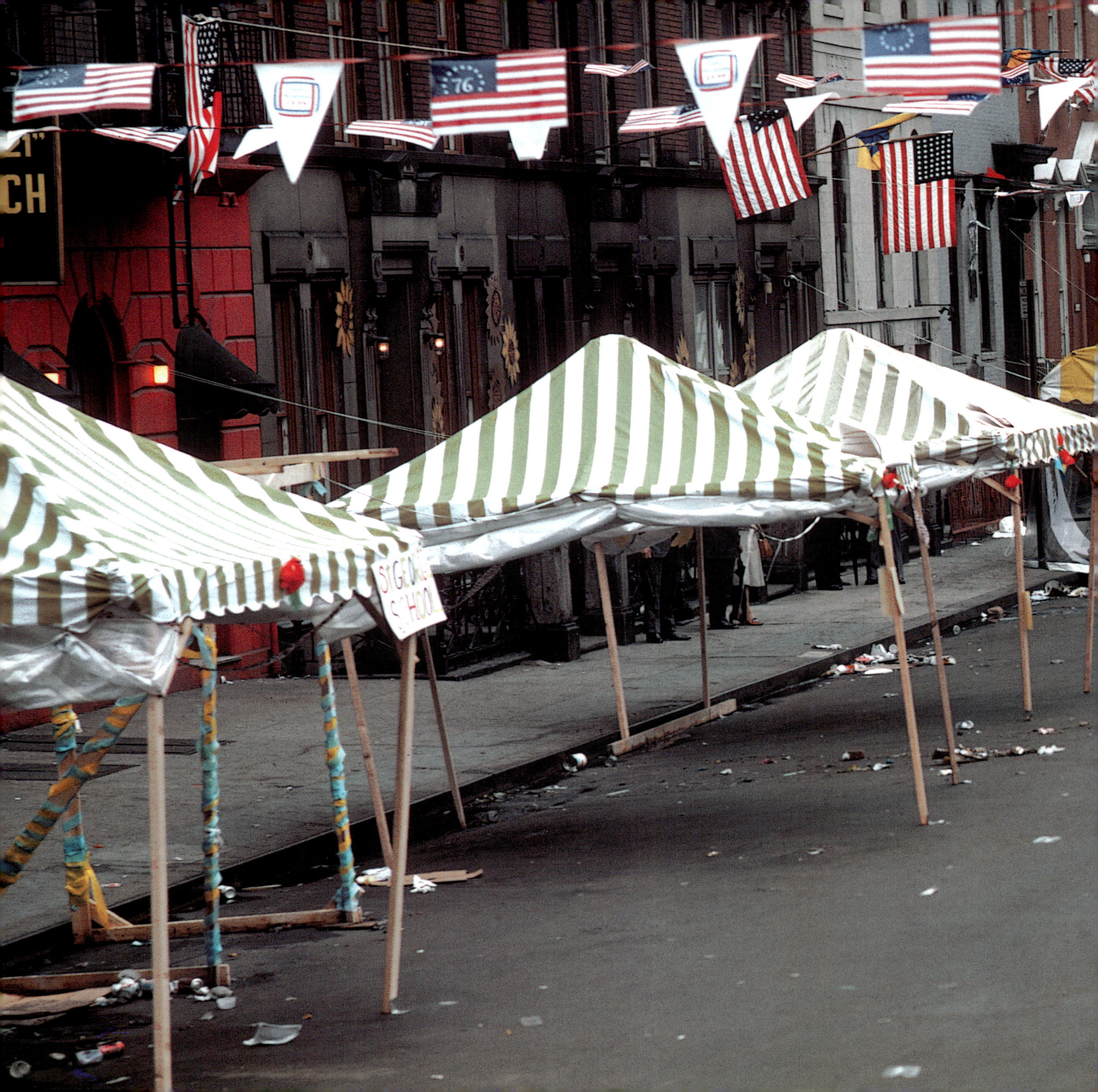
76

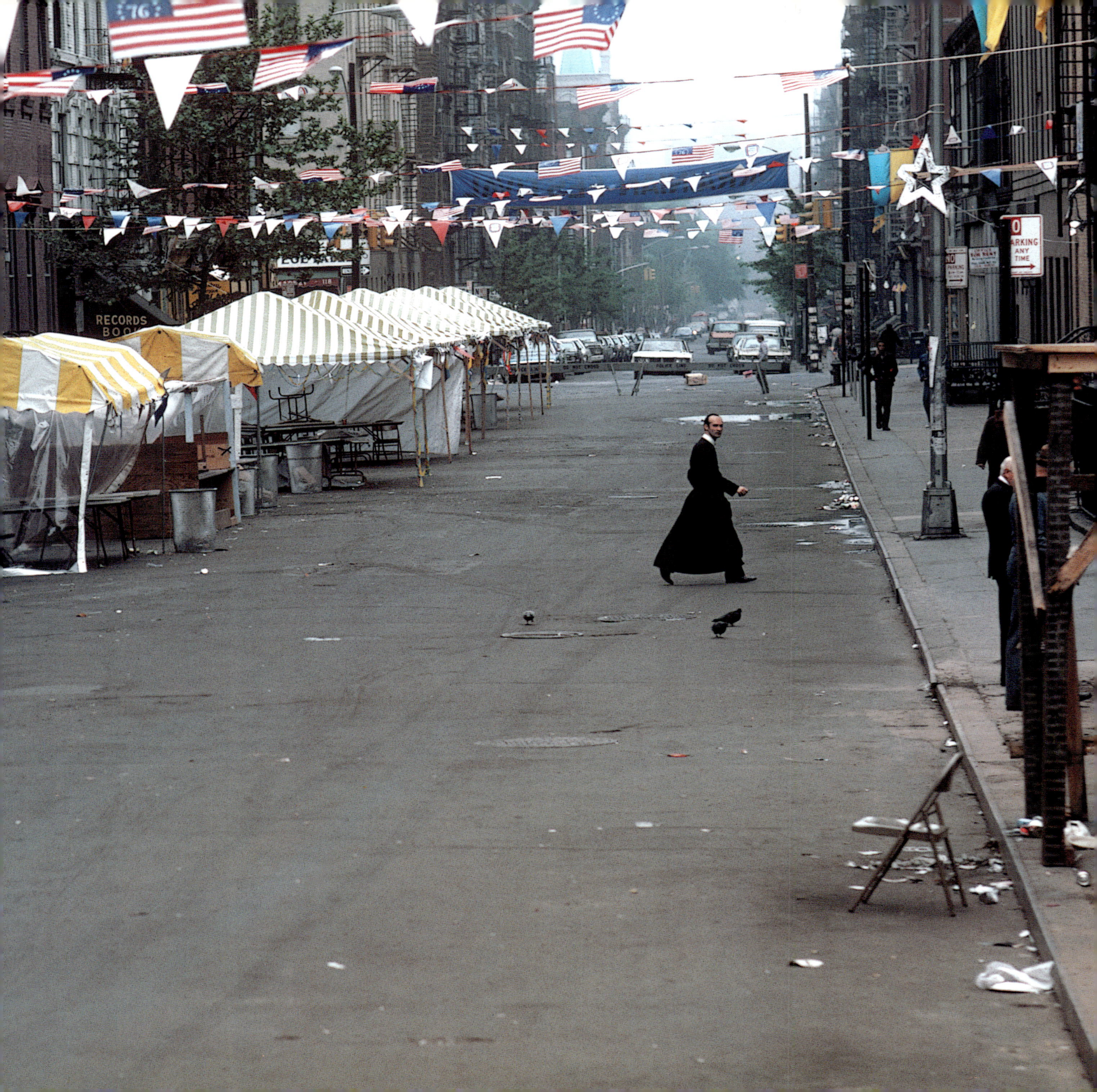

RECORDS
76
ANY TIME

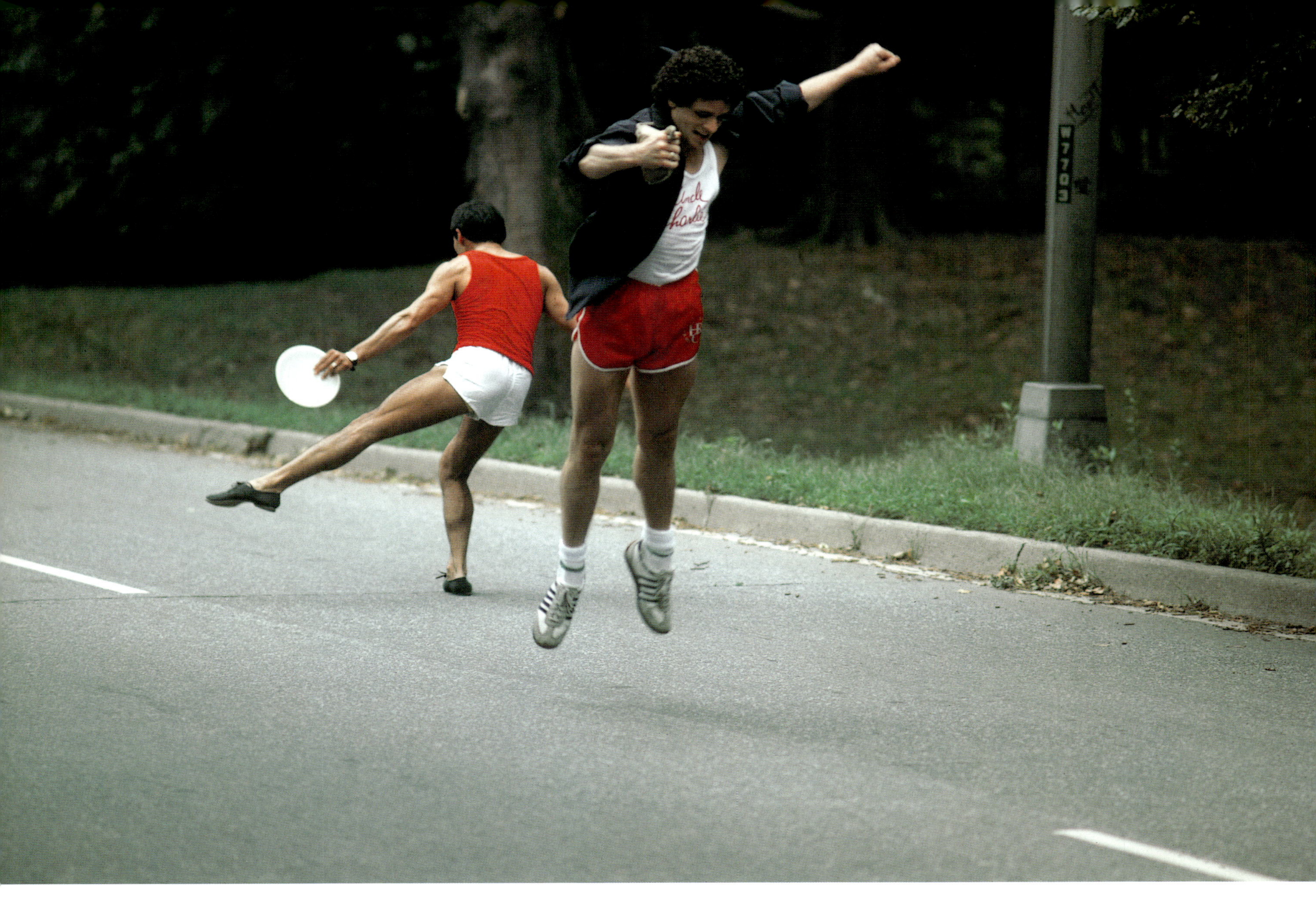
W7703

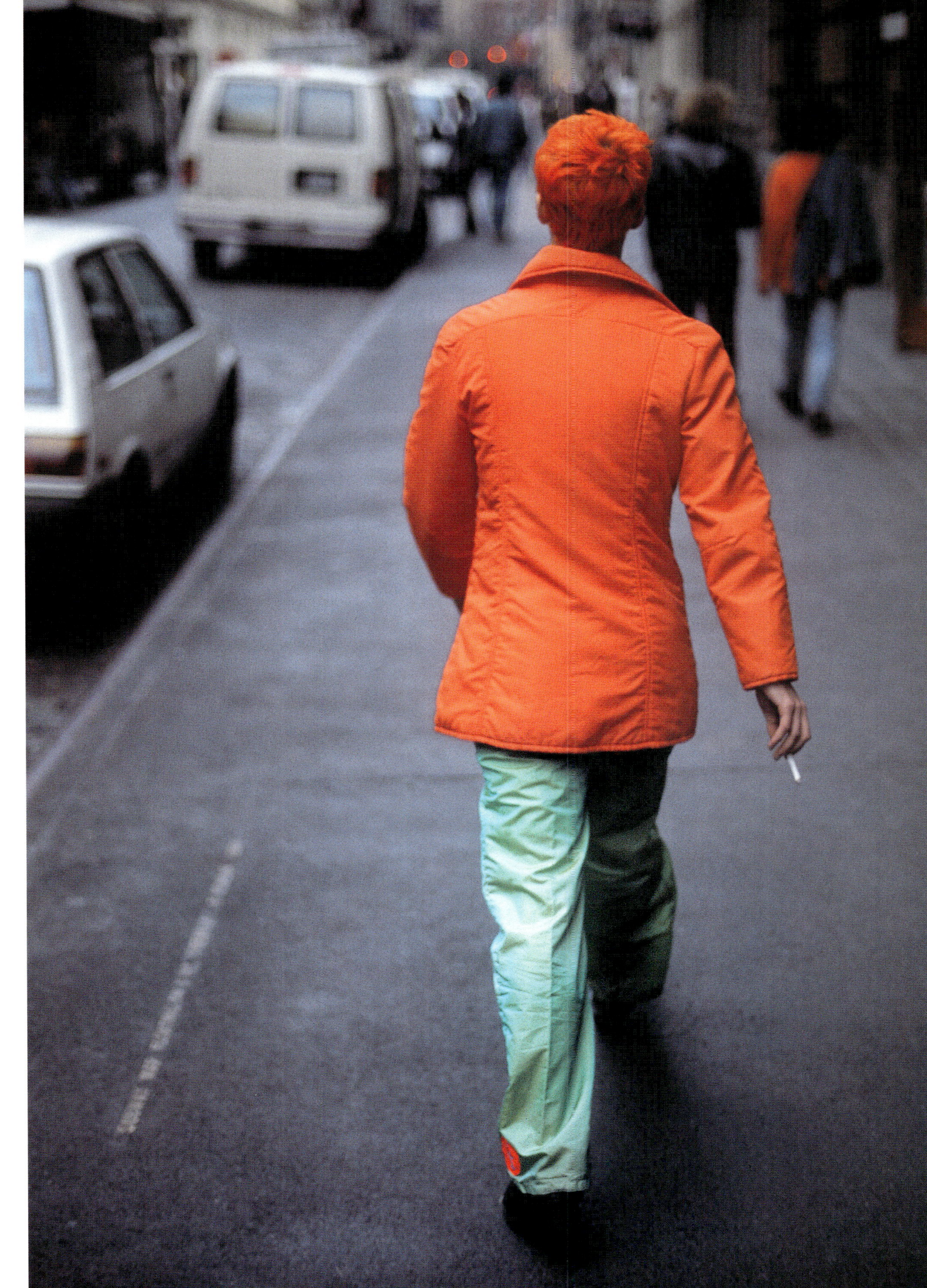

Rockefeller Center wall near 50th Street.

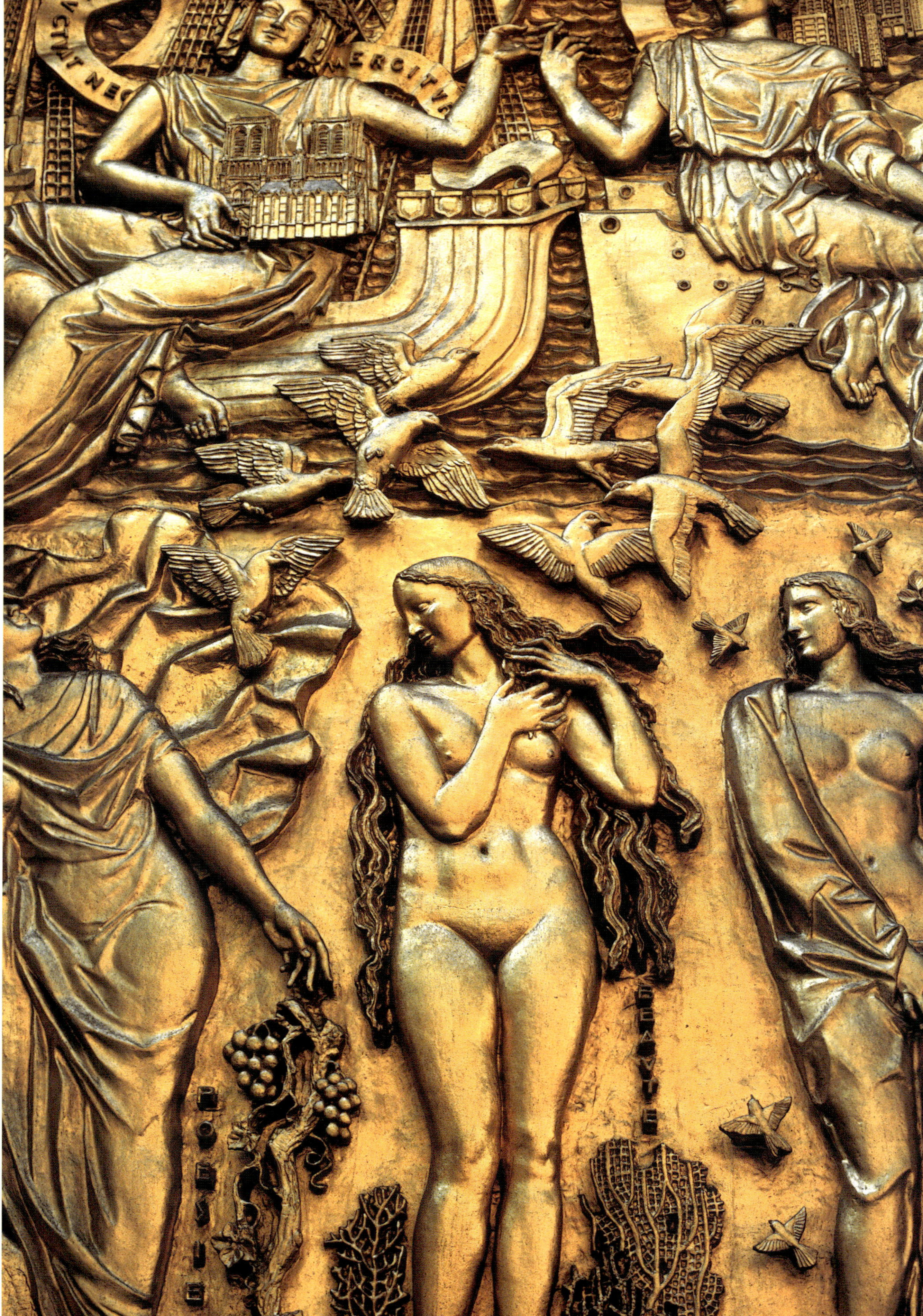

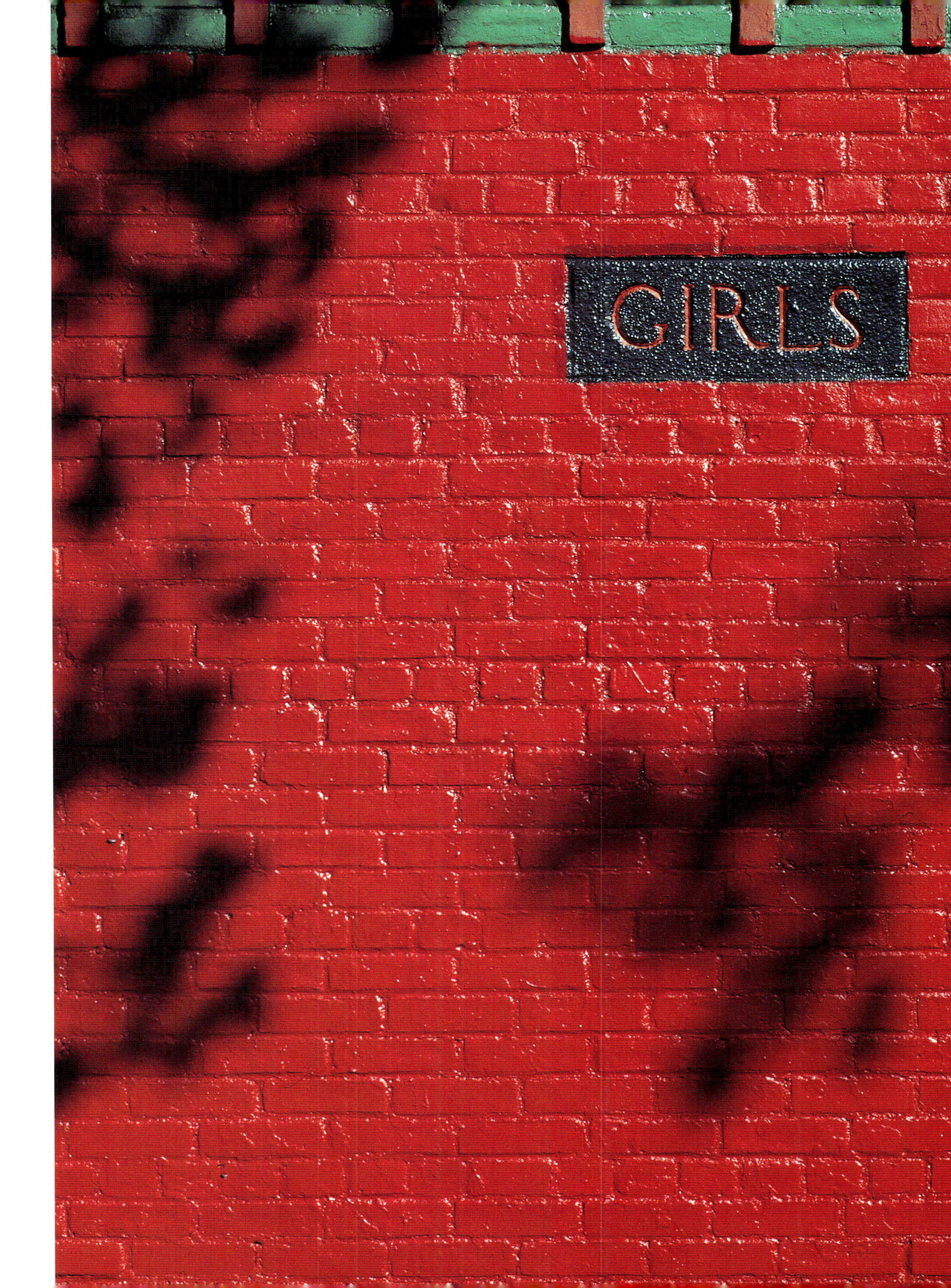
GIRLS

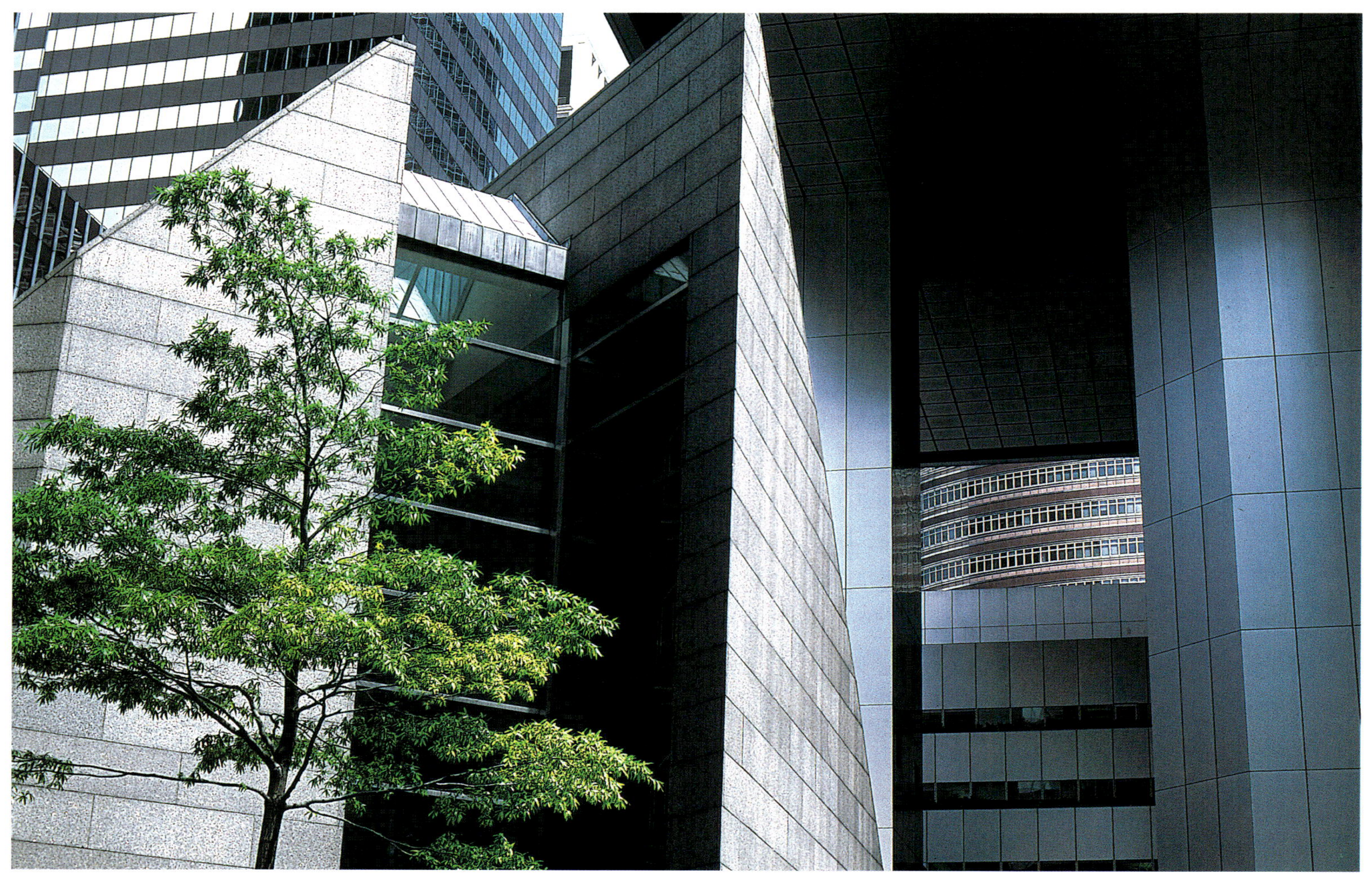

Street level view of Citicorp Building, with Philip Johnson's Lipstick building just visible in background.

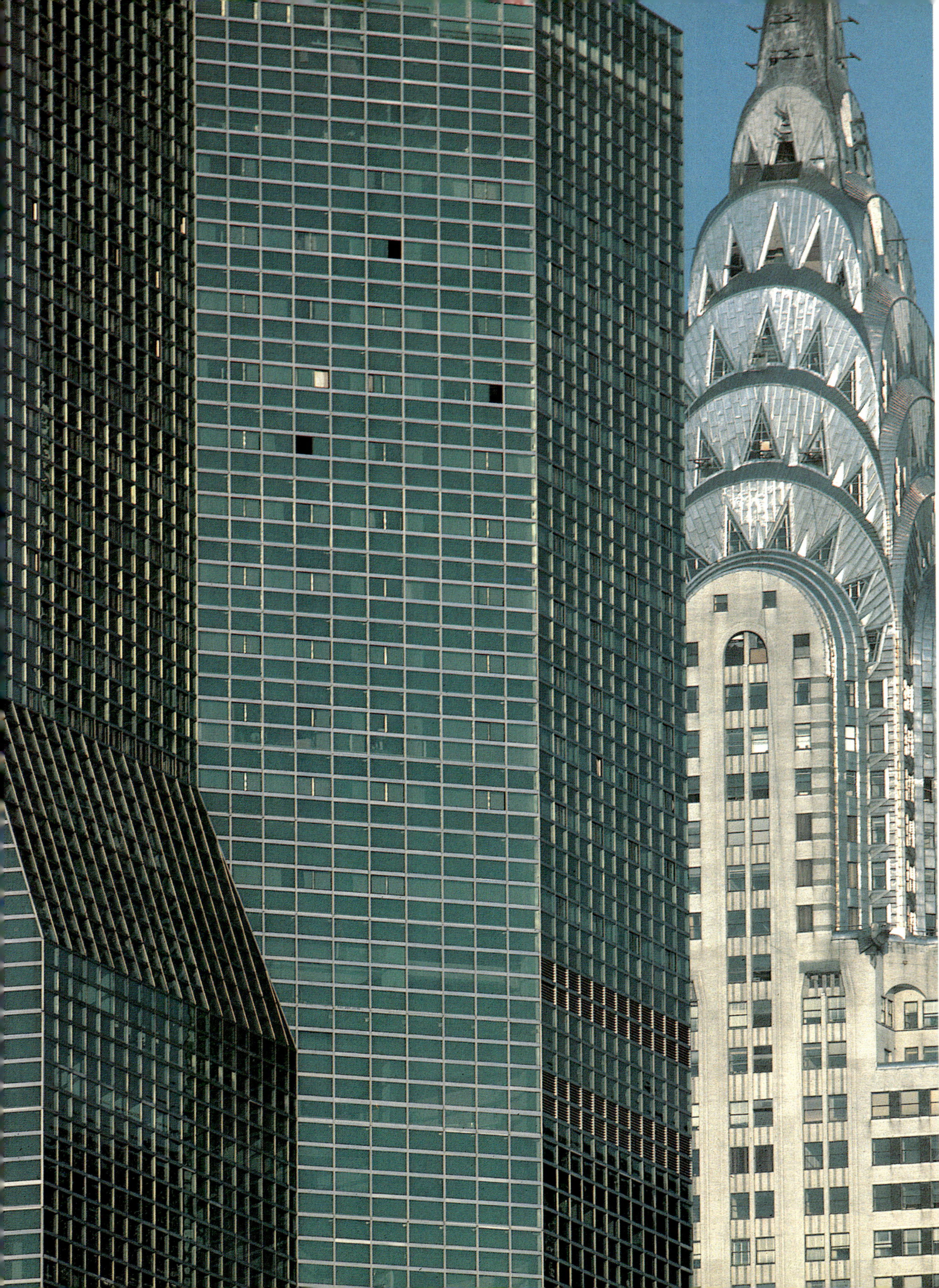

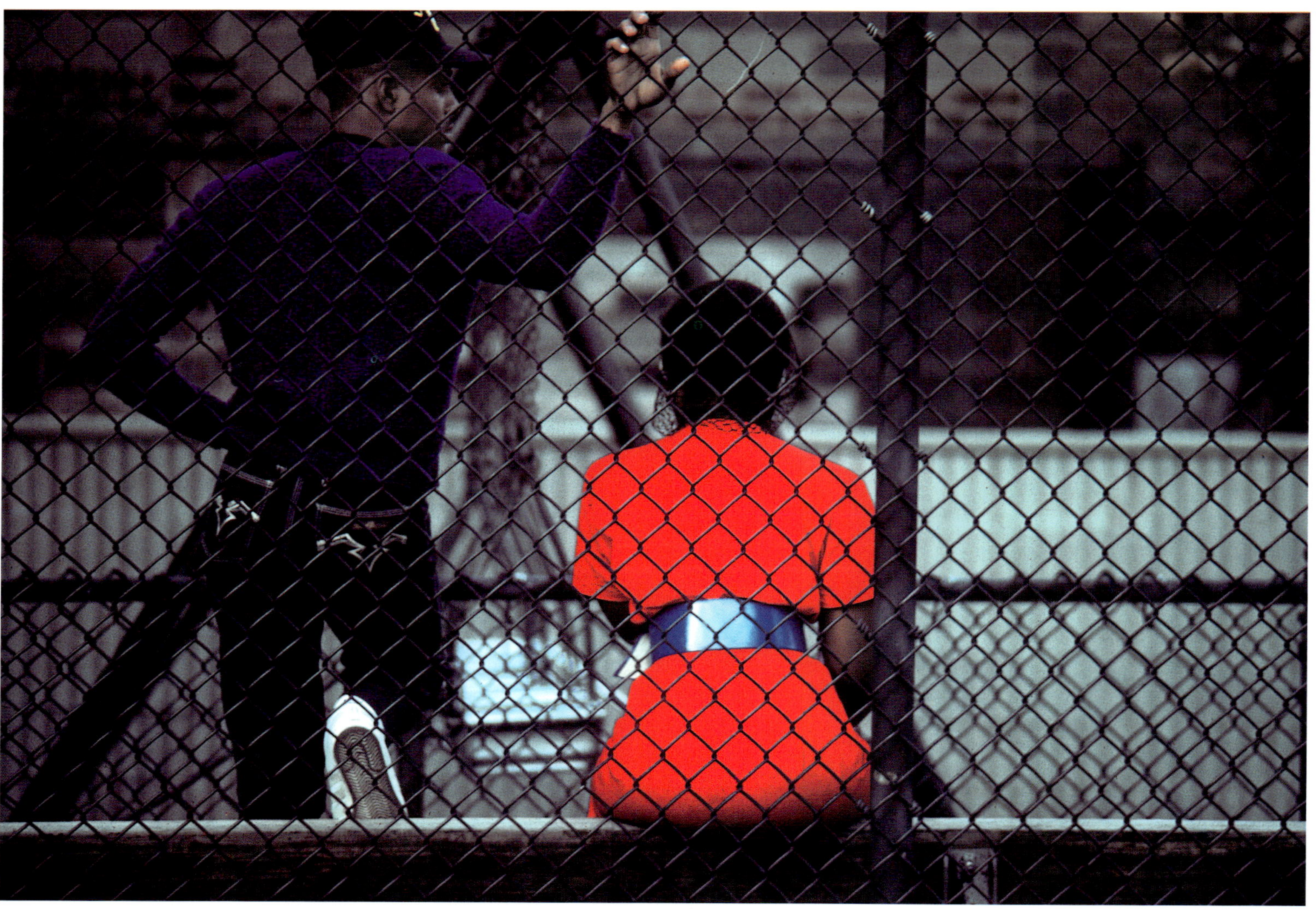

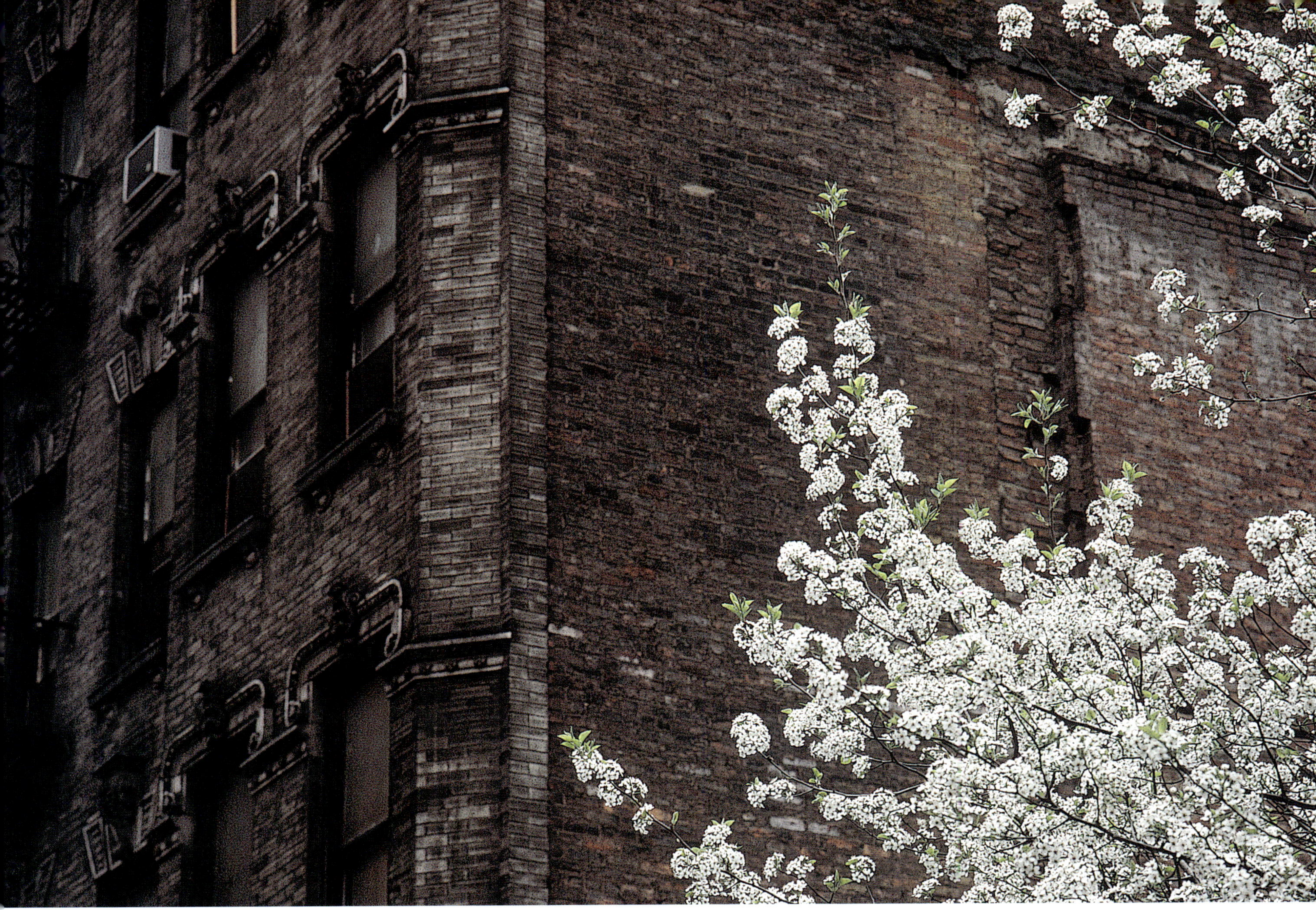

Signs of spring in New York. You mustn't blink.

It only lasts a few days.

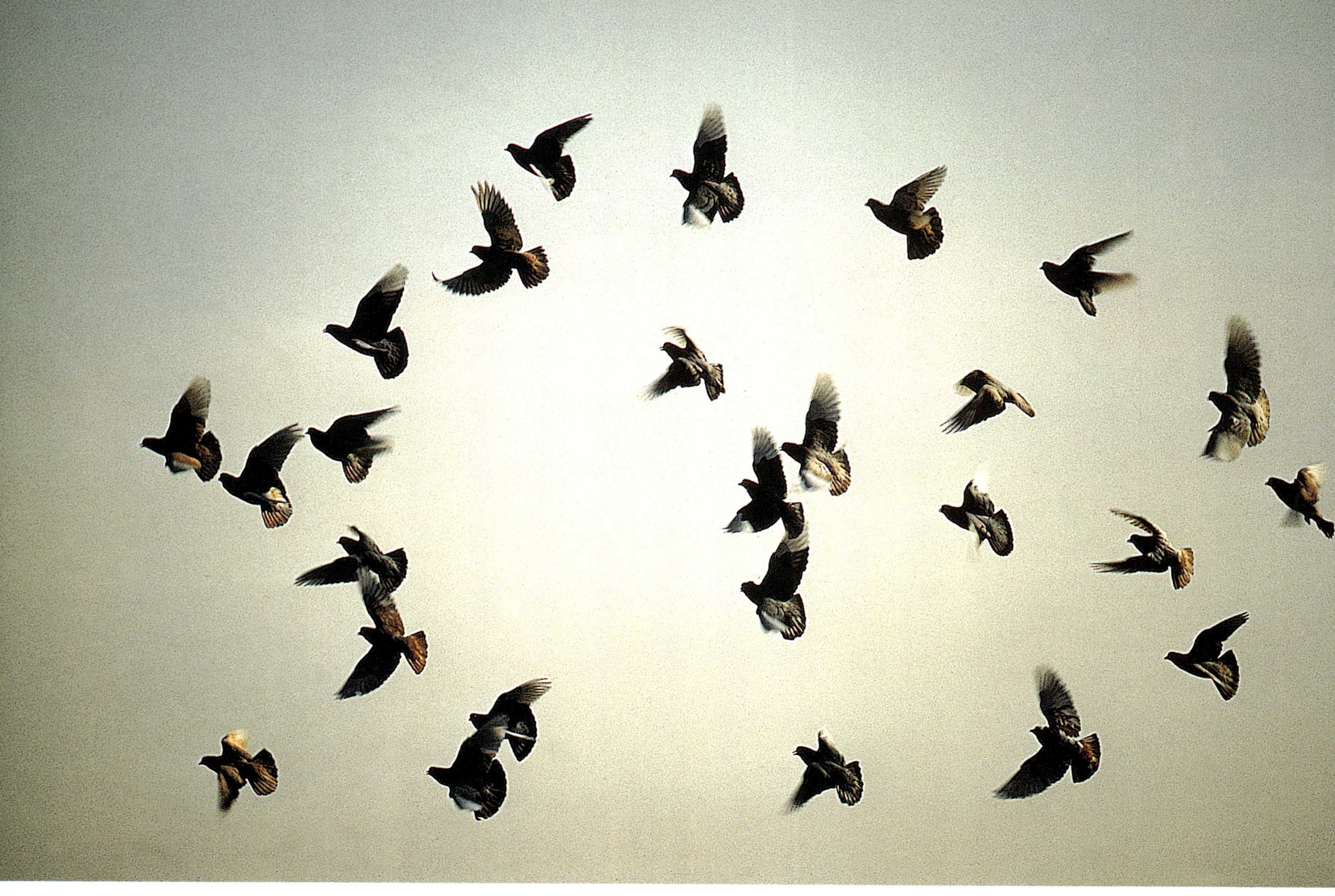

I loved shooting this flock of pigeons. My favorite of thousands of such images. It's still not perfect. Some guys are out of position. They know who they are.

Summer in

New York.

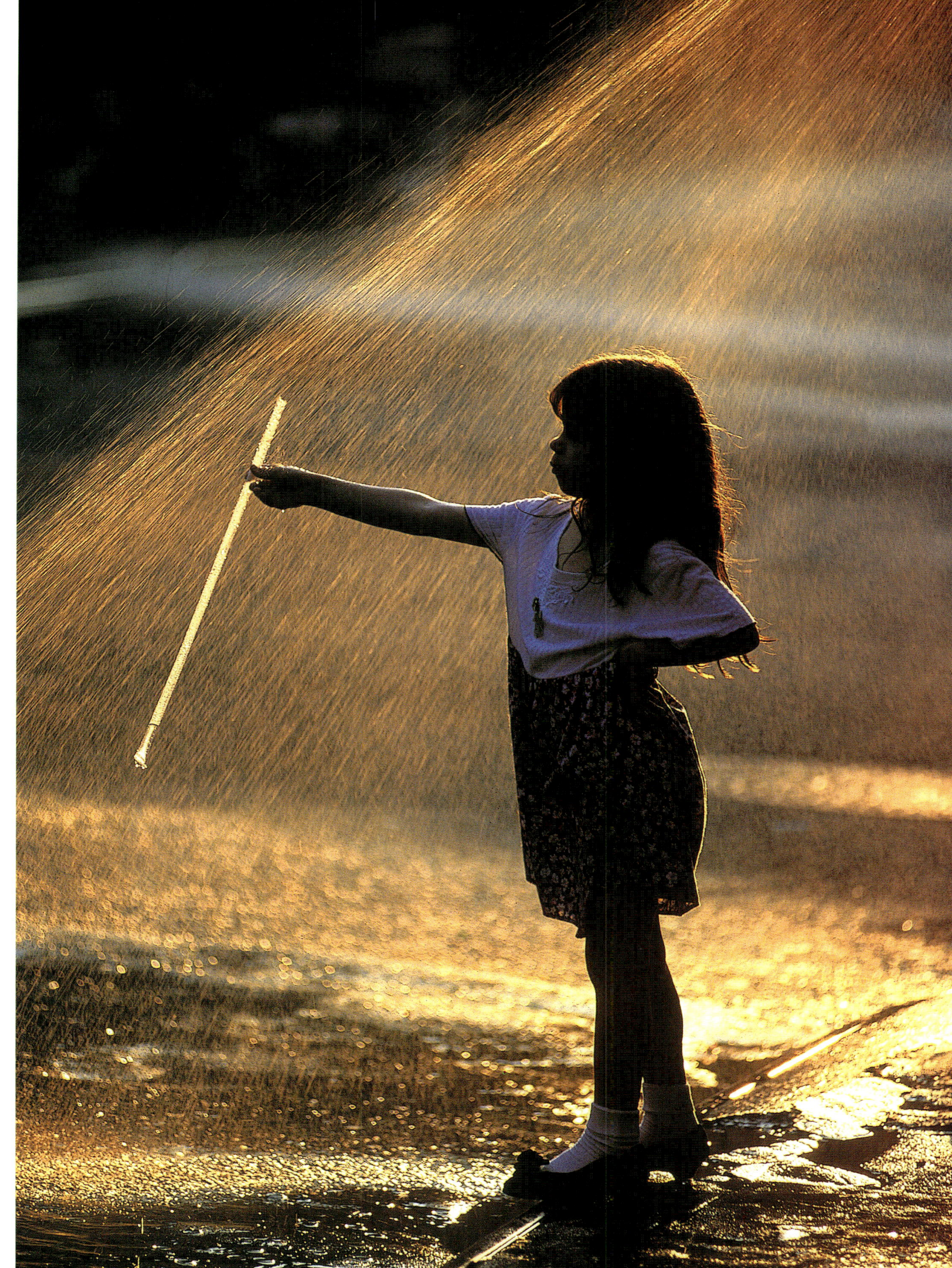

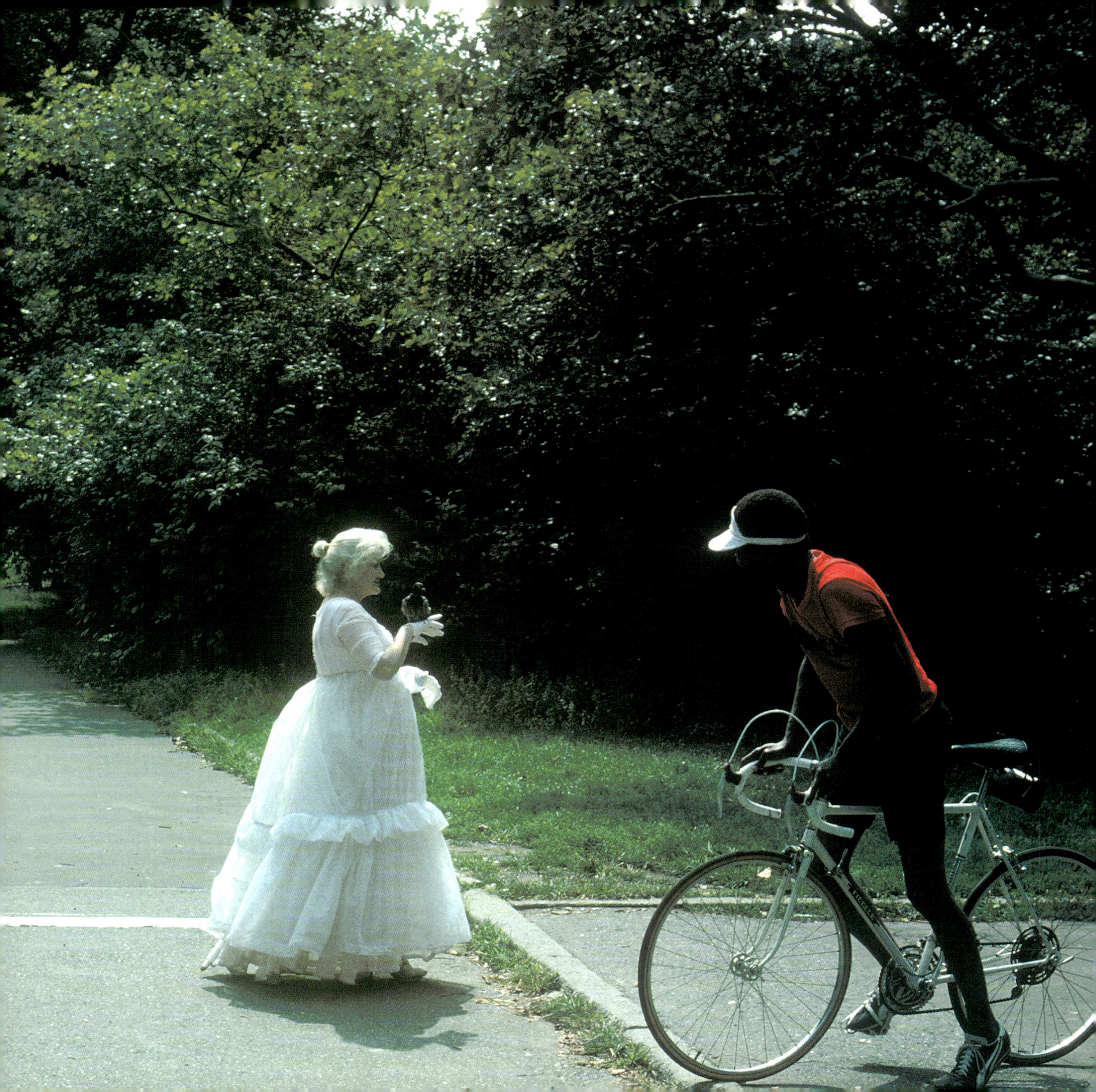

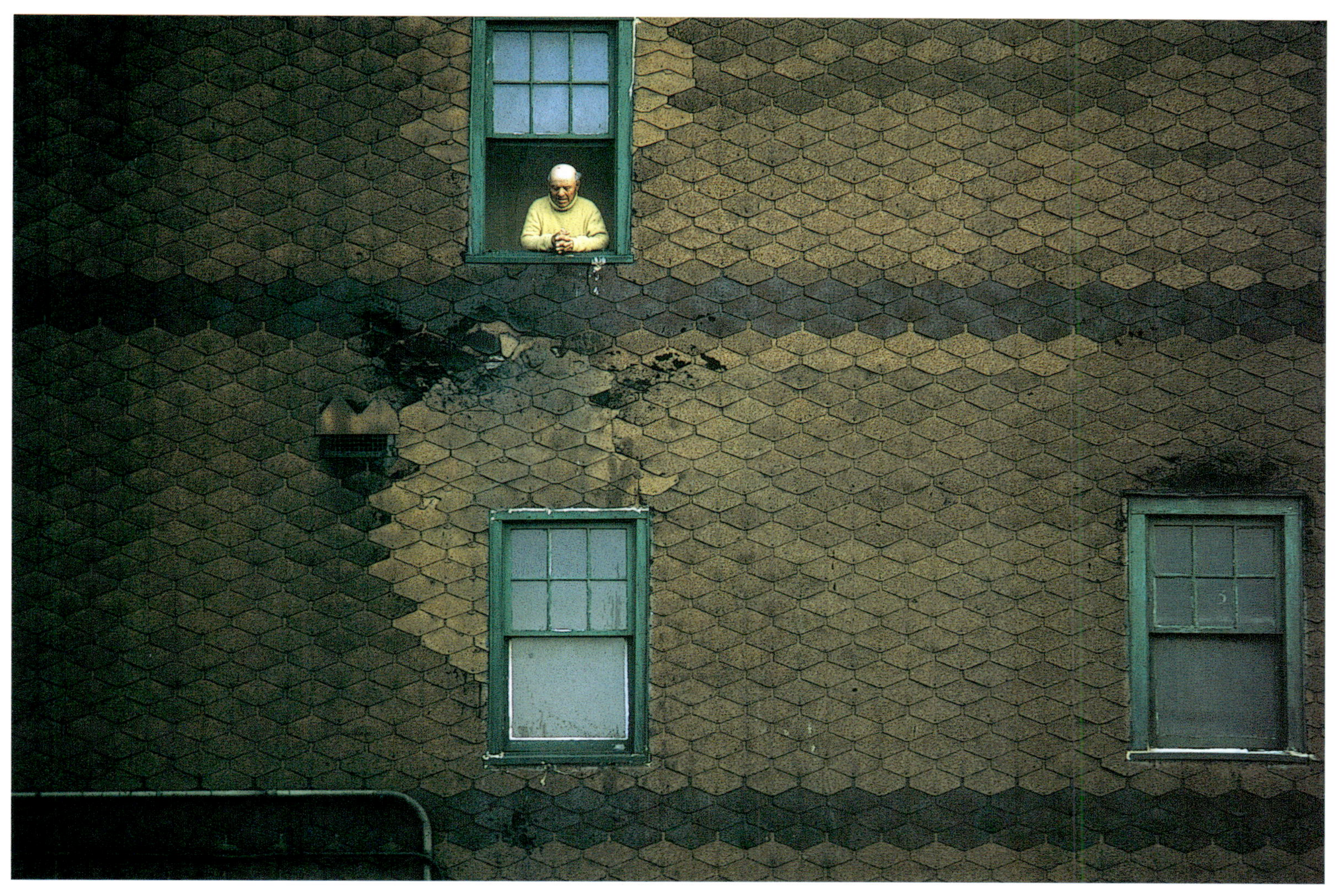

An old two-story shingled wall house
in Coney Island, now long gone.

St. Patrick's Day parade.

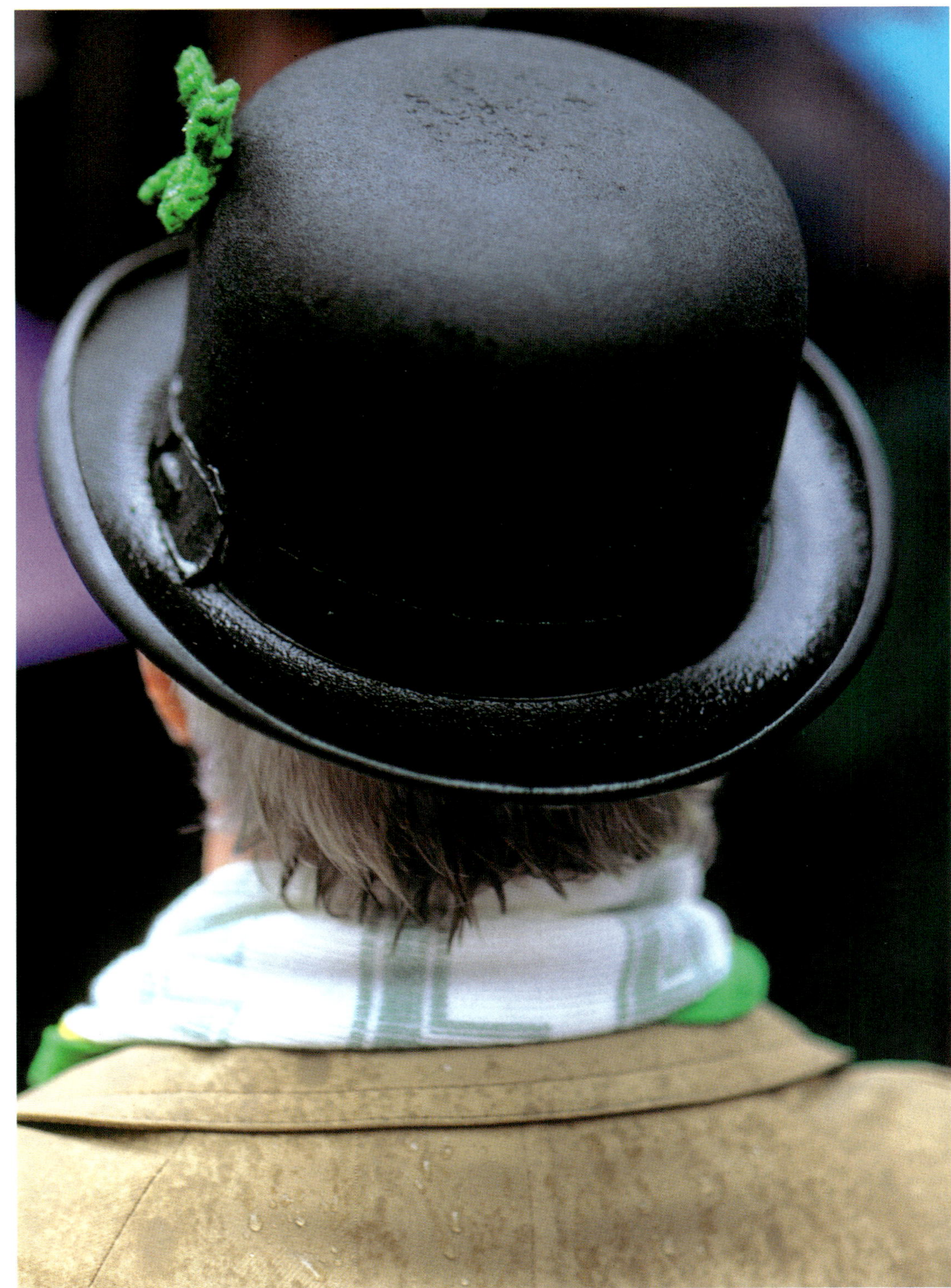

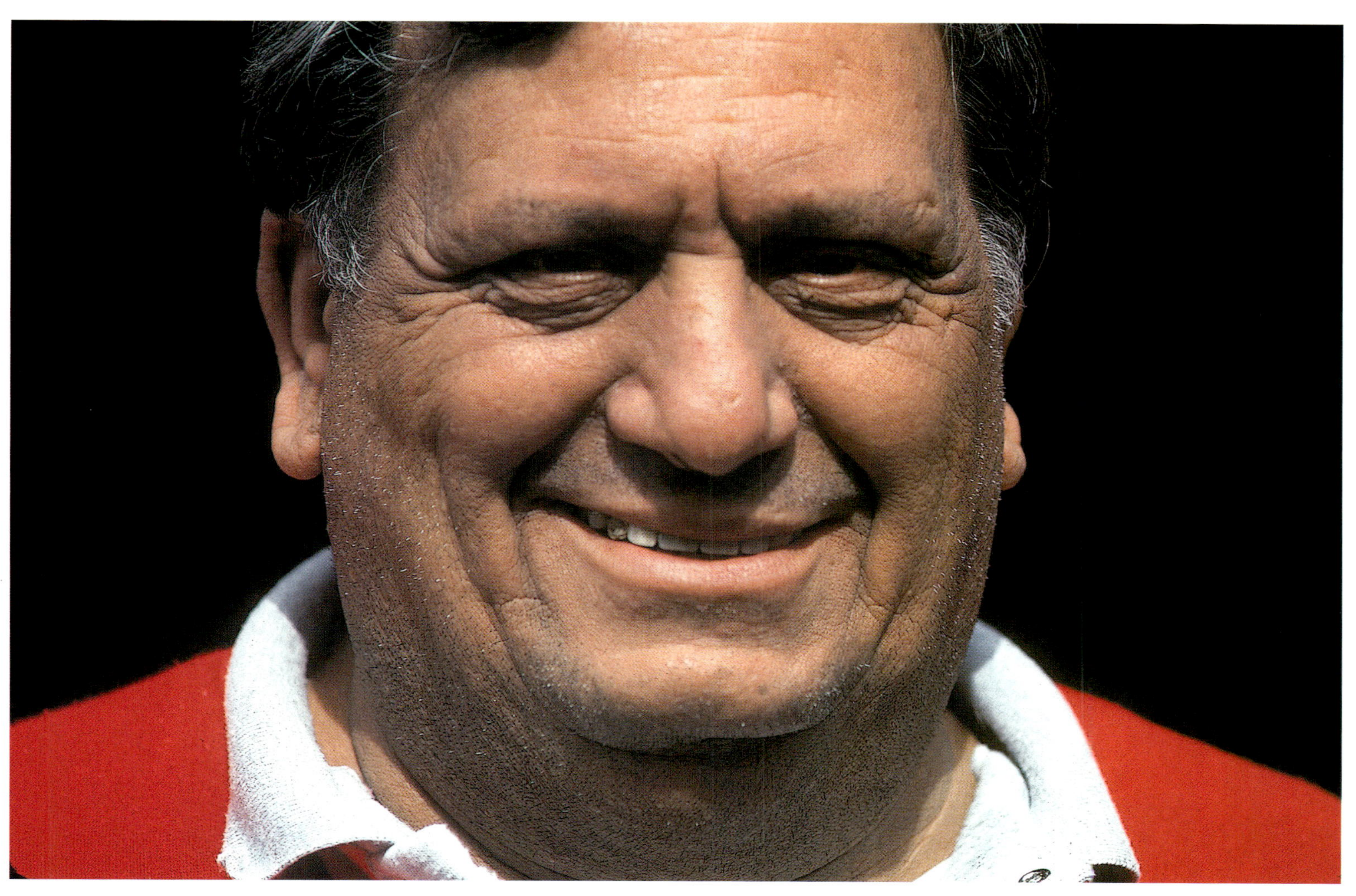

John Carbone, an old friend with a used office furniture business on Canal Street.

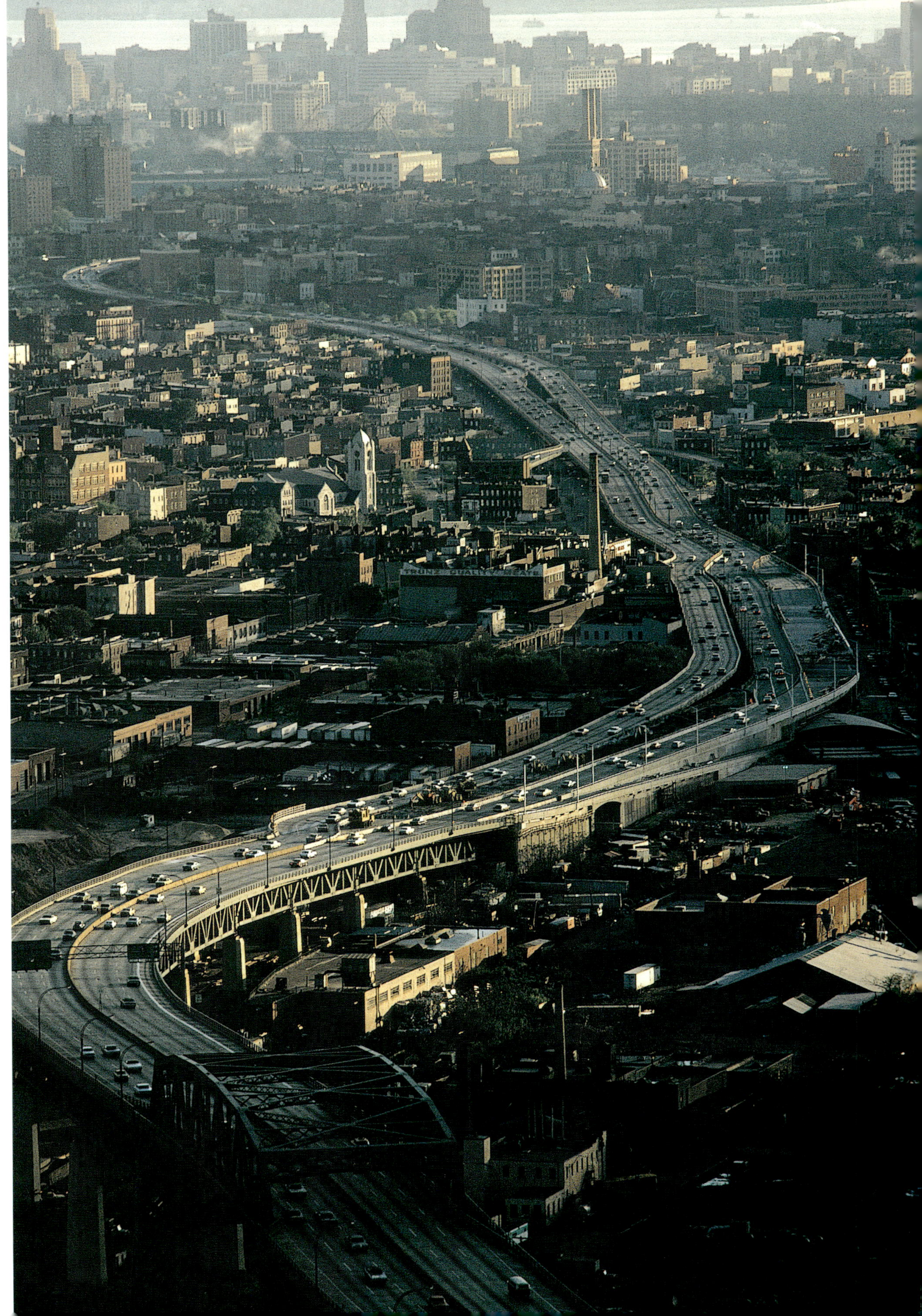

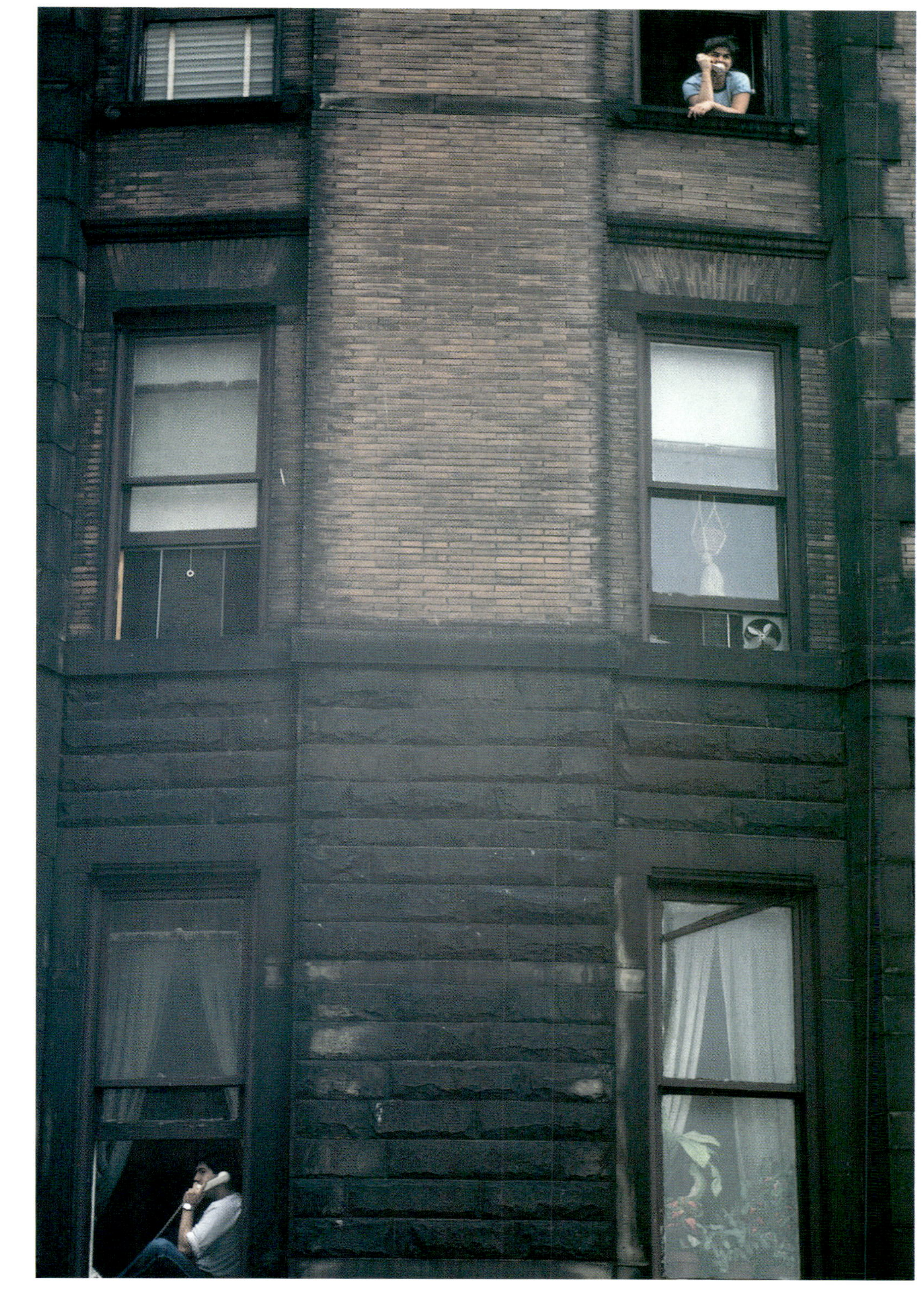

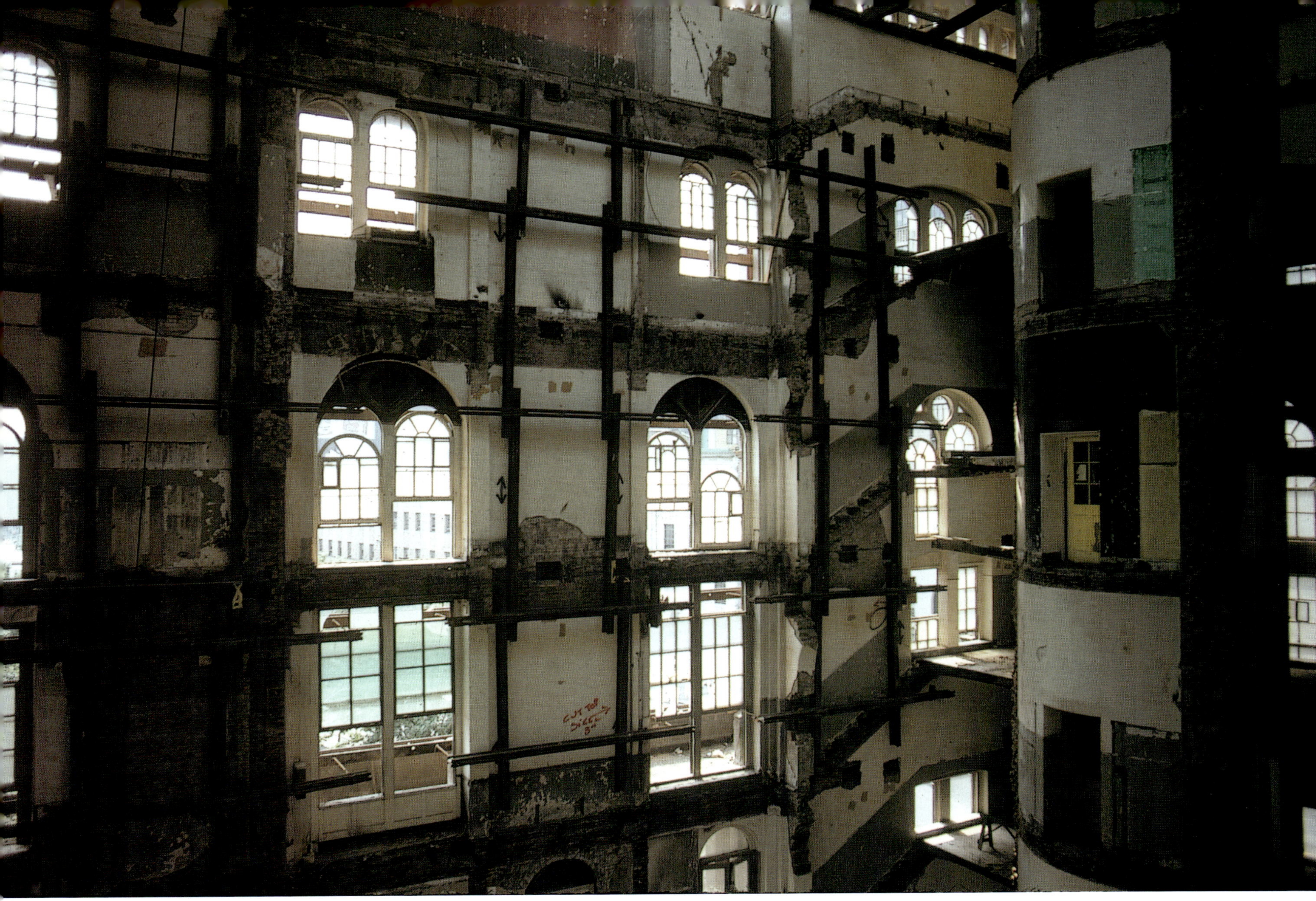

Interior renovation of Cooper Union, the first free school in New York.

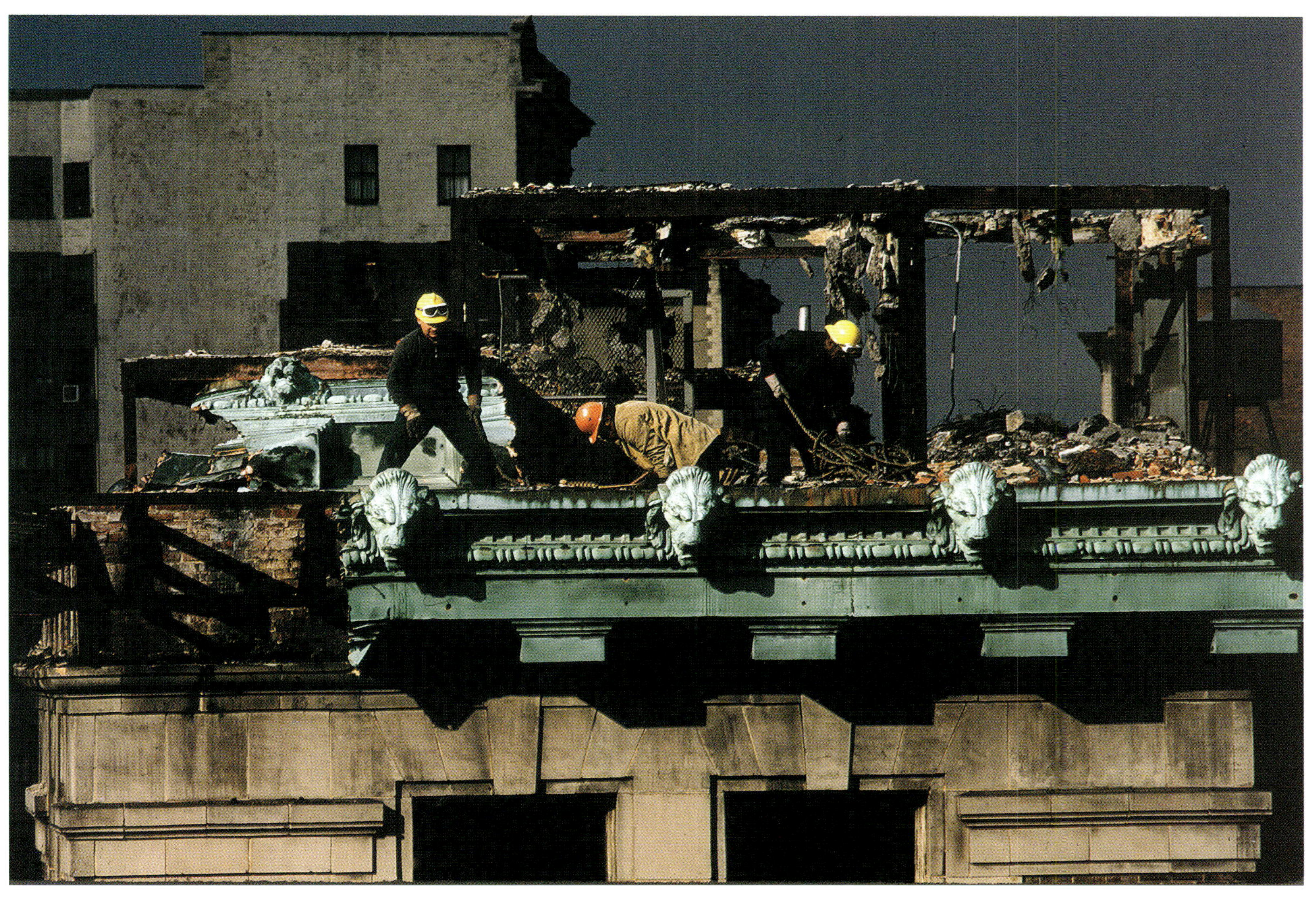

School being demolished to make way for an apartment house in Little Italy.

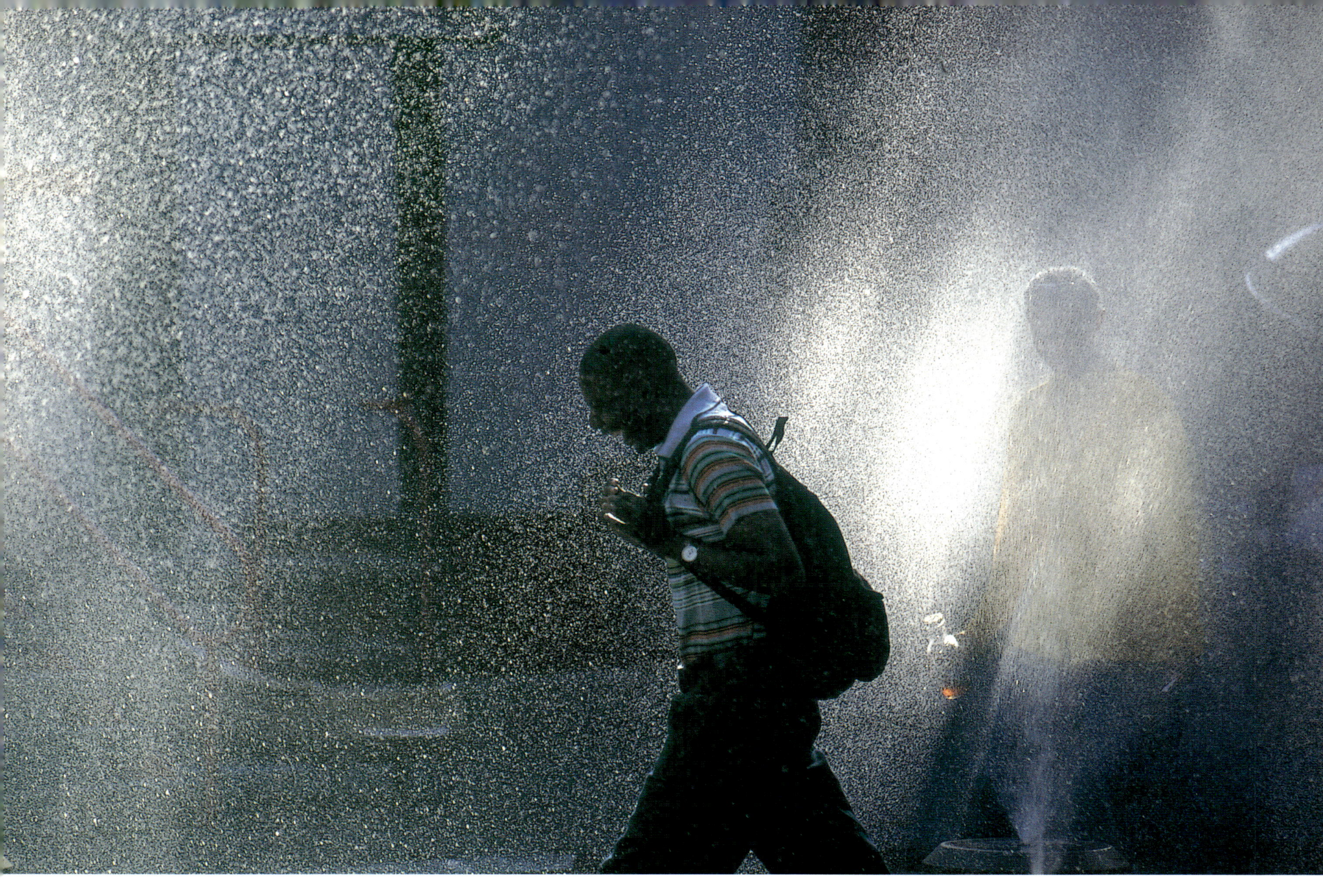

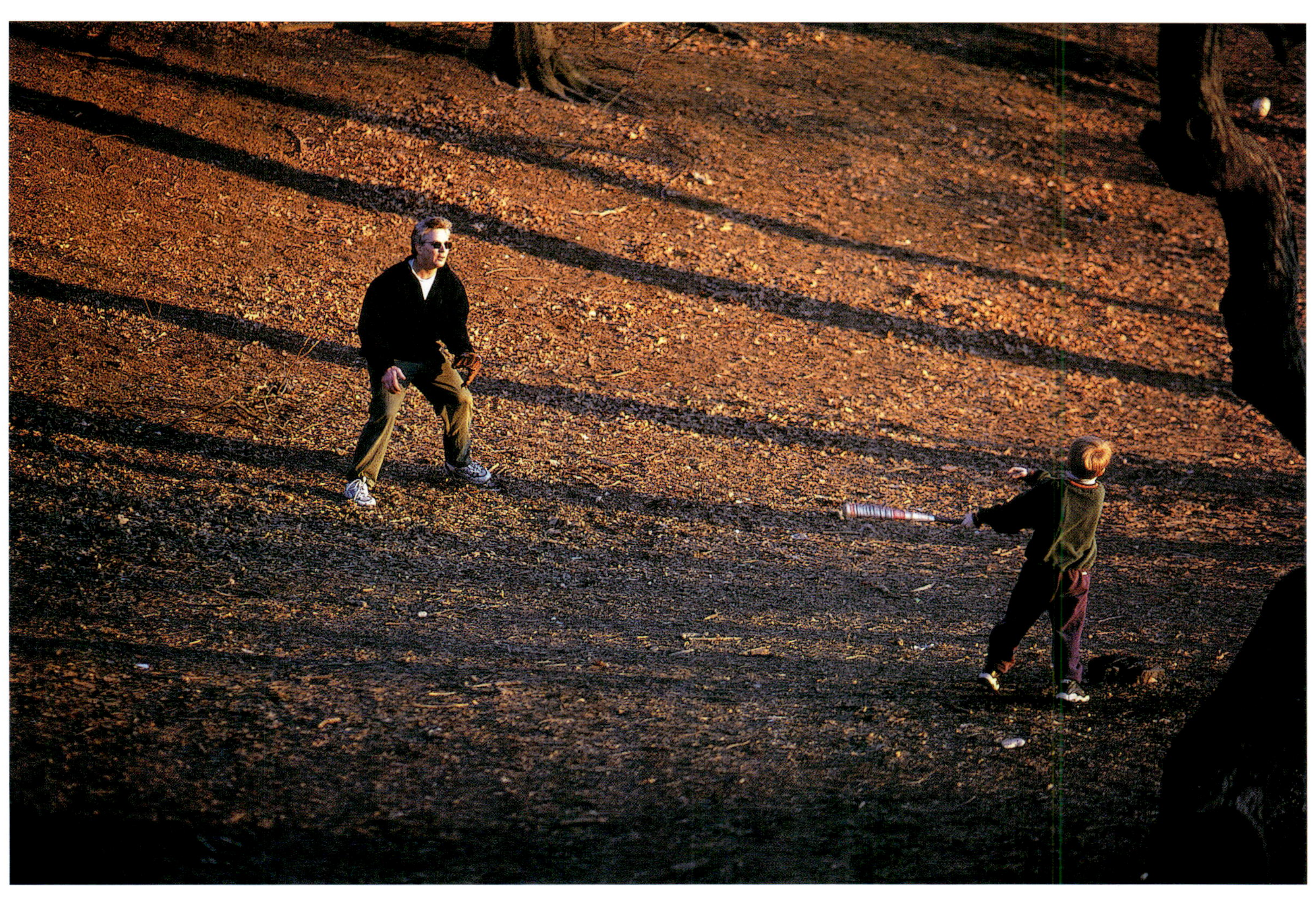

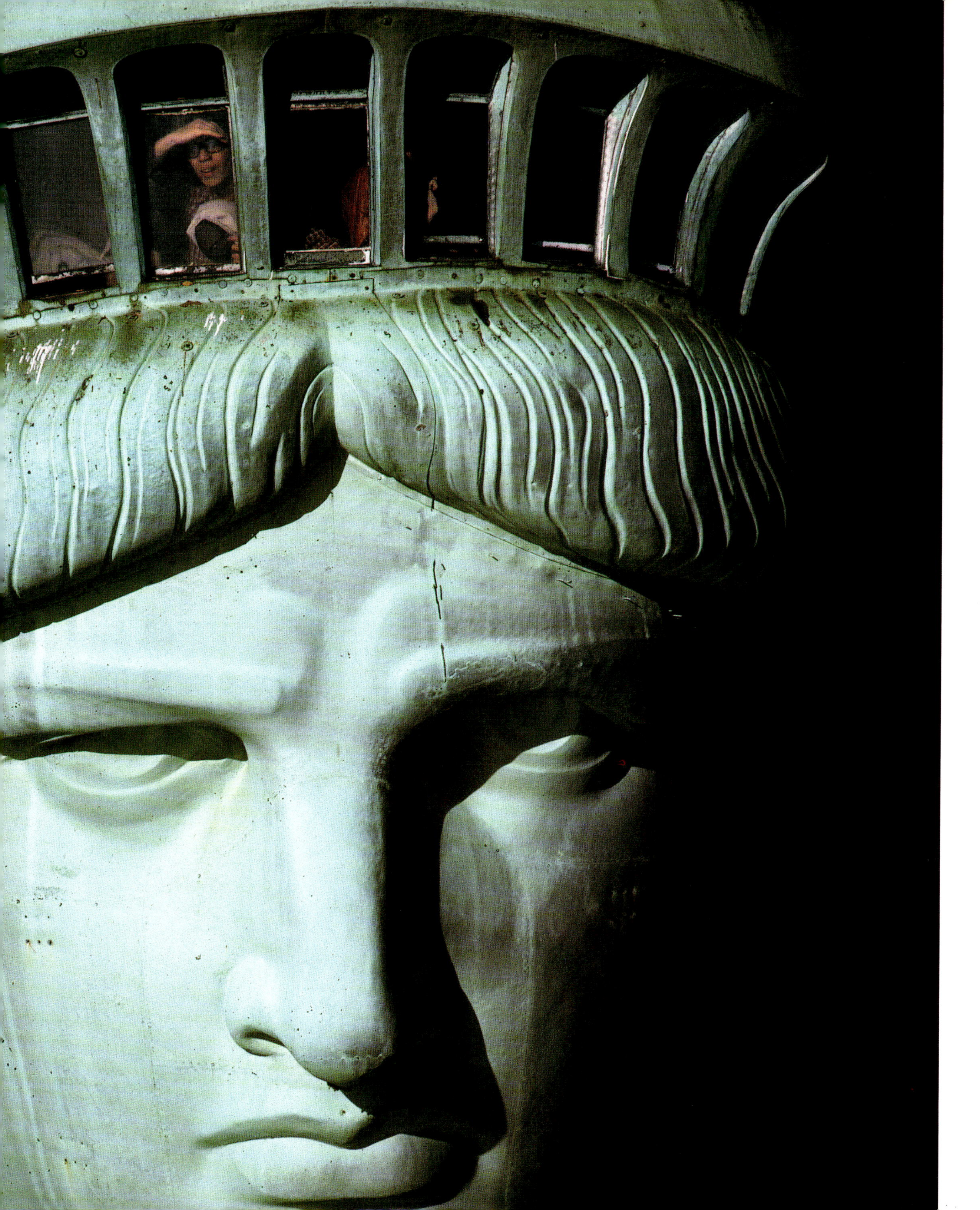

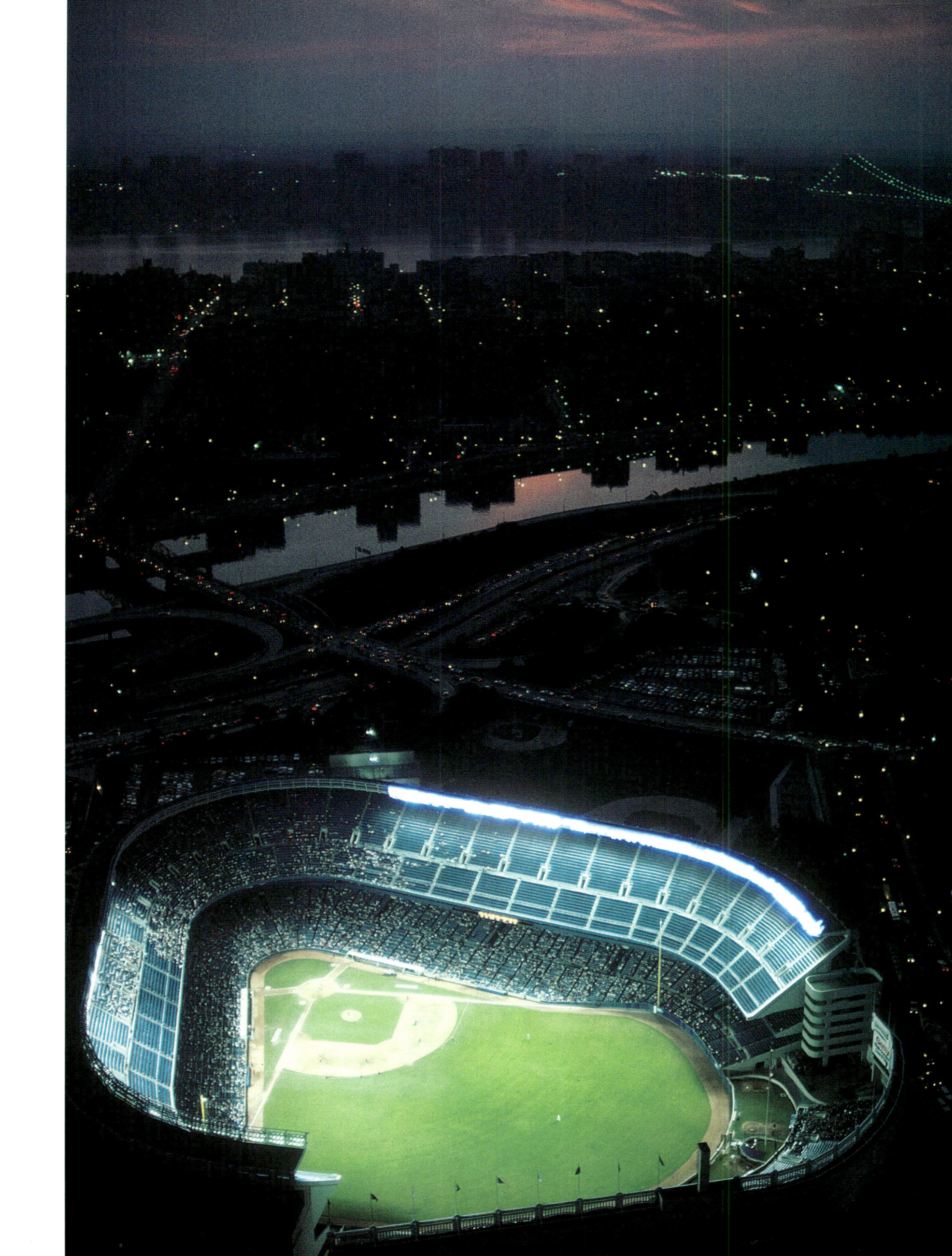

Yankee

Stadium.

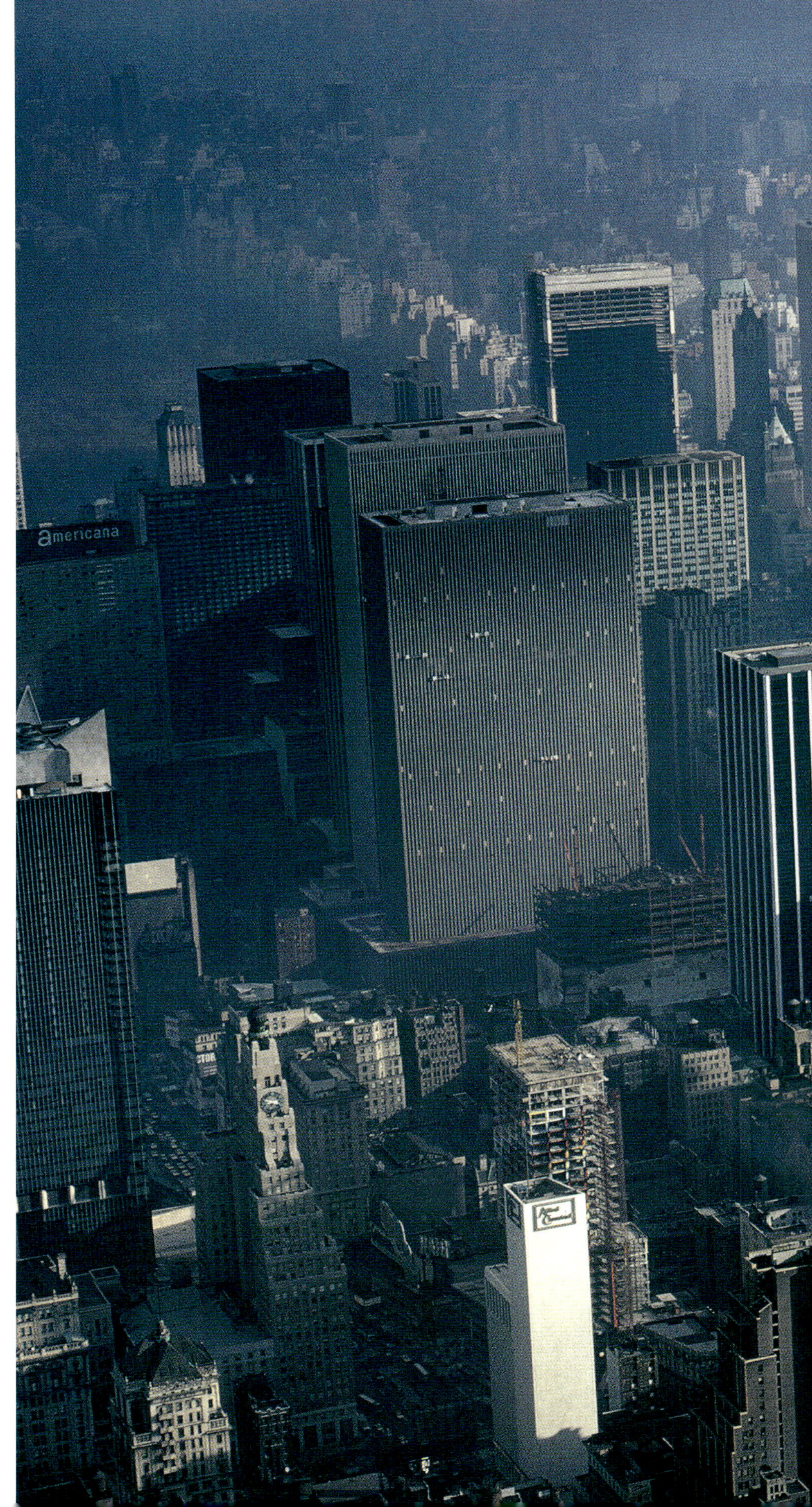
americana

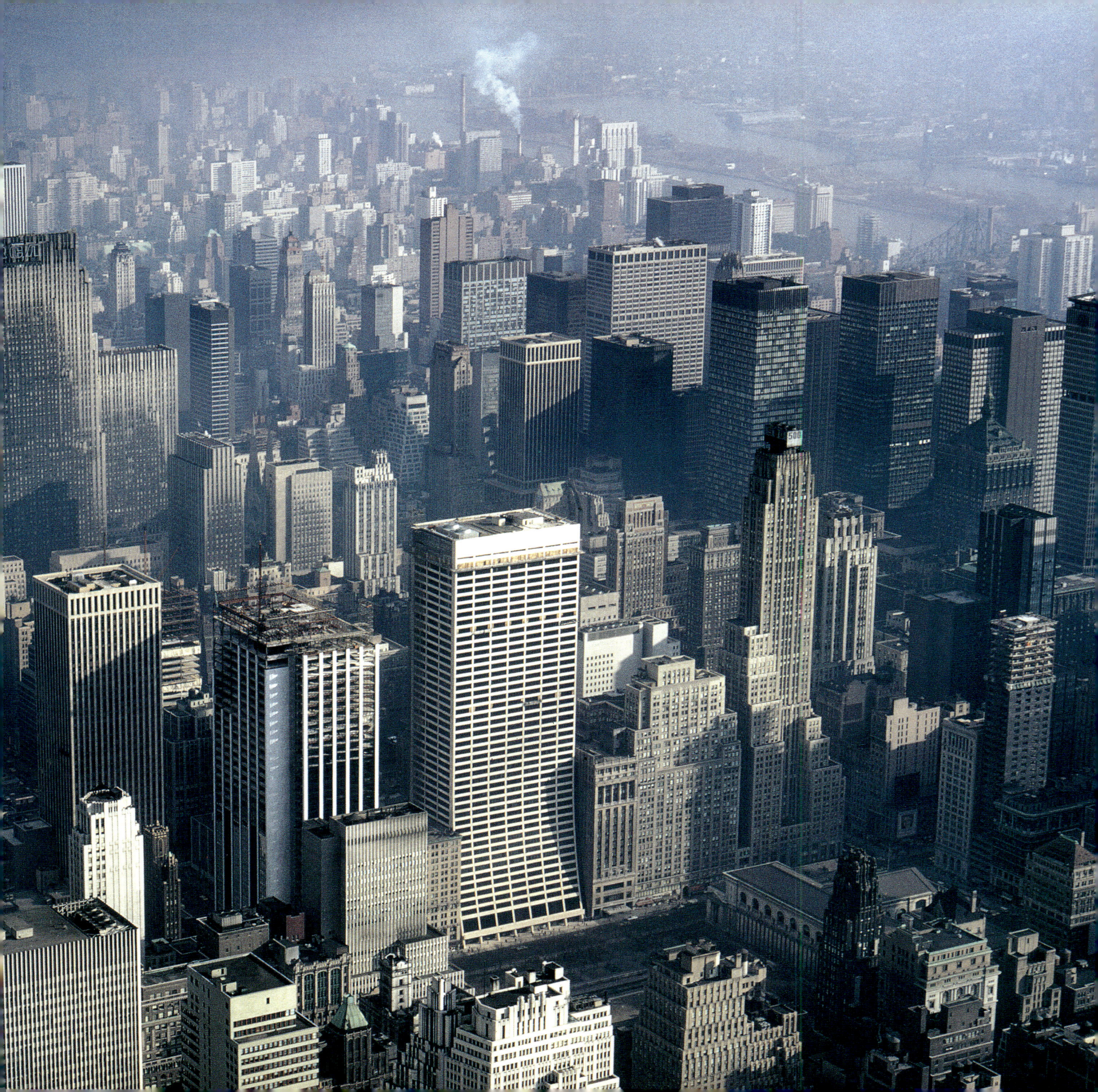

Roosevelt Island and Manhattan, from Queens.

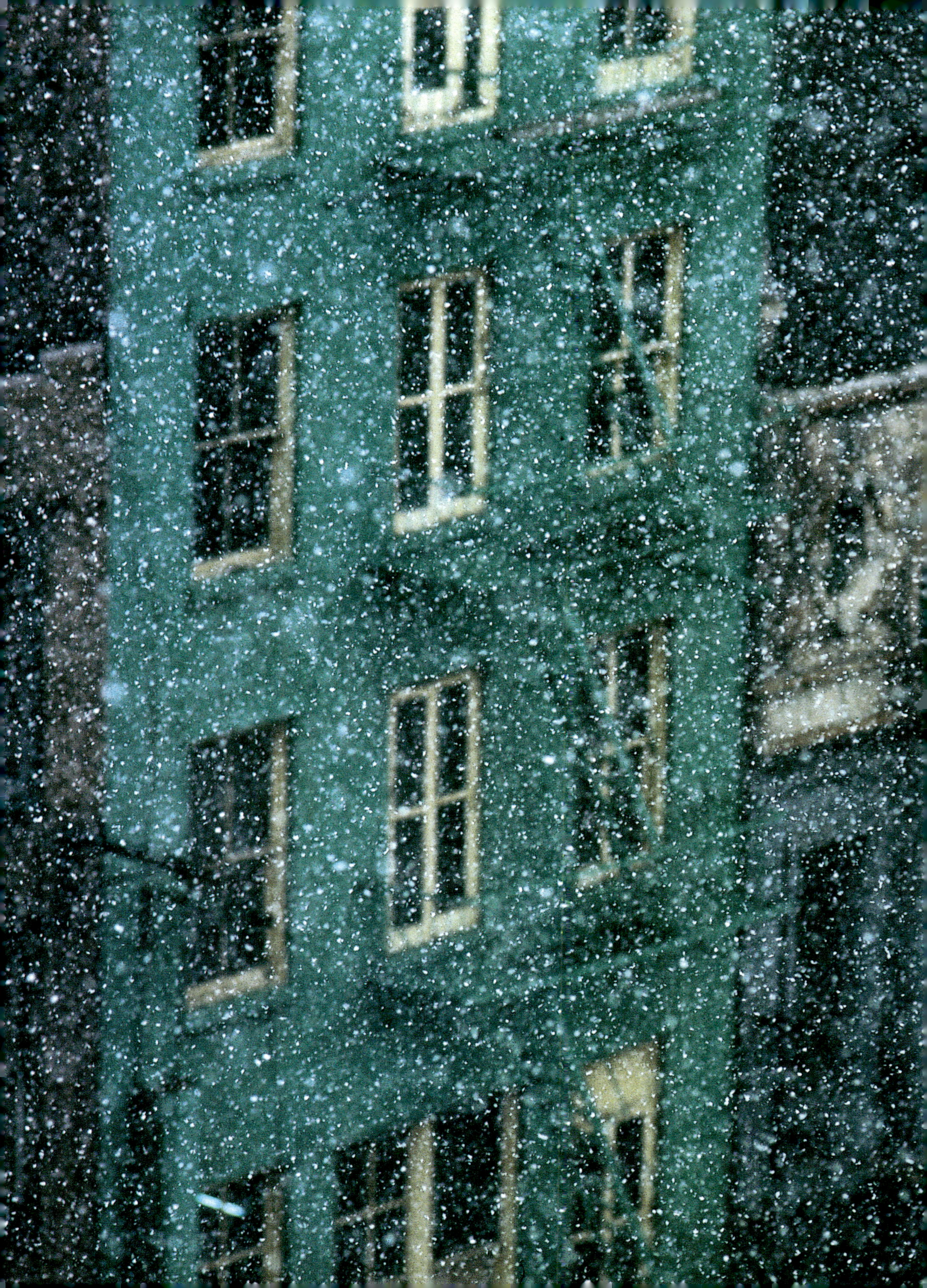

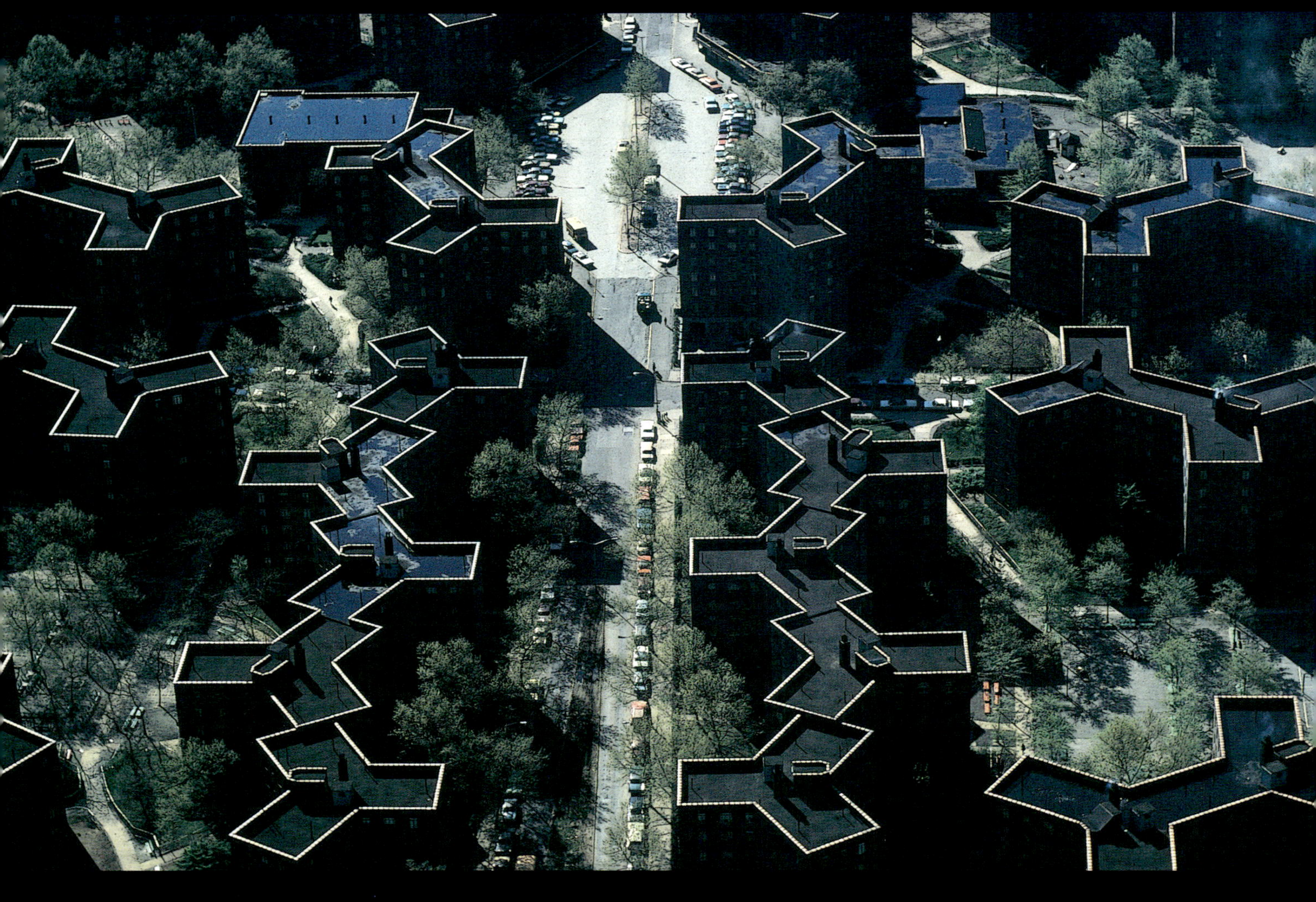

Lillian Wald housing project on the Lower East Side.

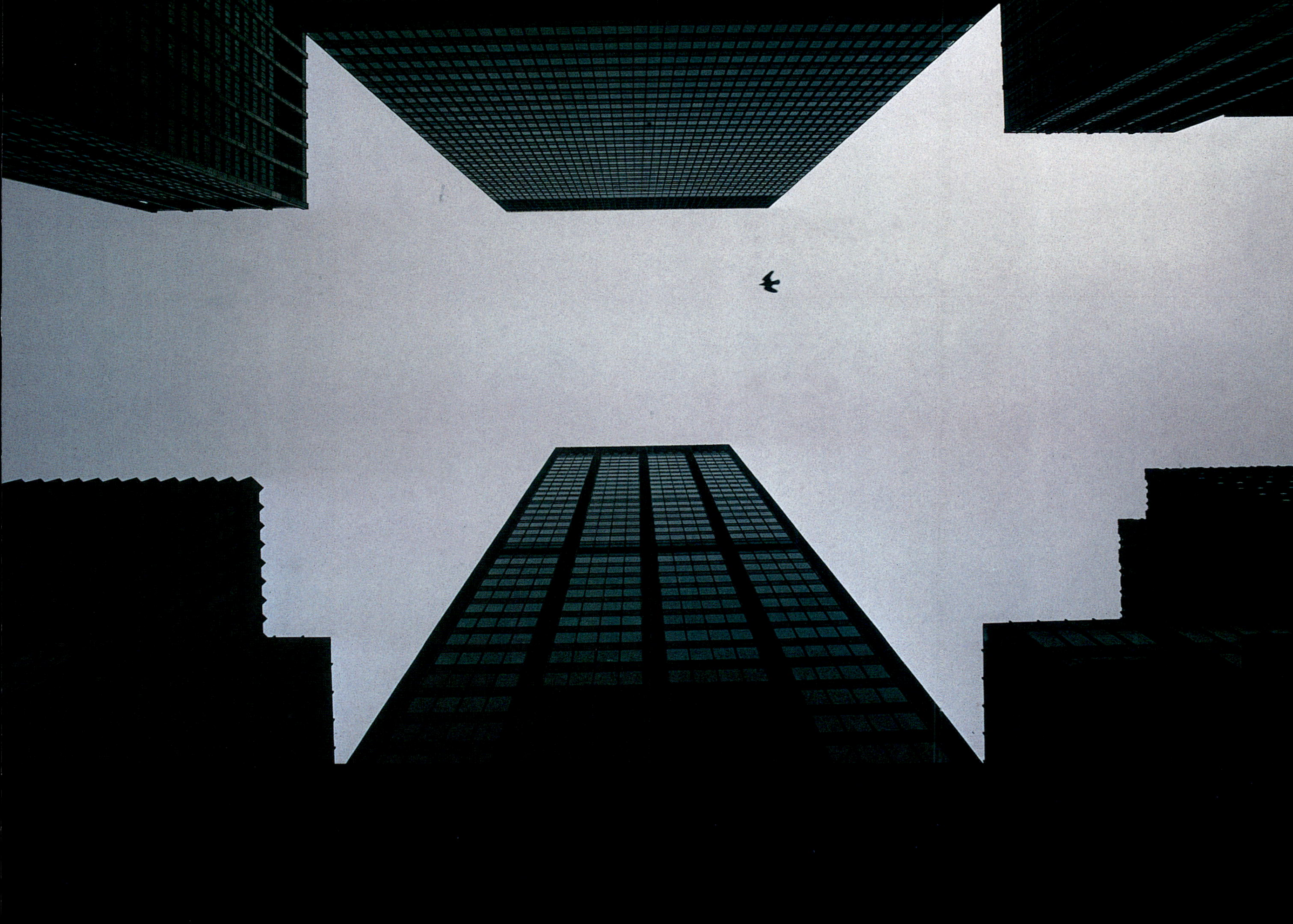

Shooting straight up on 6th Avenue near 50th Street.

Chinese New Year in Chinatown.

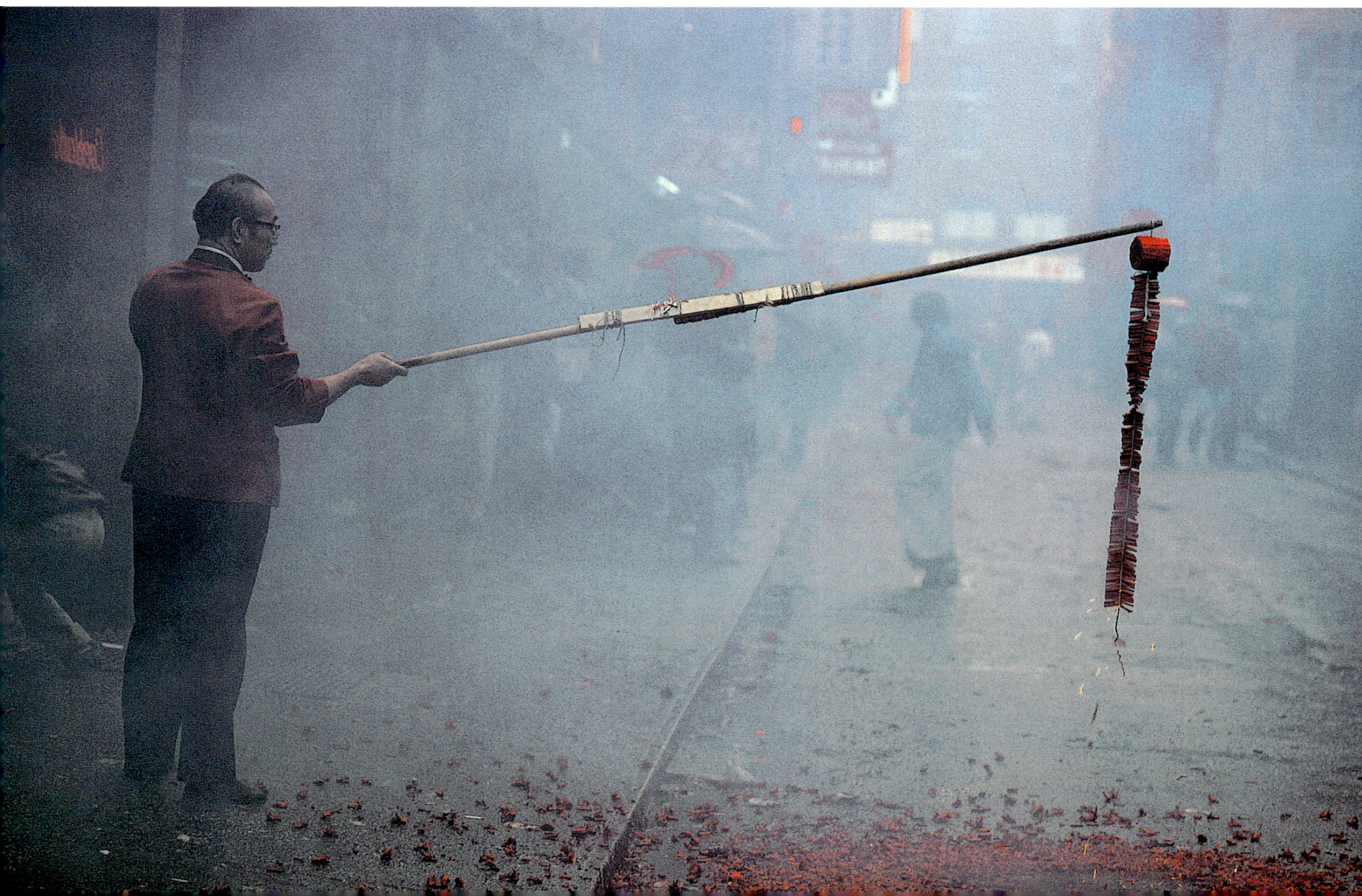

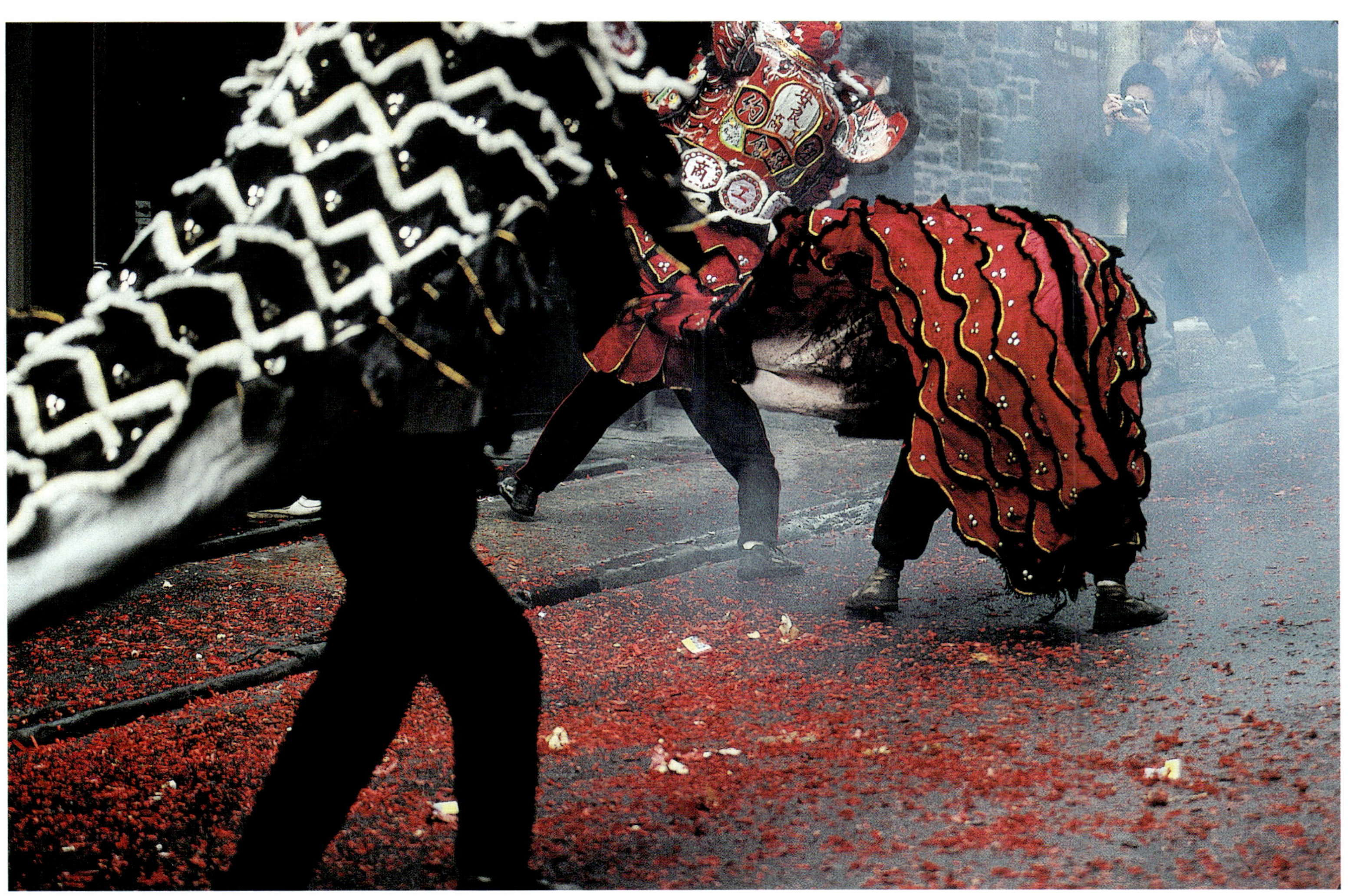

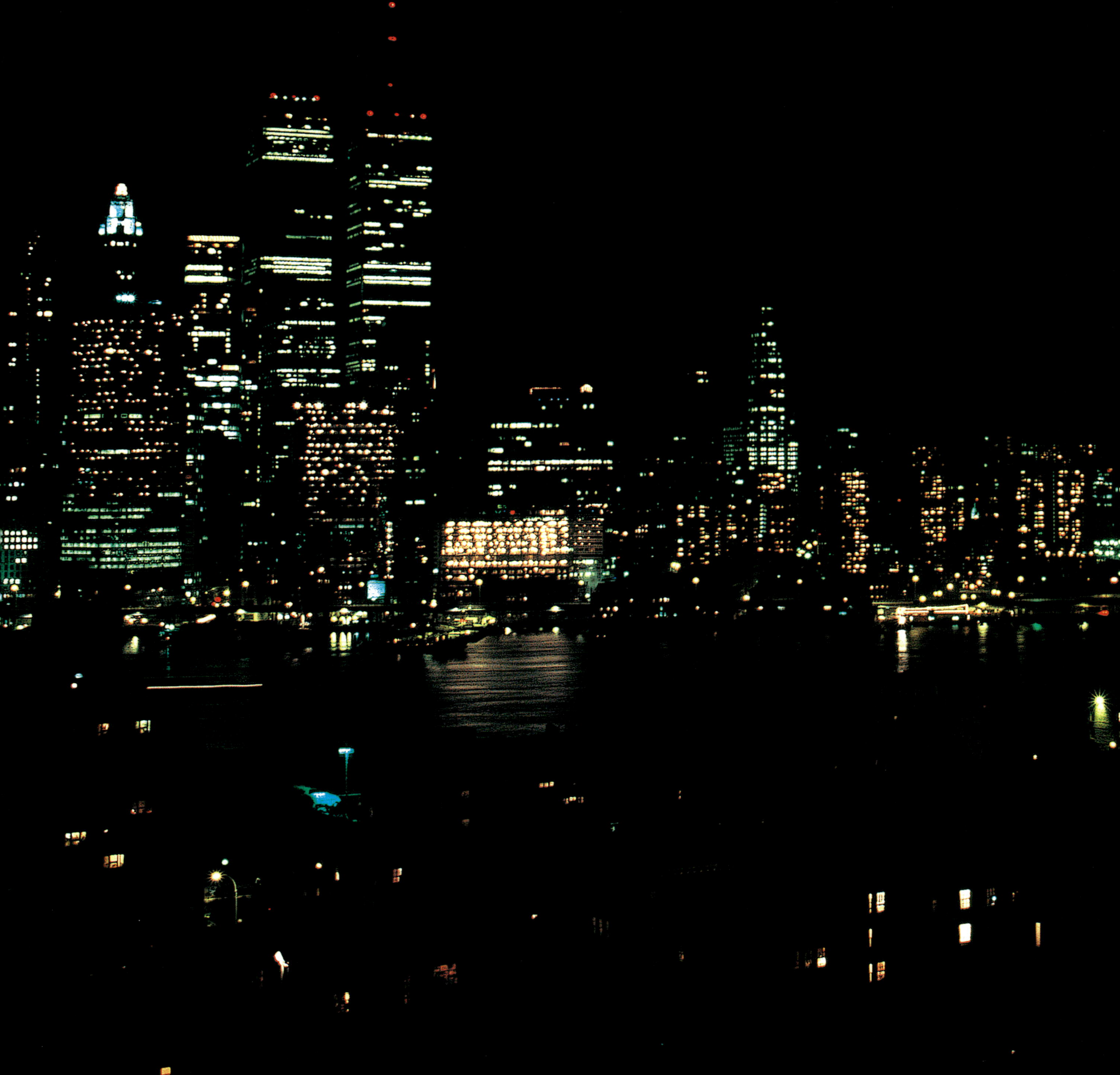

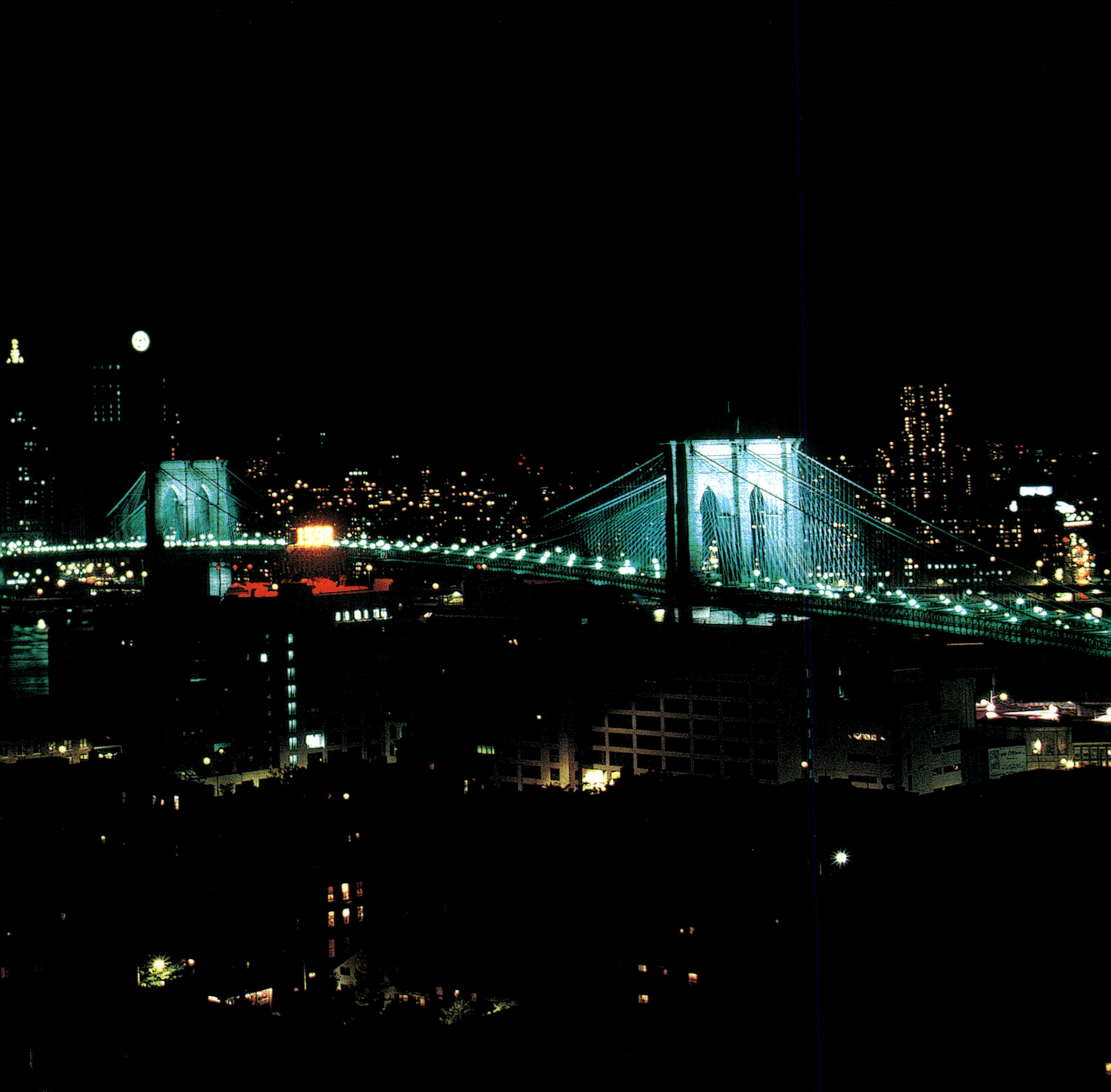

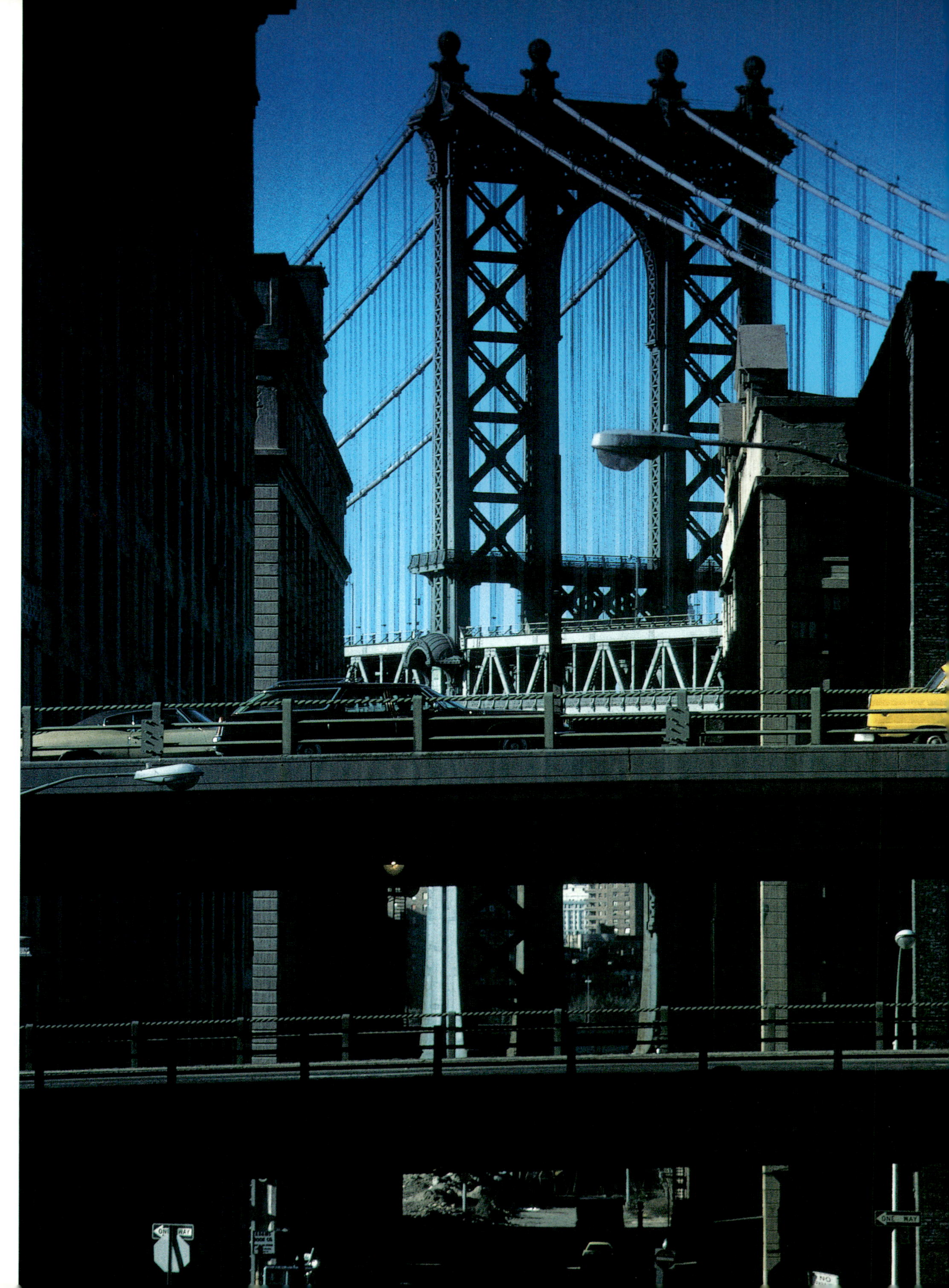

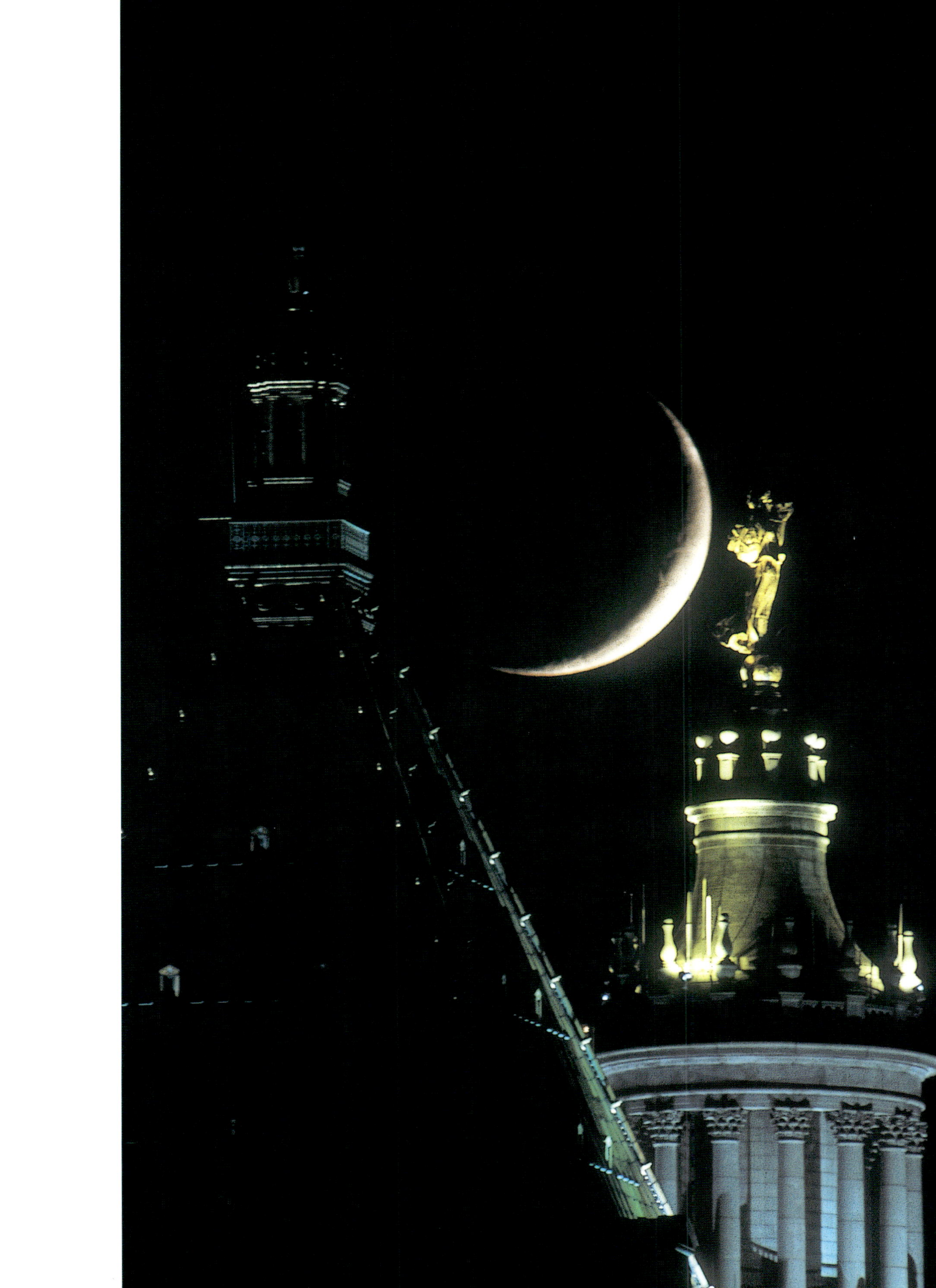

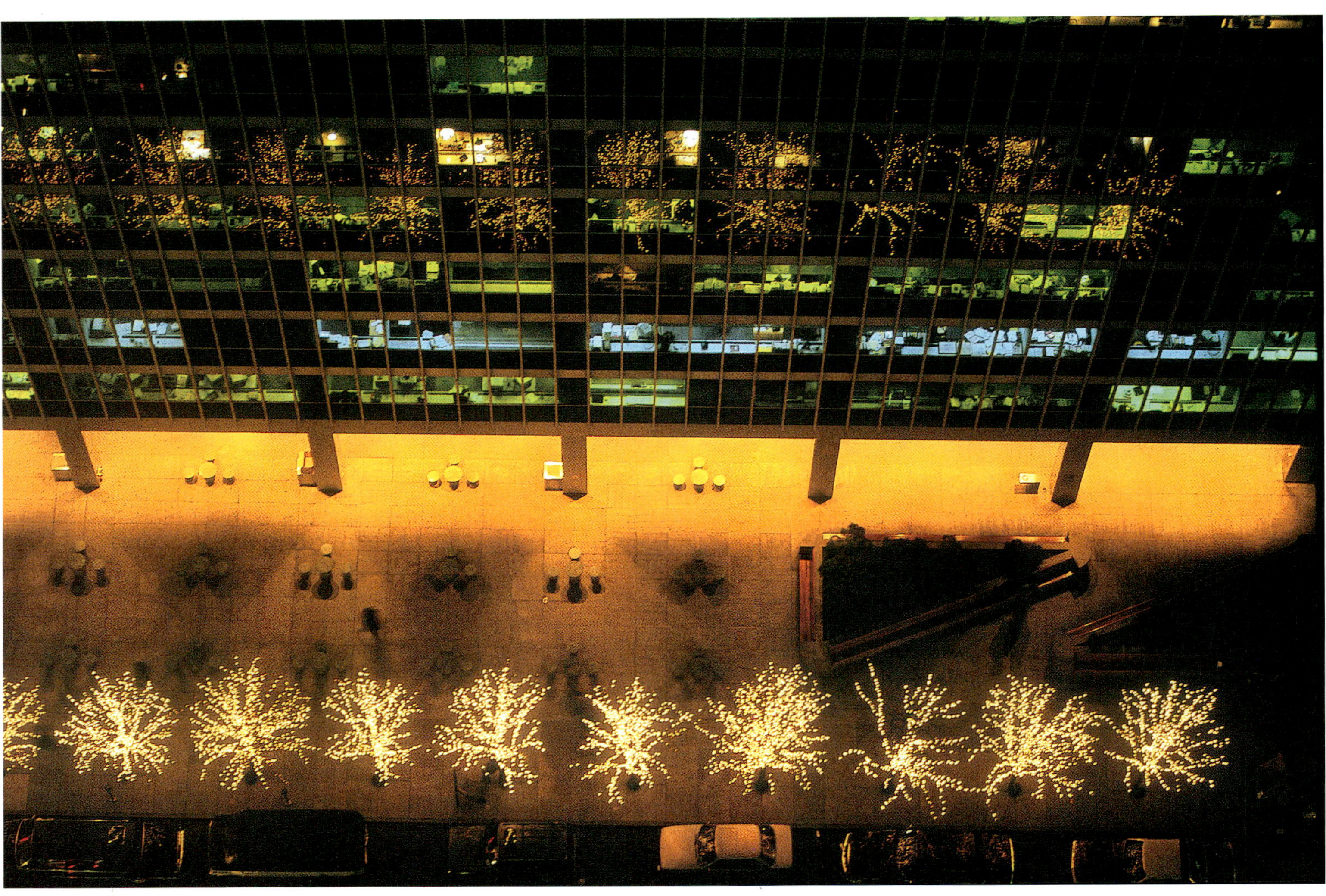

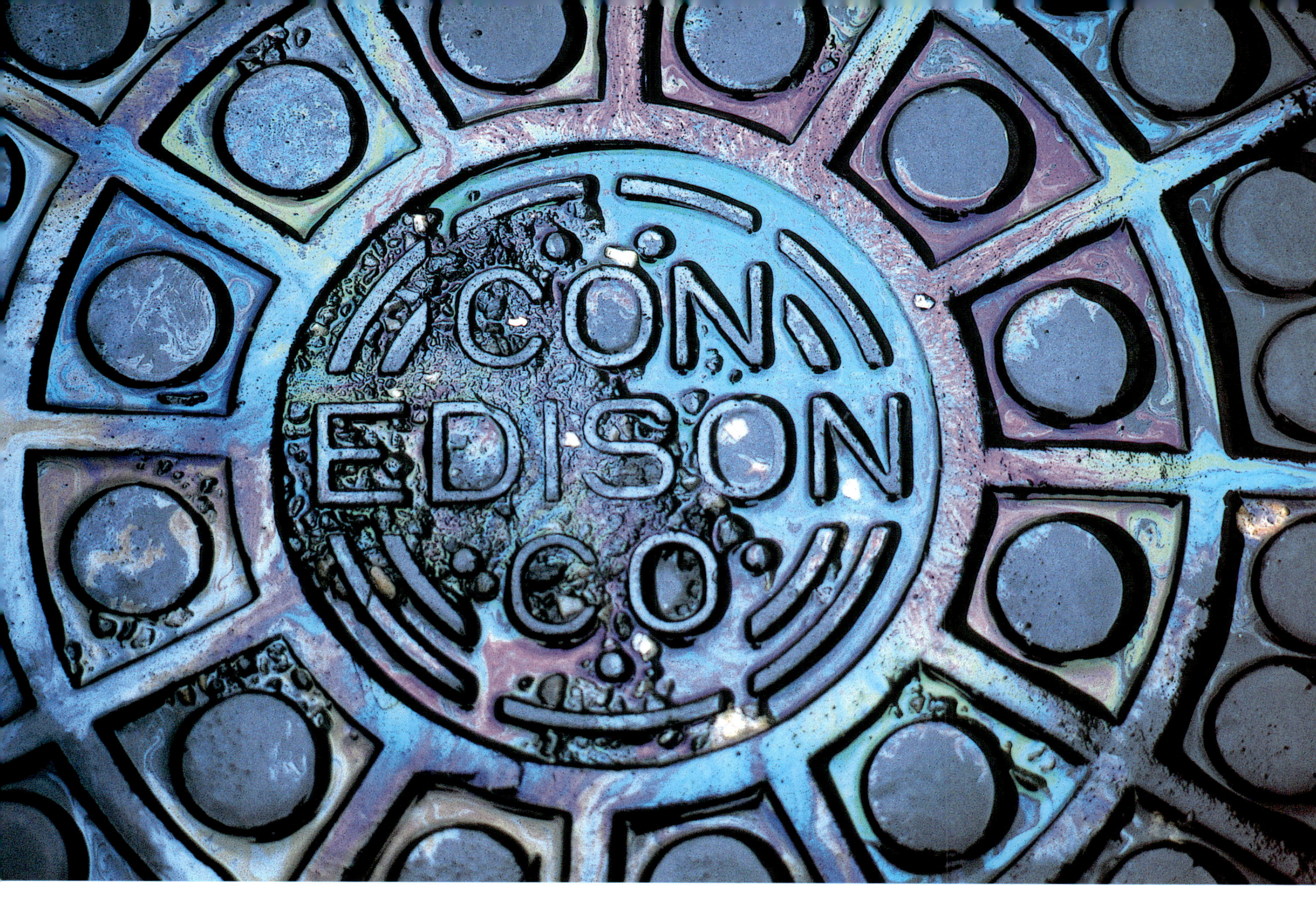
CON
EDISON
CO

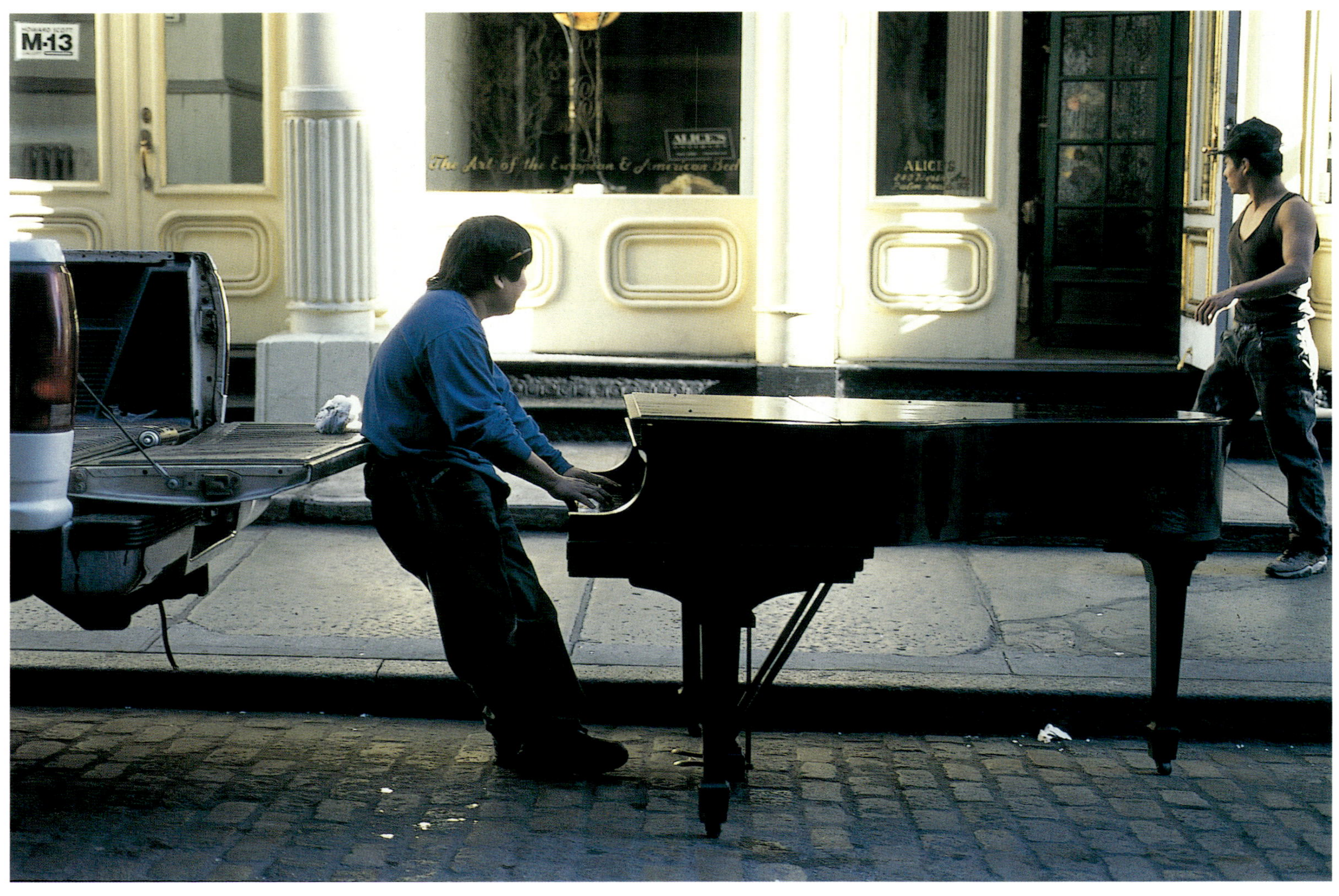

A little afternoon music by a piano mover on a SoHo side street.

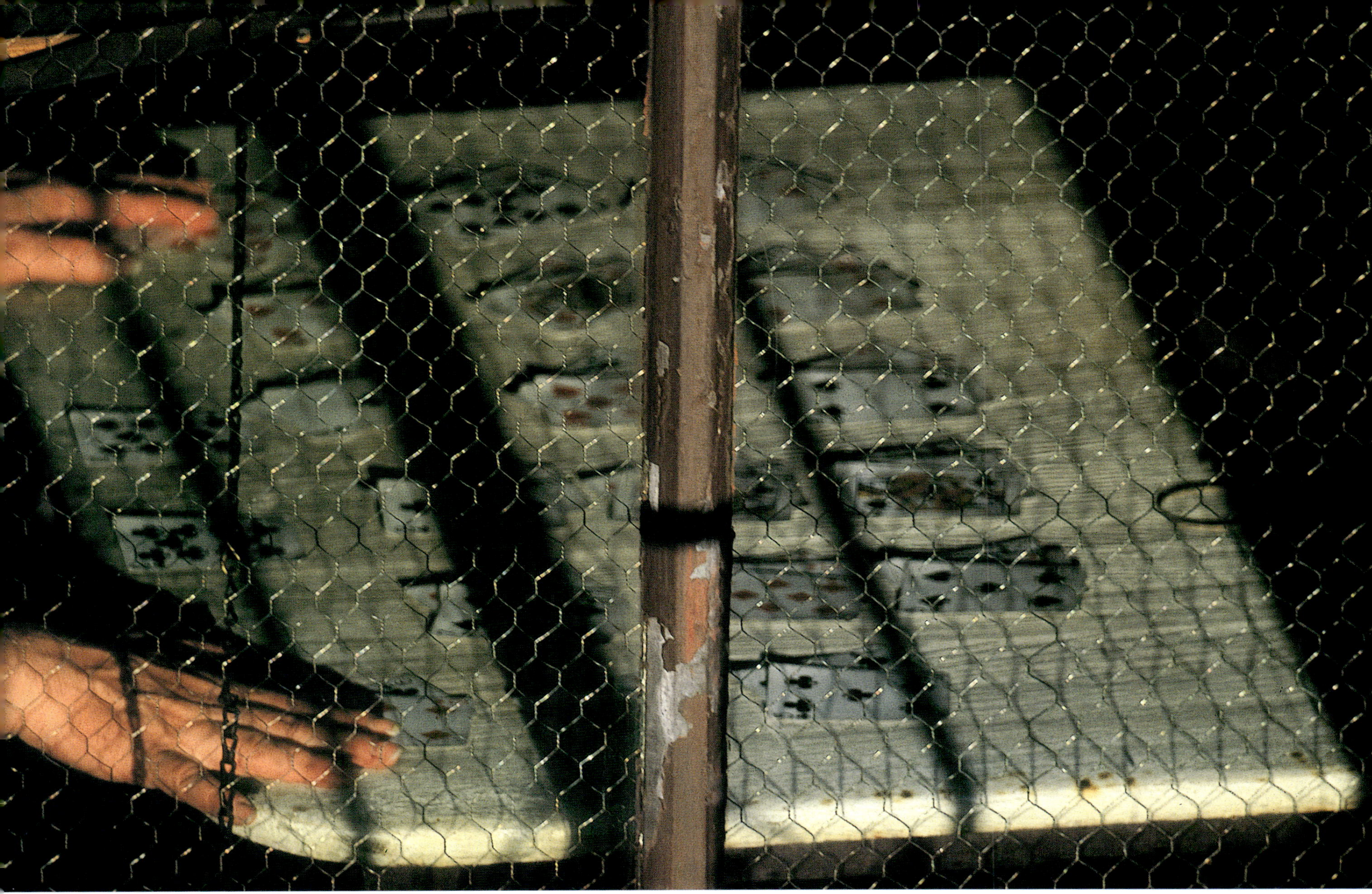

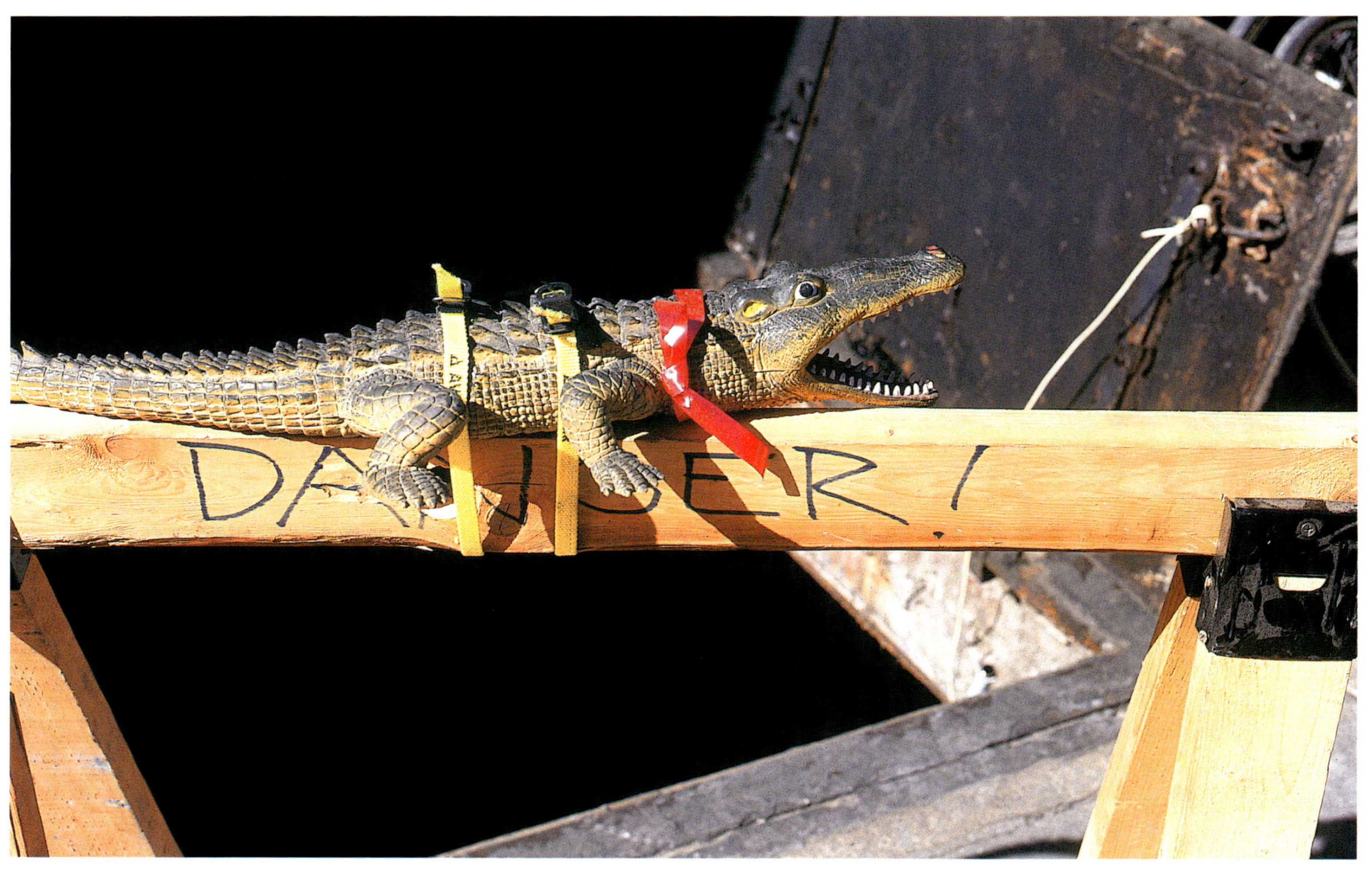

The moving hand writes. And having written, moves on…

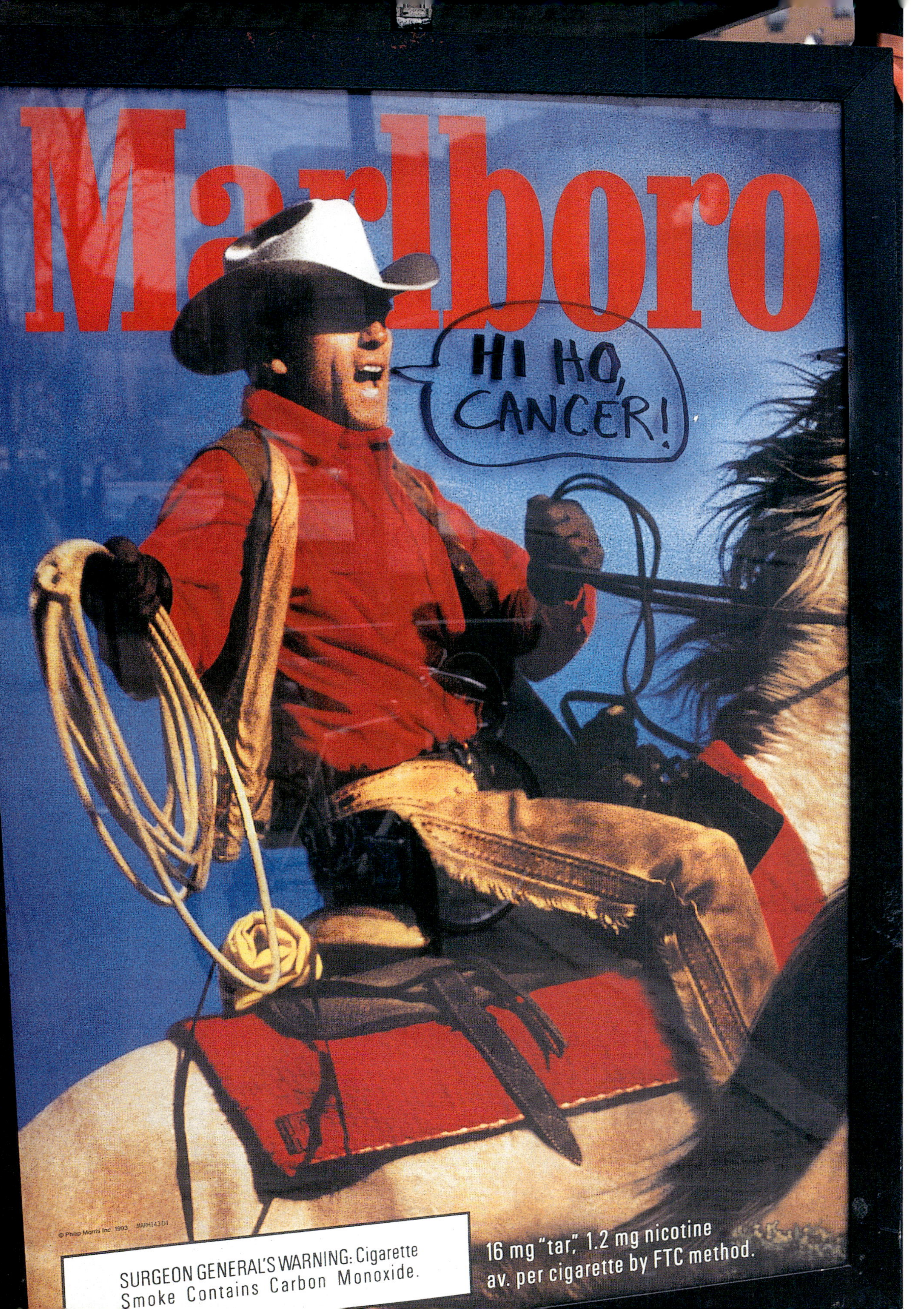
Marlboro
HI HO, CANCER!
SURGEON GENERAL'S WARNING: Cigarette Smoke Contains Carbon Monoxide.
16 mg "tar," 1.2 mg nicotine av. per cigarette by FTC method.

New Yorkers can ignore anything except a chance to watch a lightning-fast towaway guy do his job.

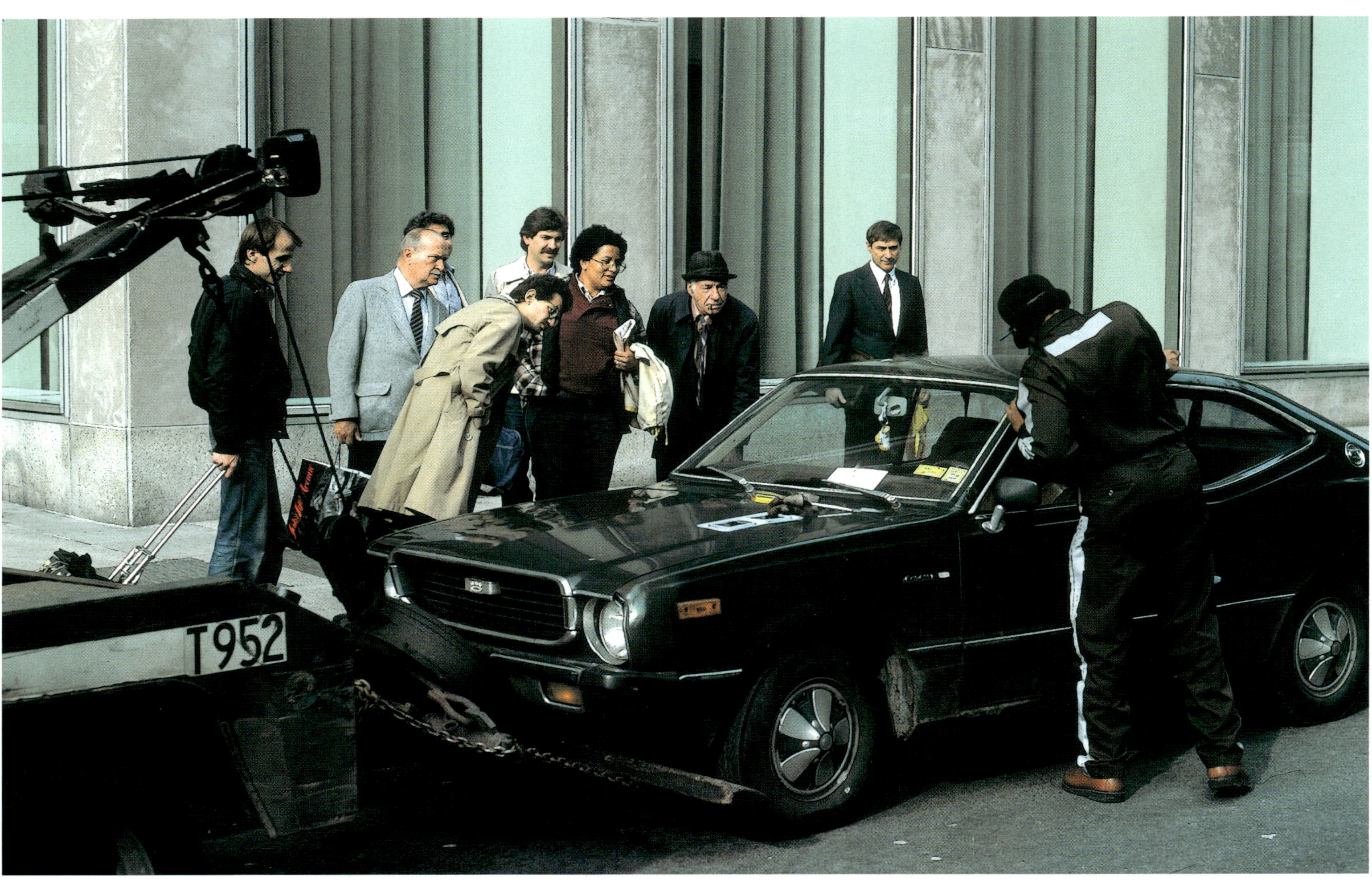

Trust me. There *is* a restaurant nearby.

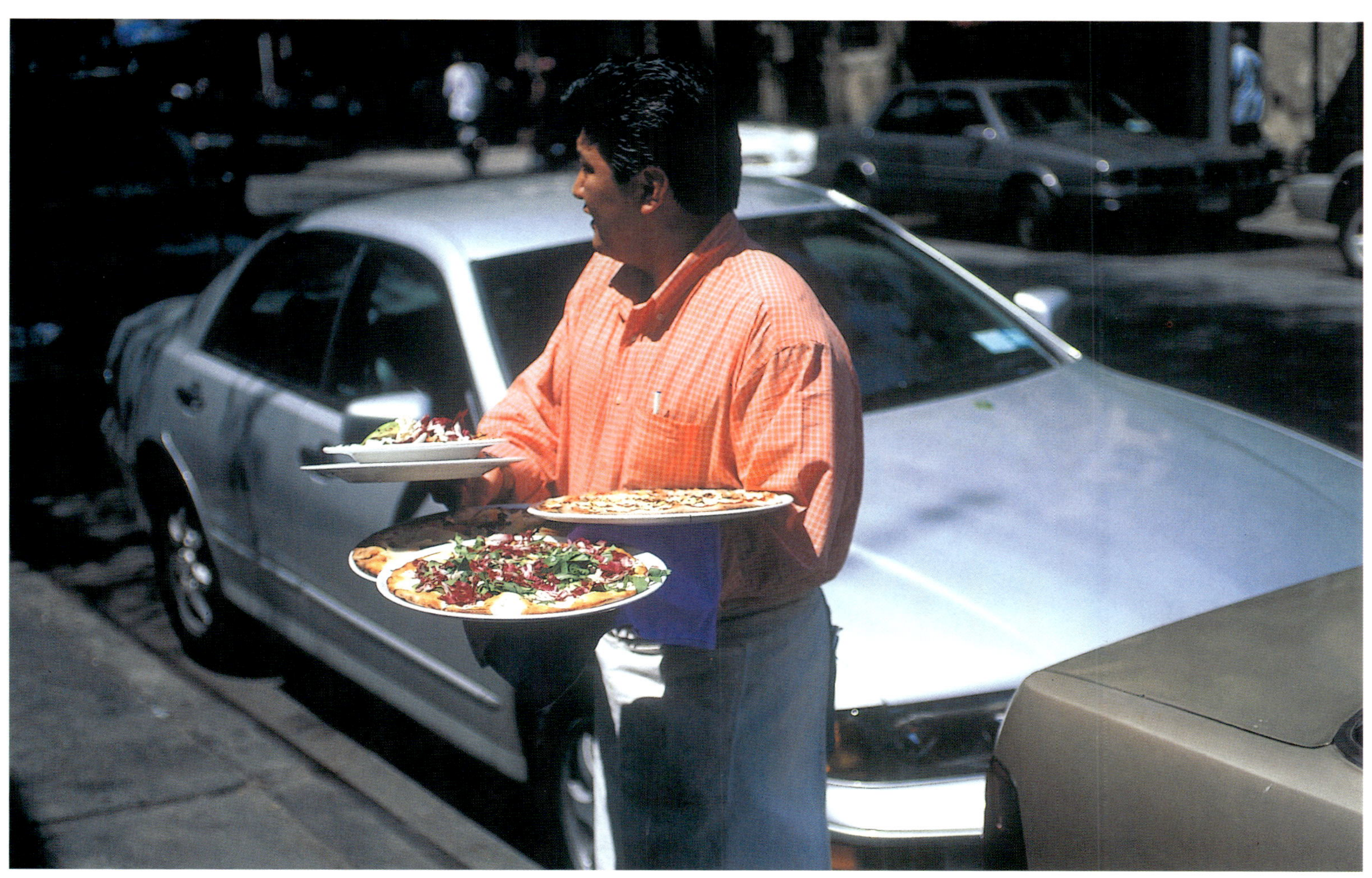

West Indian parade in Brooklyn.

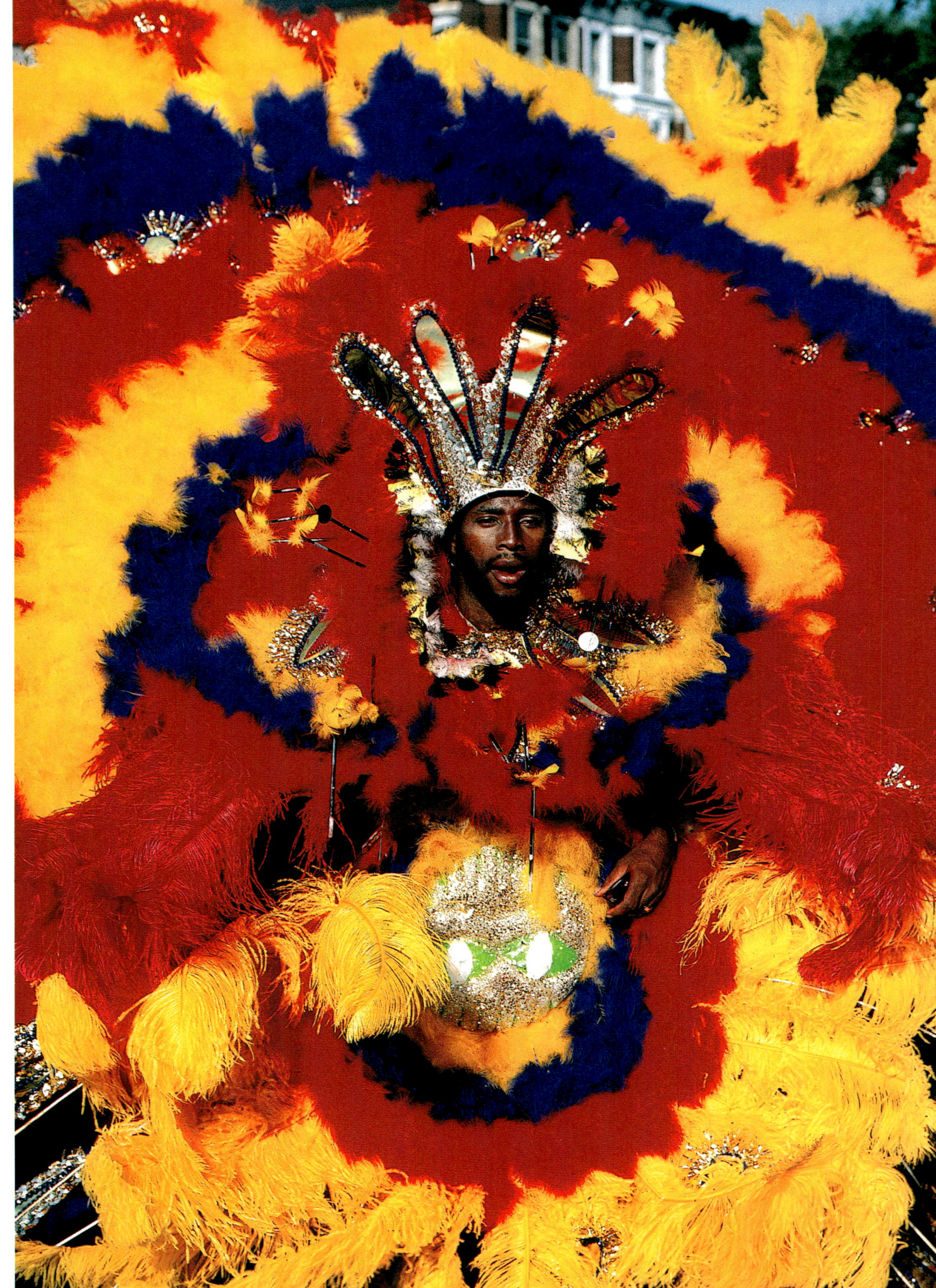

Brazilian dancers,

downtown Manhattan.

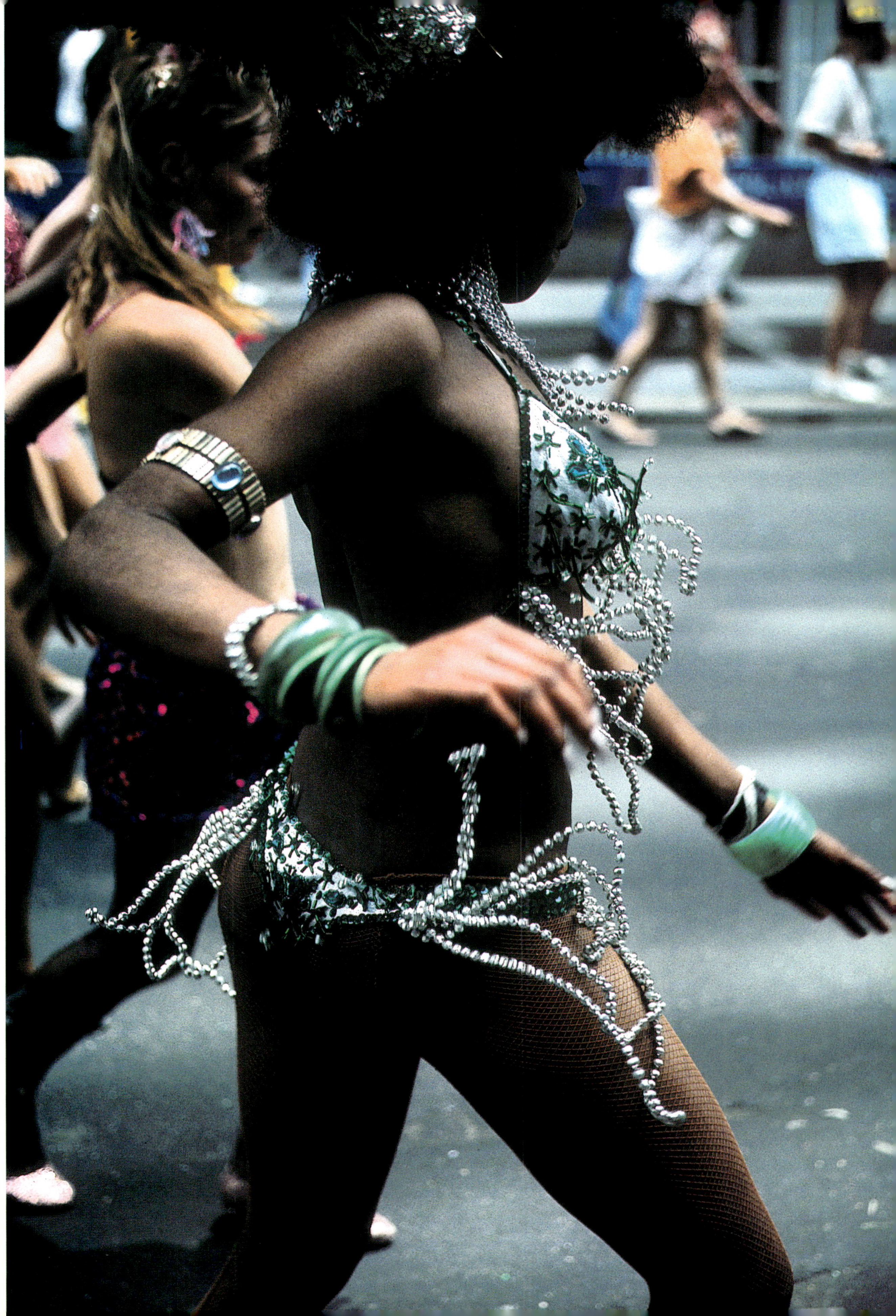

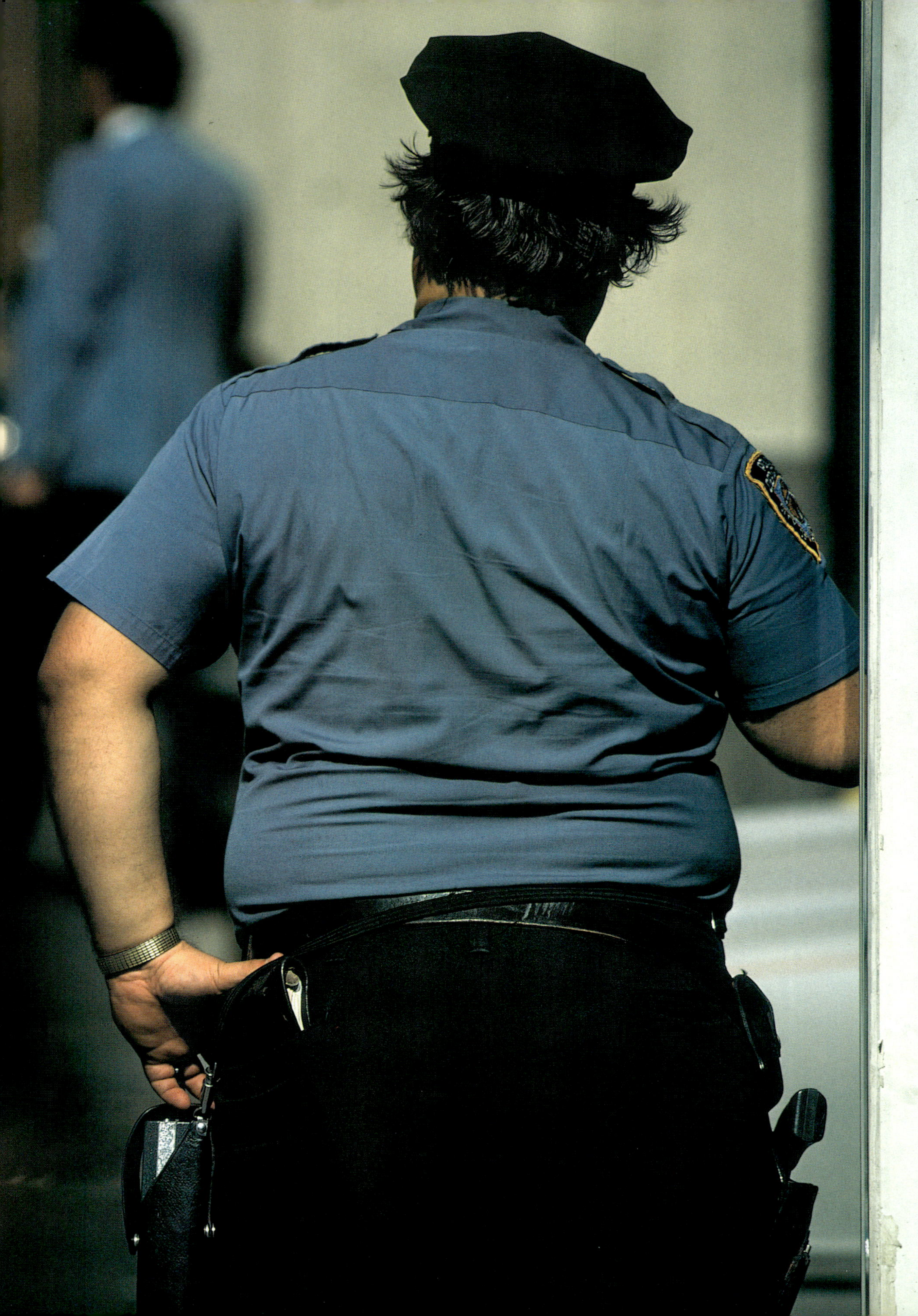

Gay Pride parade.

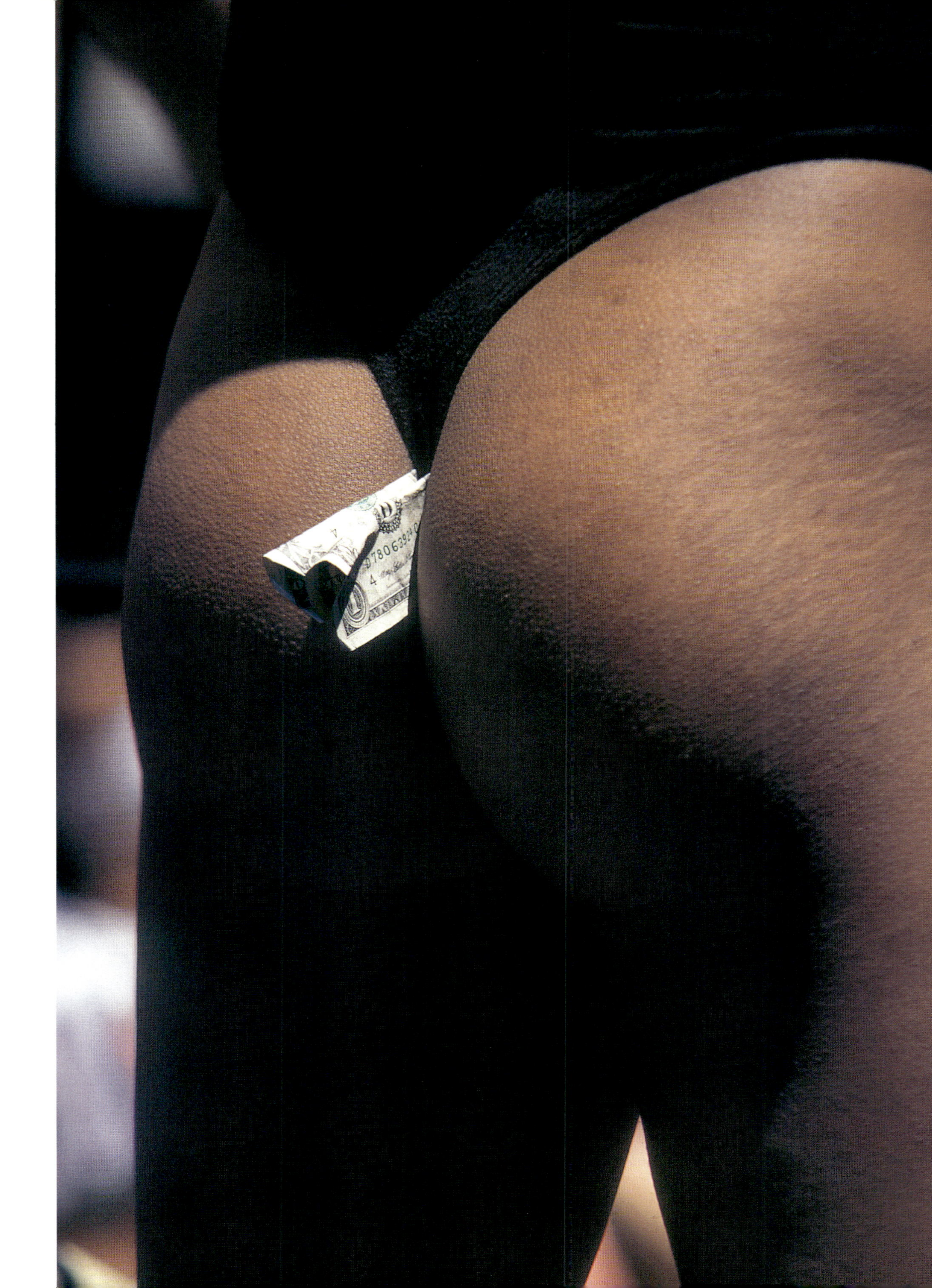

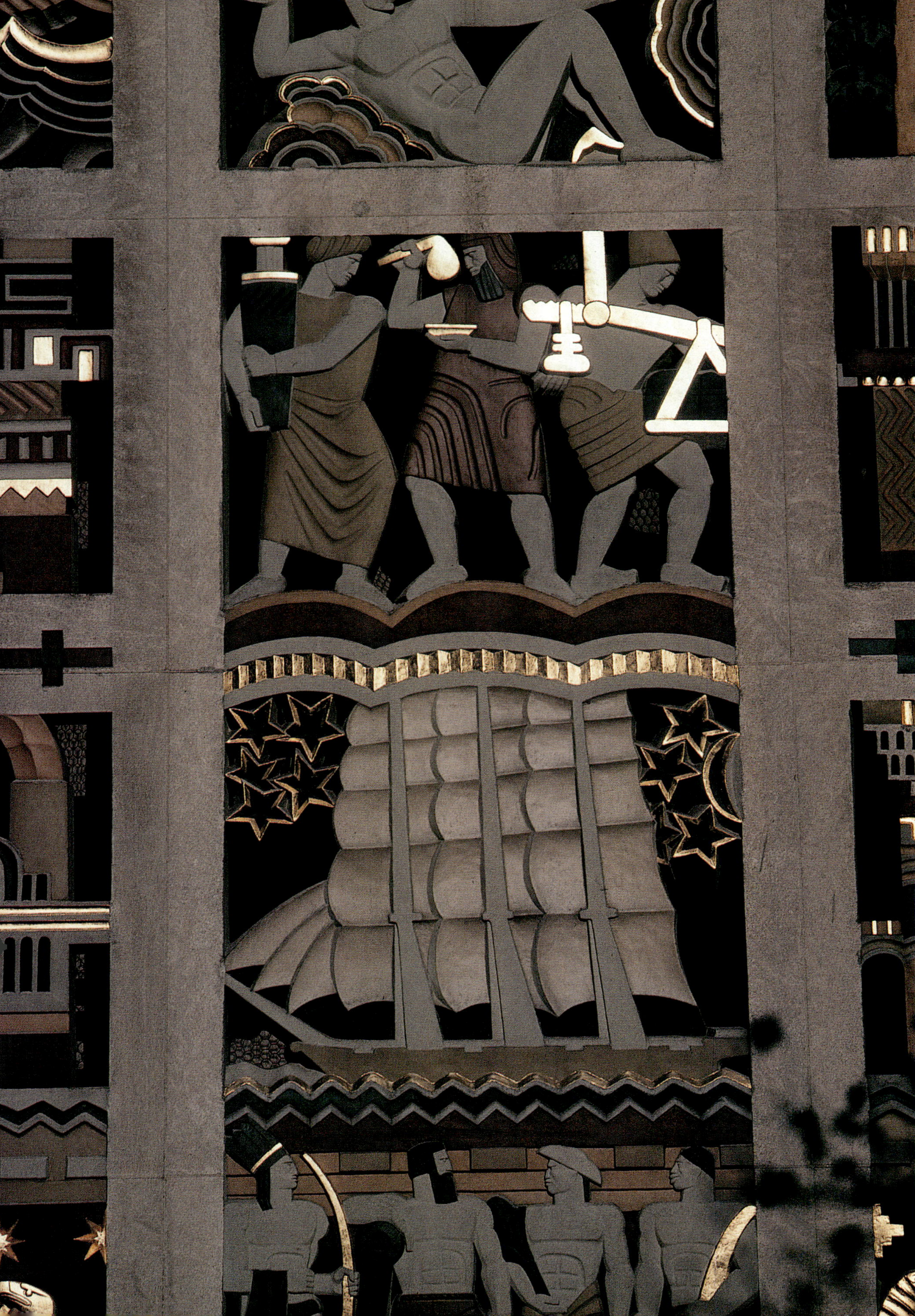

Mural at

Rockefeller Center.

A wall painting for a diner on lower 6th Avenue.

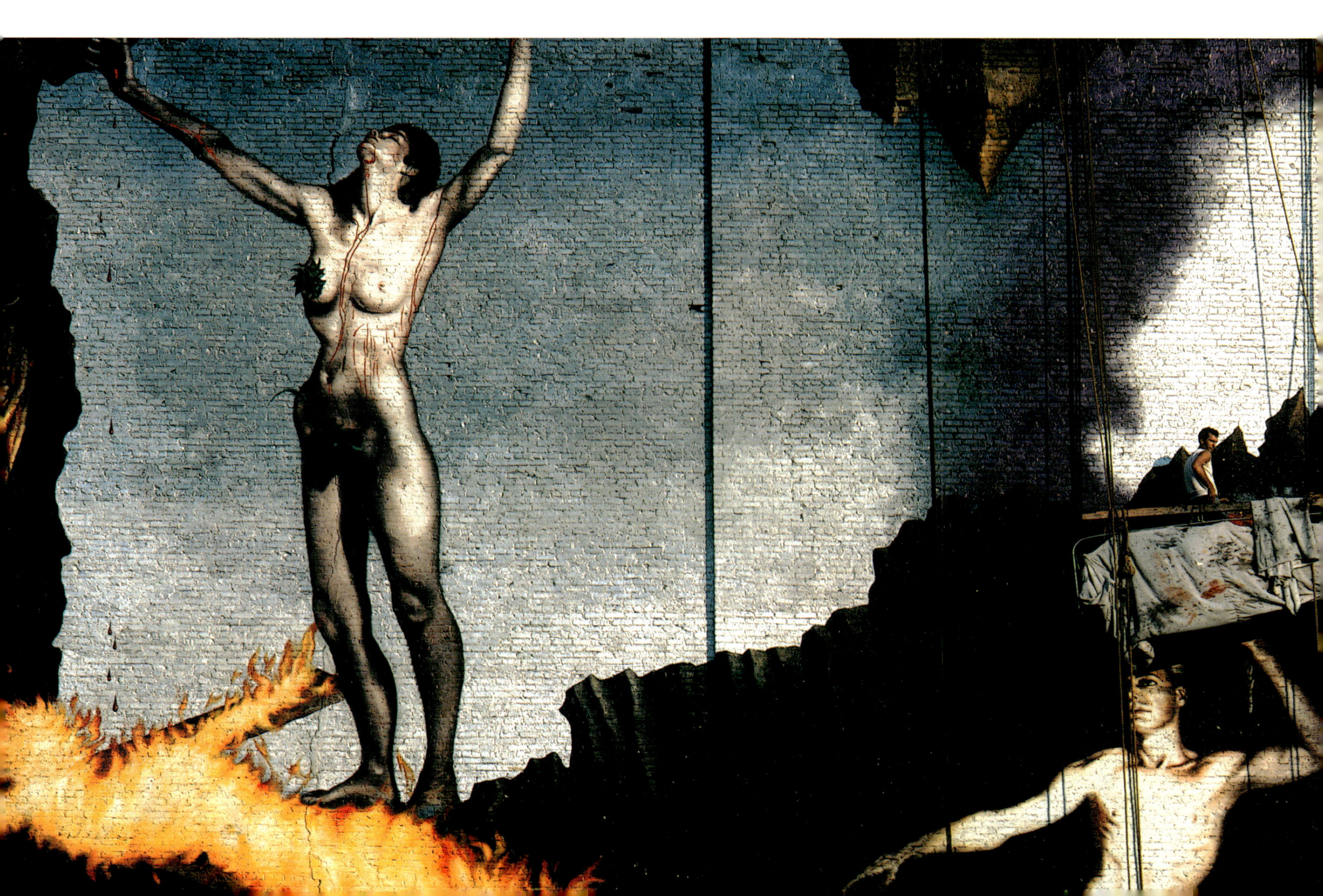

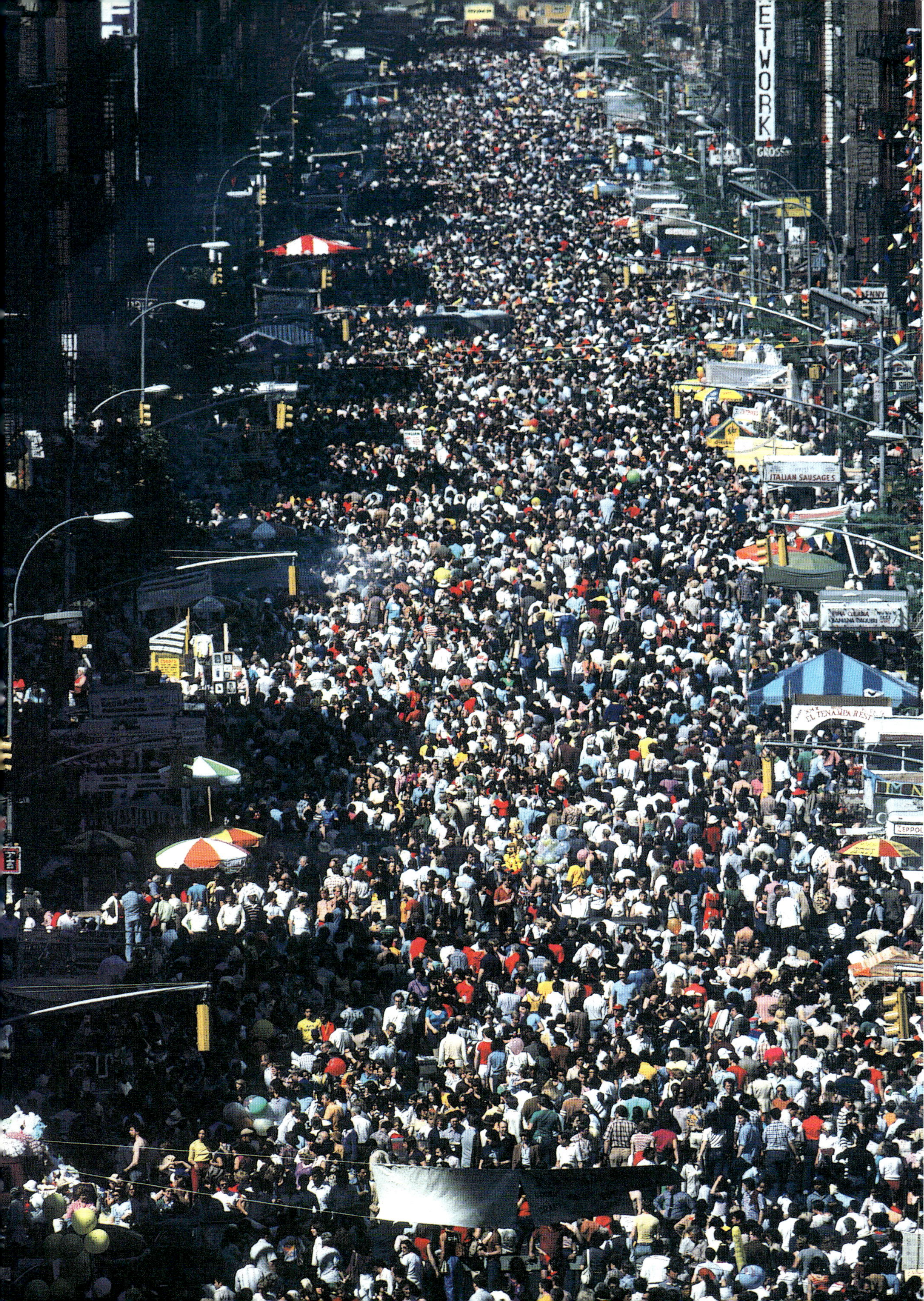

9th Avenue food festival, from 42nd to 57th Street.

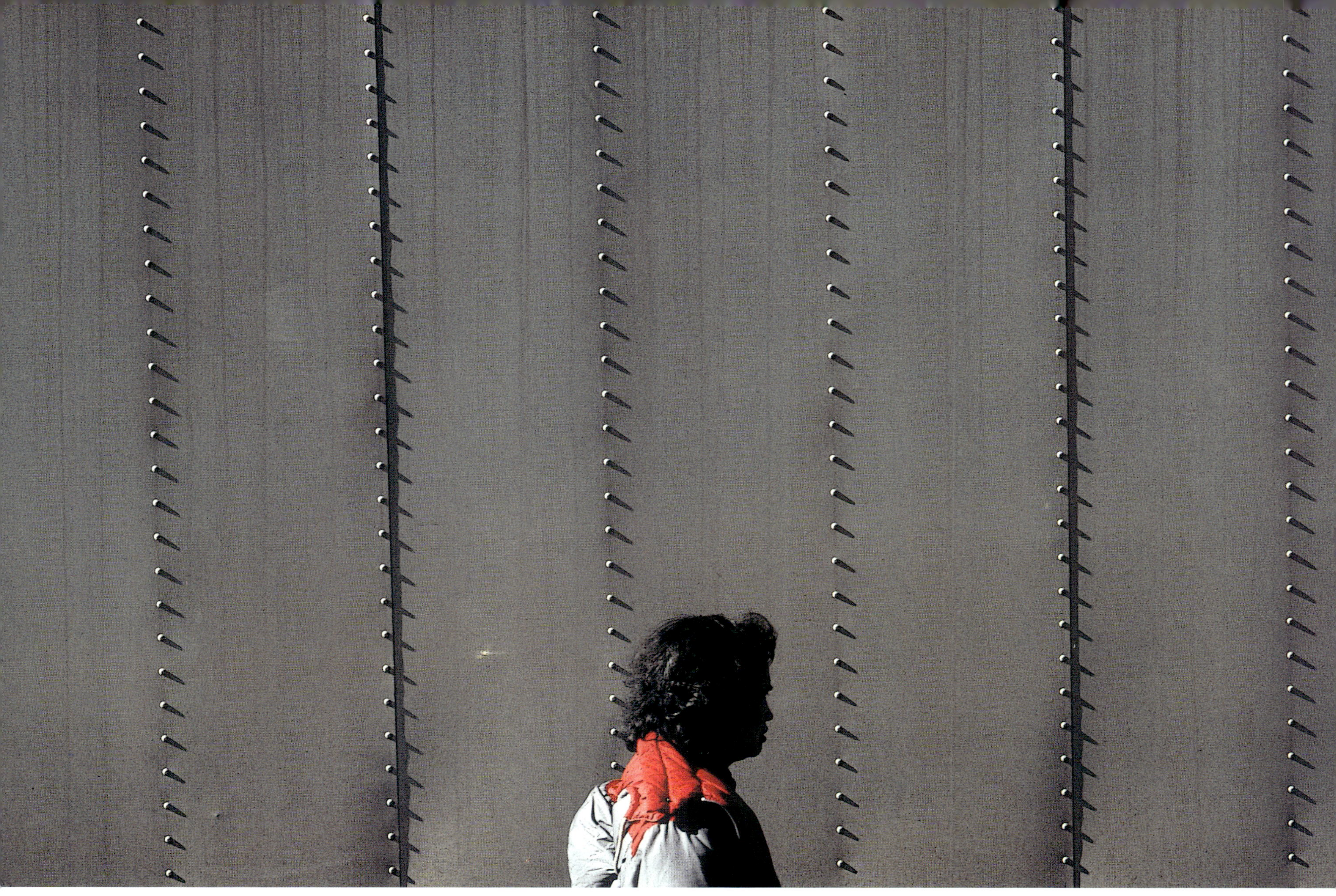

At the Statue of Liberty birthday celebration an out-of-towner, seeing all the lights from the crafts on the water, mistook them for house lights and said, "I always thought the statue was on the water."

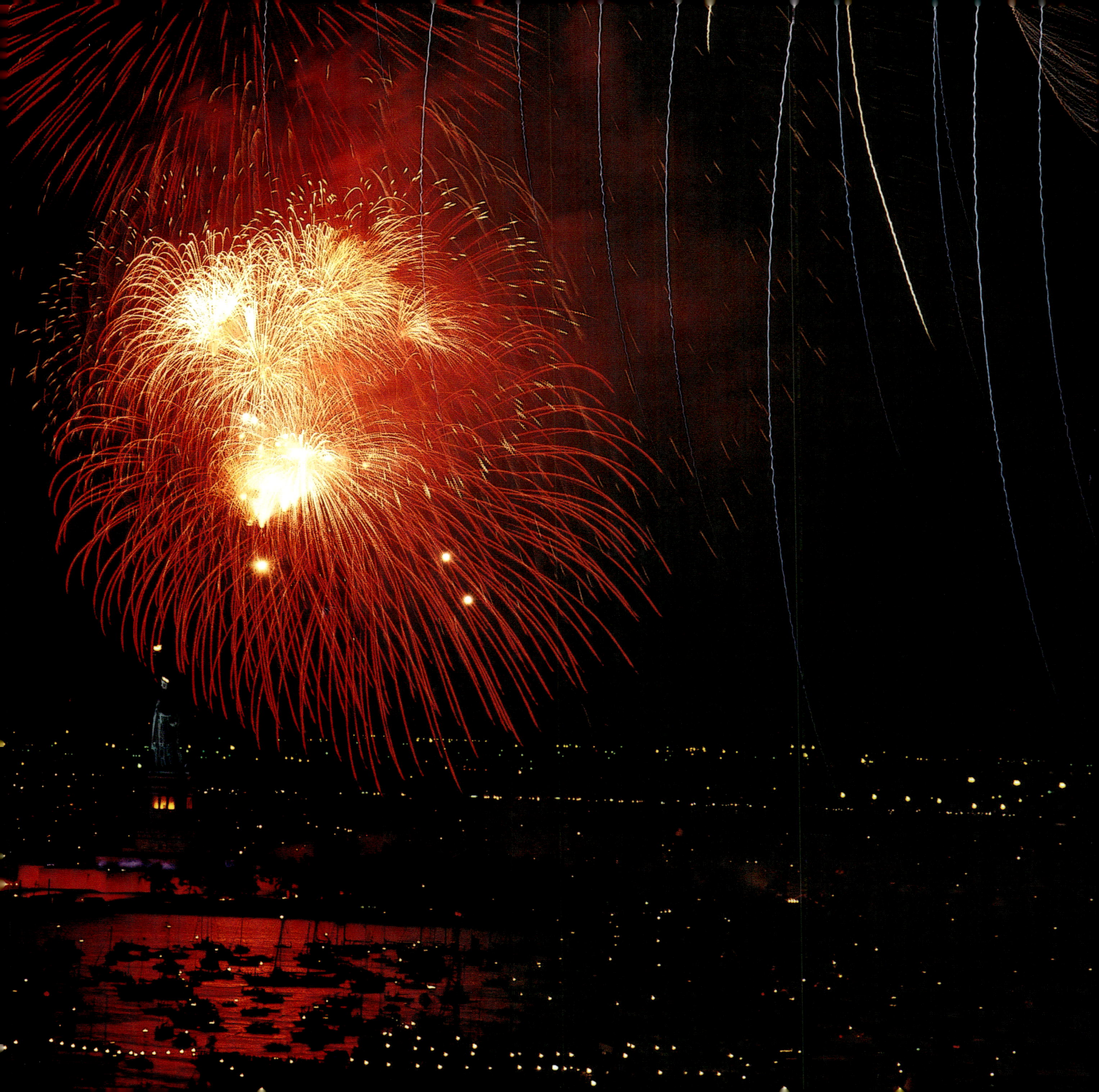

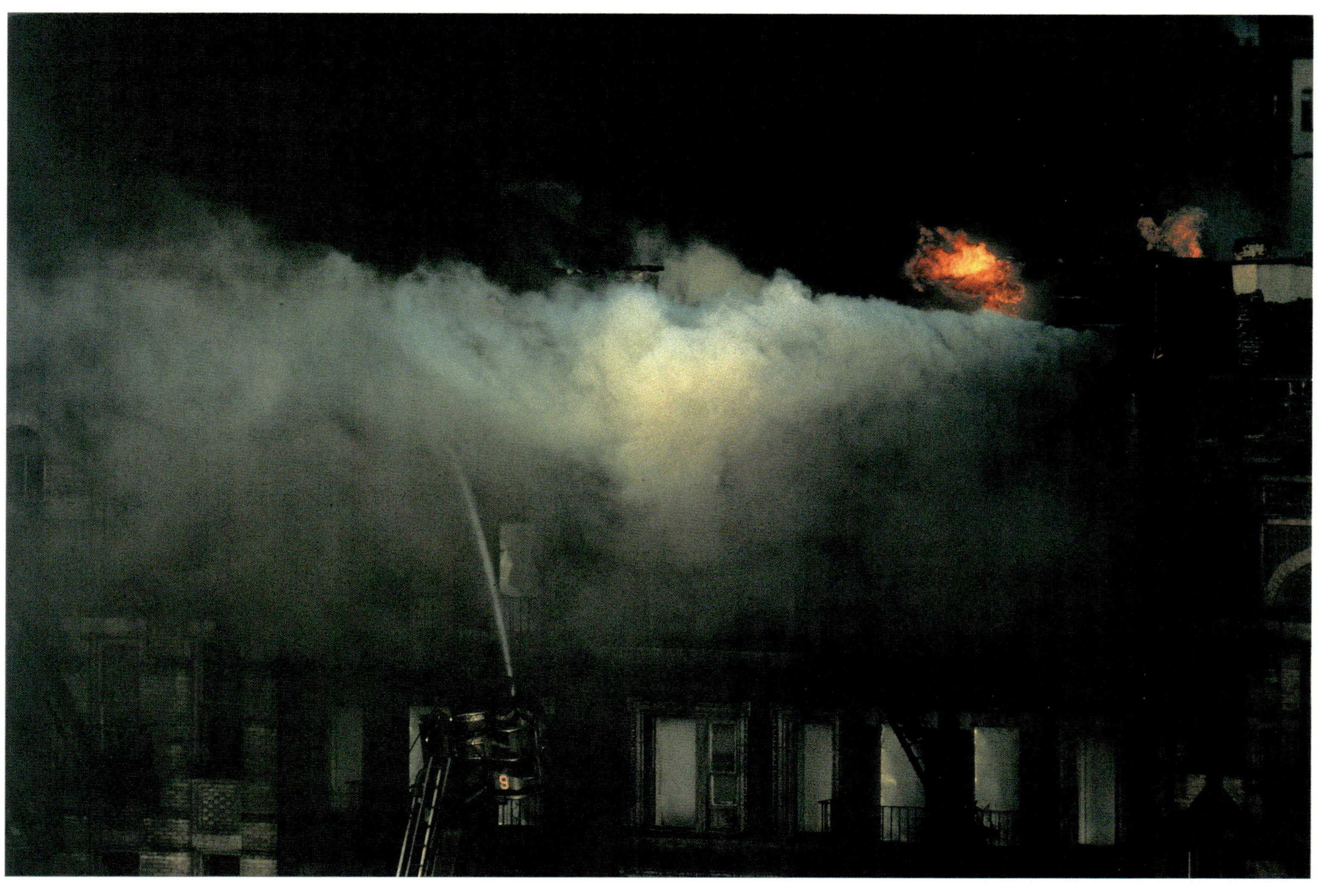

I have a reputation for being a "white cloud"—someone who drives along with firemen and never sees house fire.

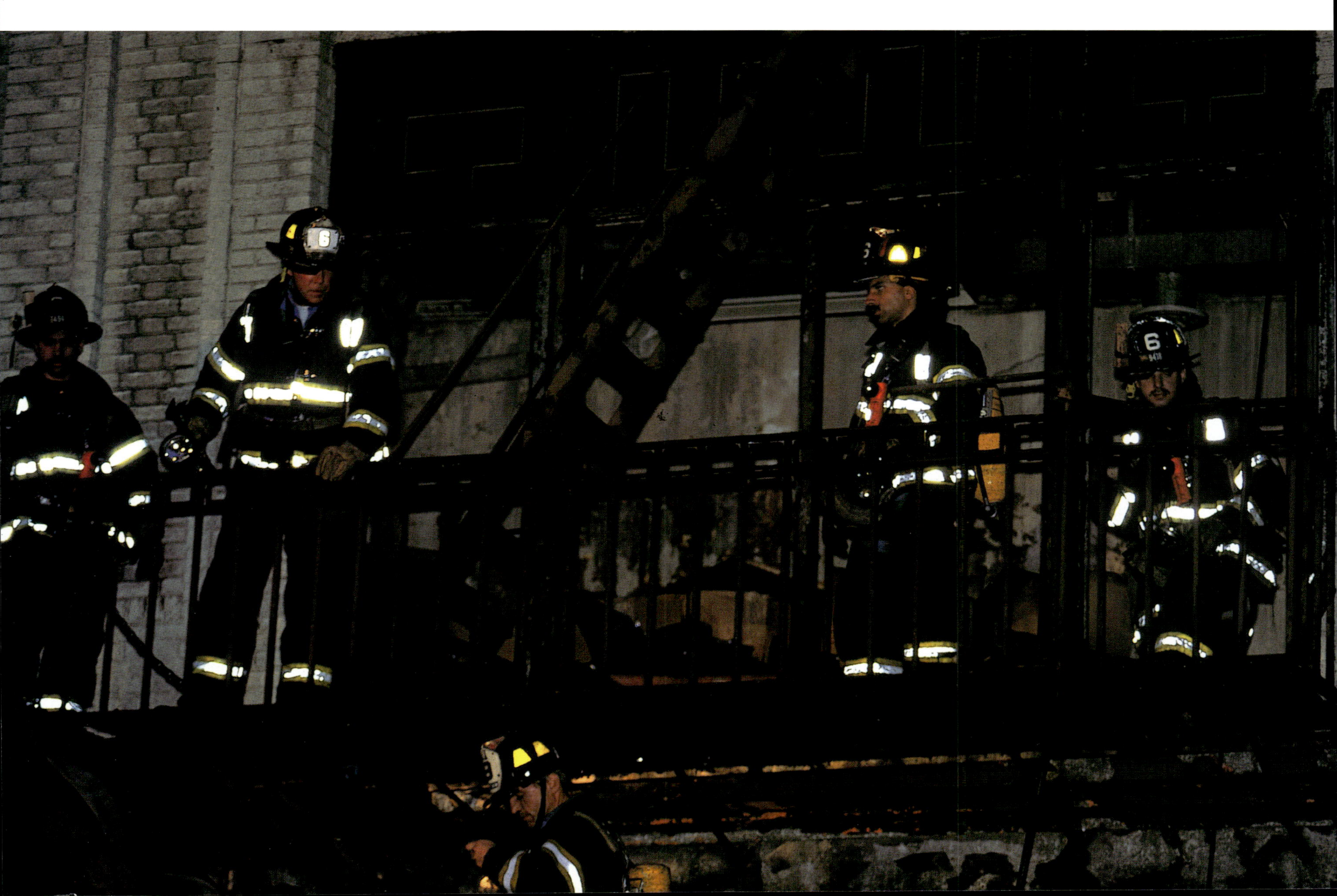

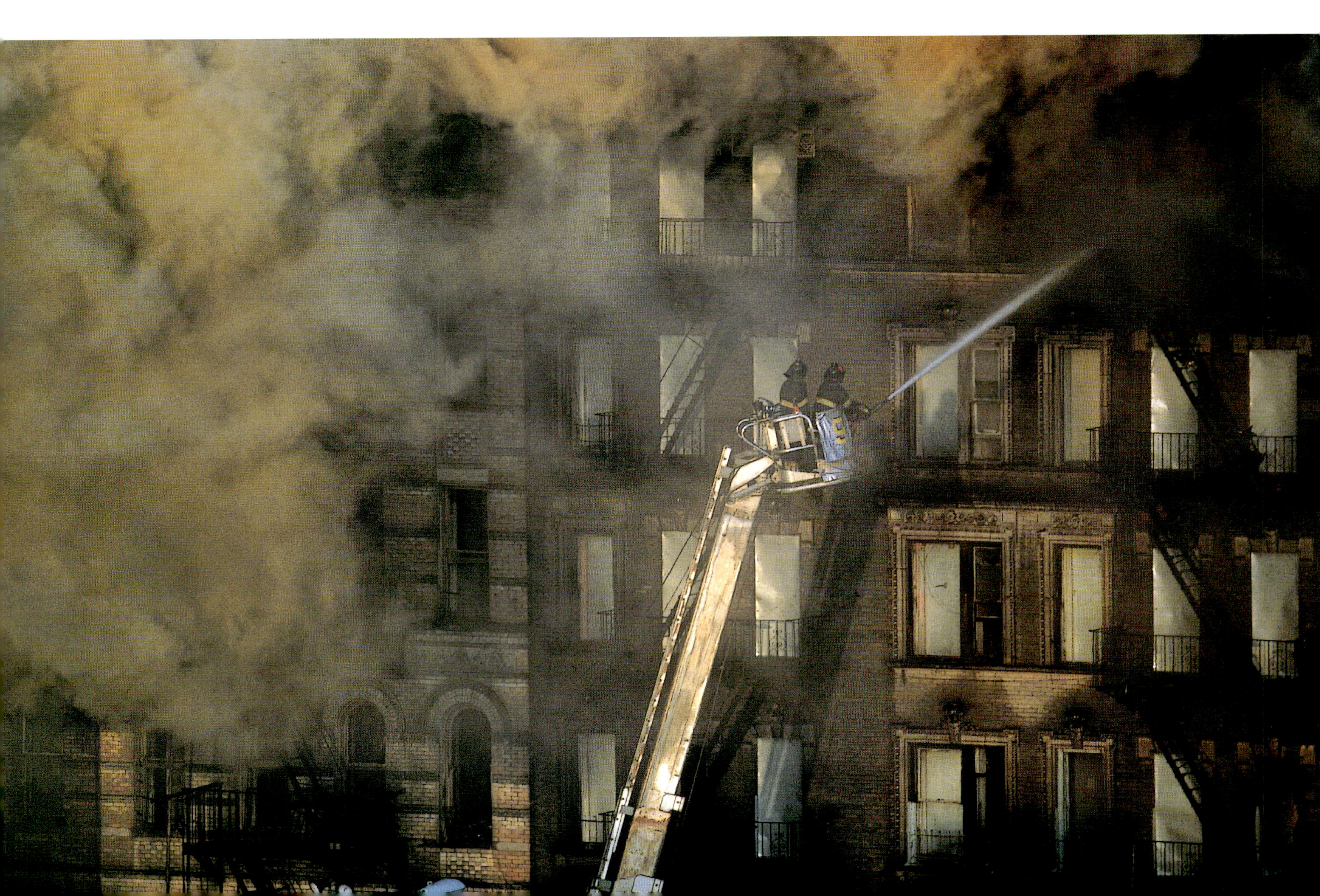

This wasn't a fire, but an explosion of steam pipes that spread asbestos over a number of buildings.

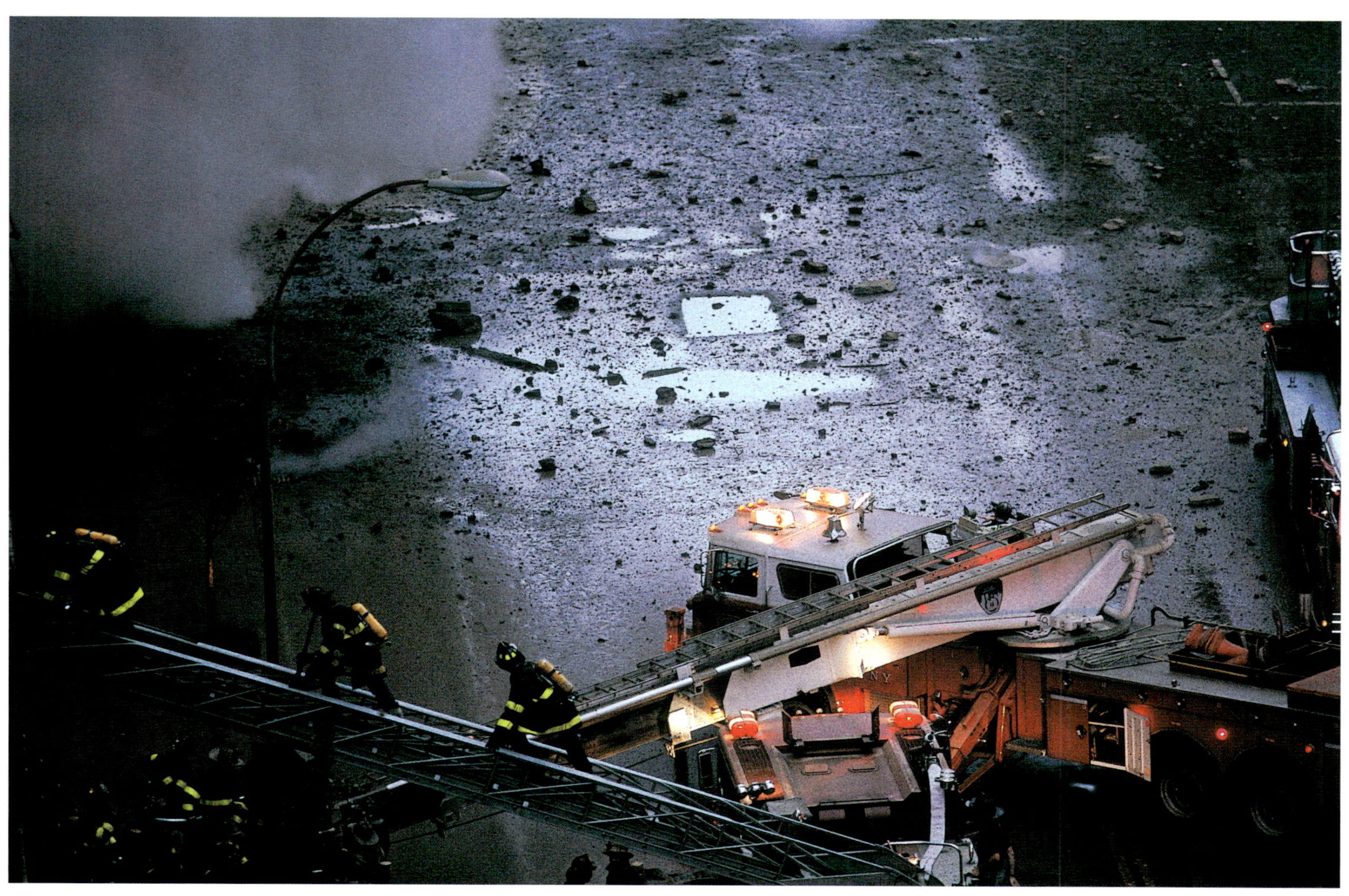

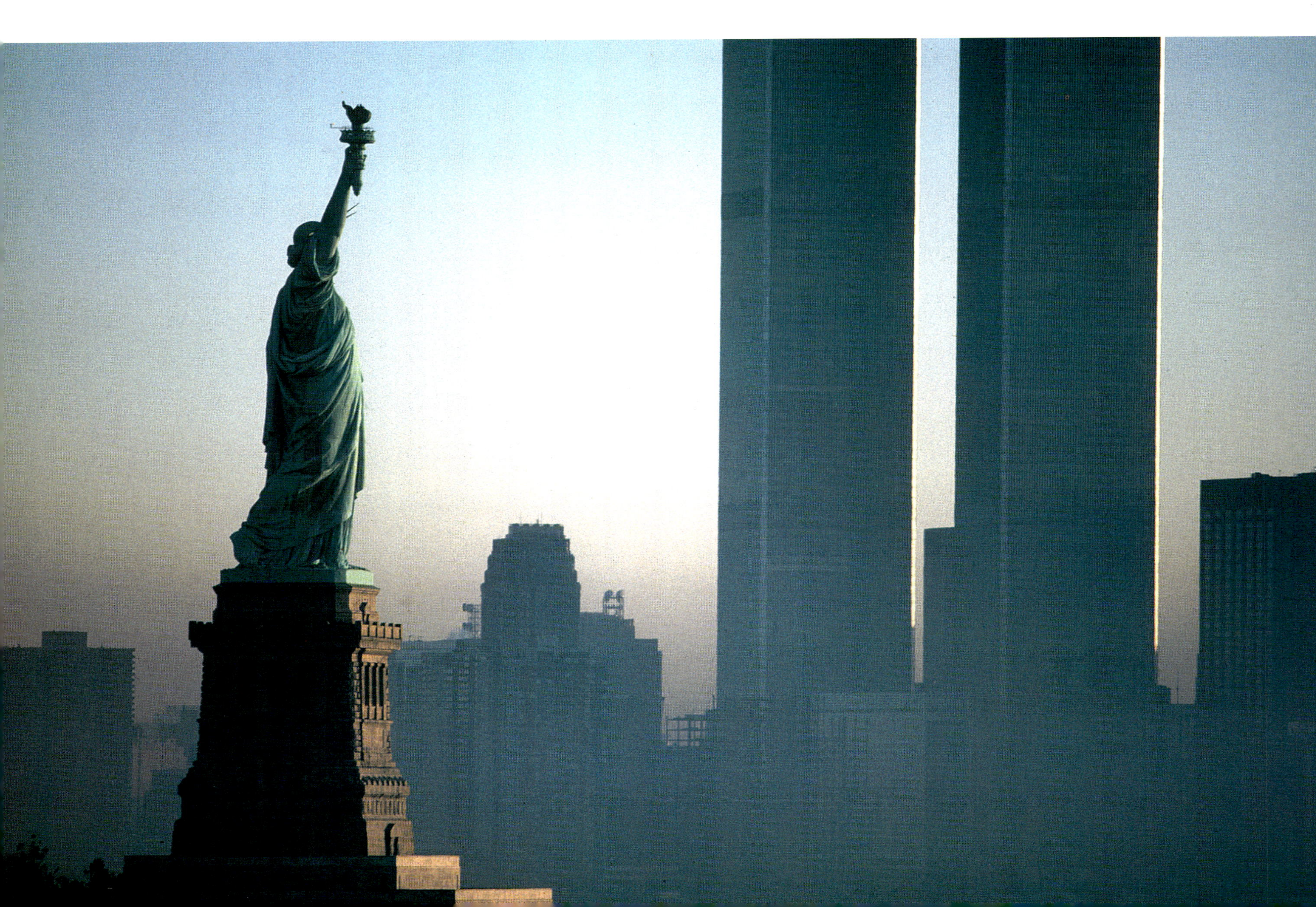

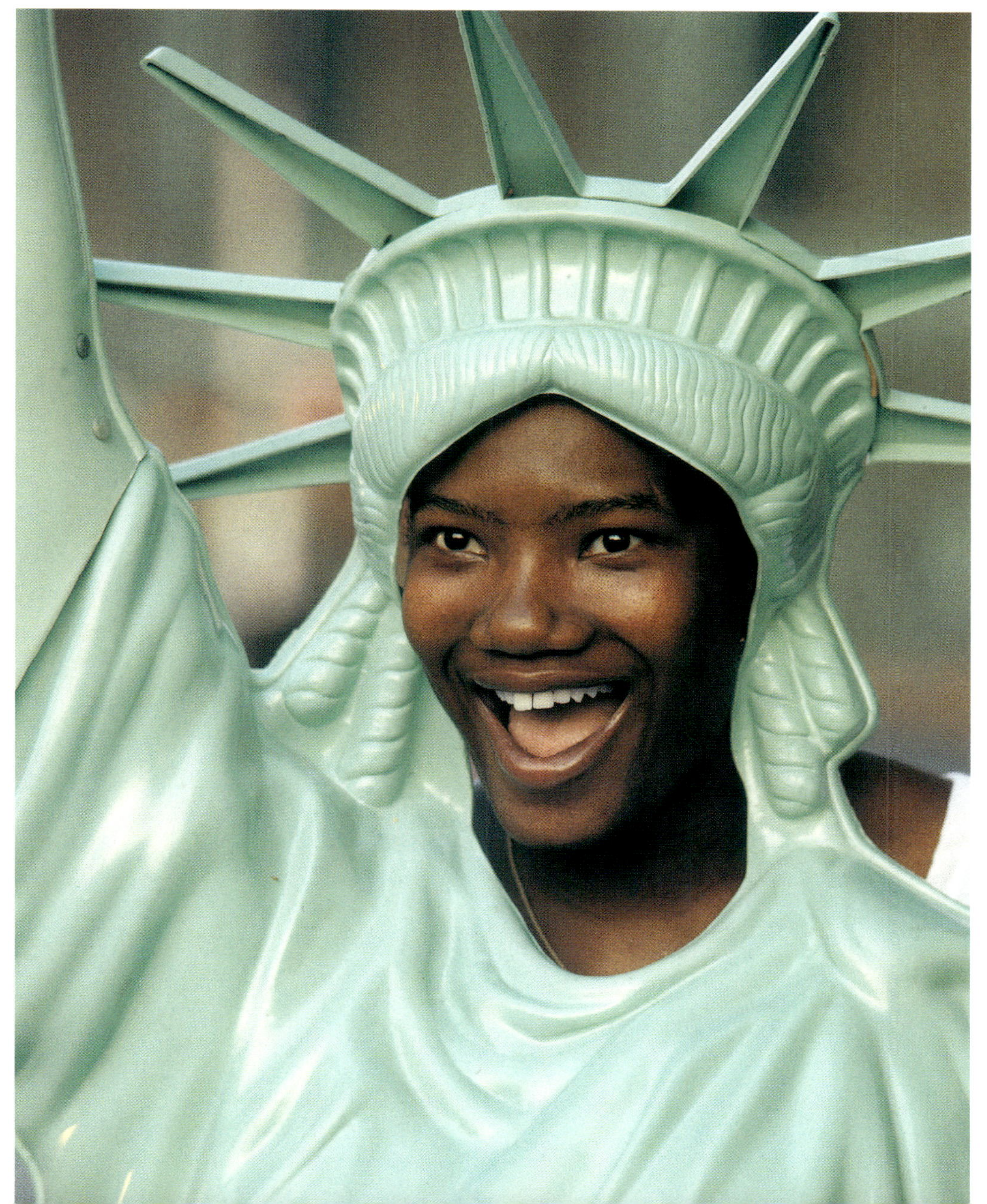

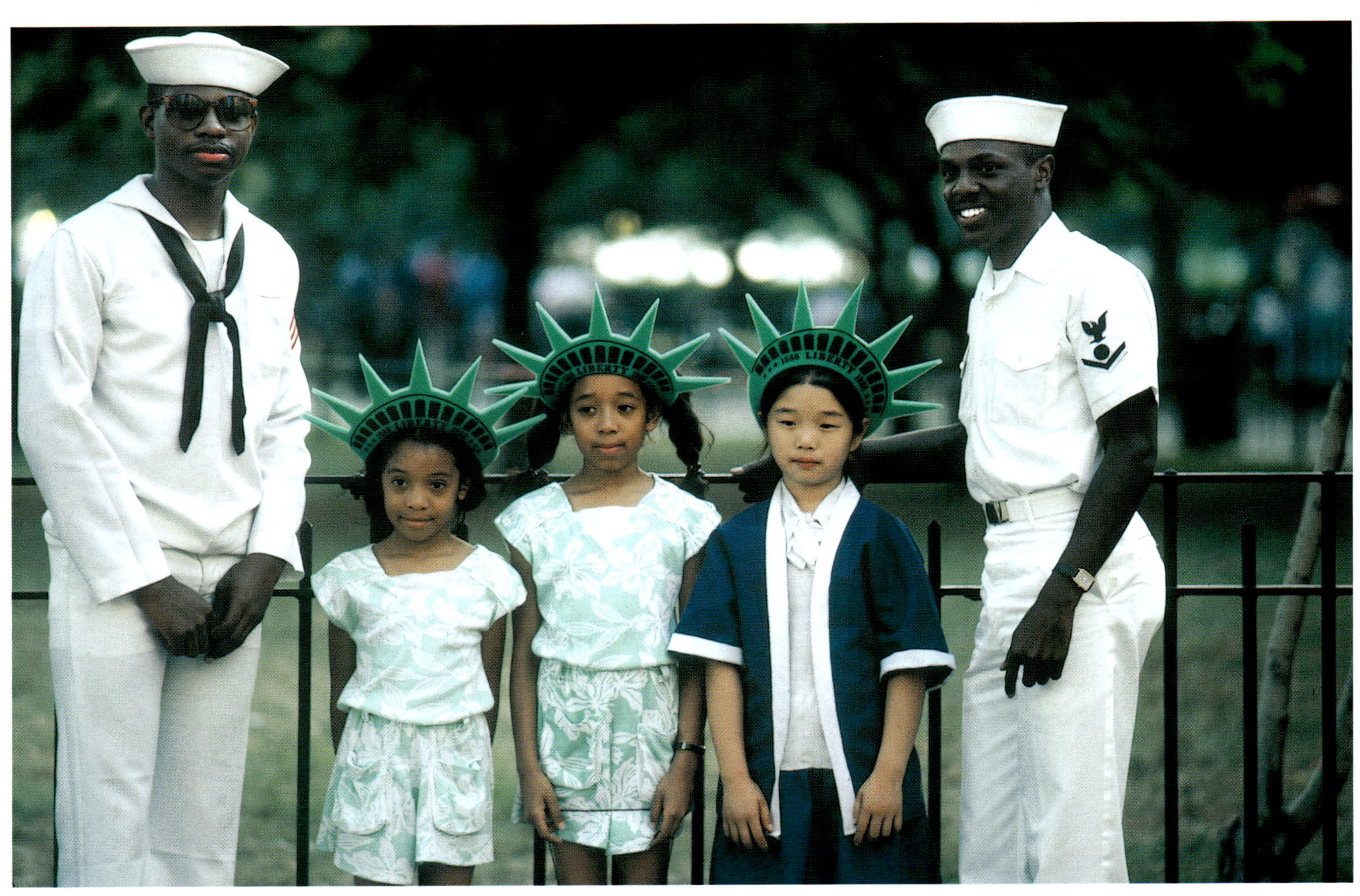
LIBERTY
1886 LIBERTY

Statue of Liberty restoration.

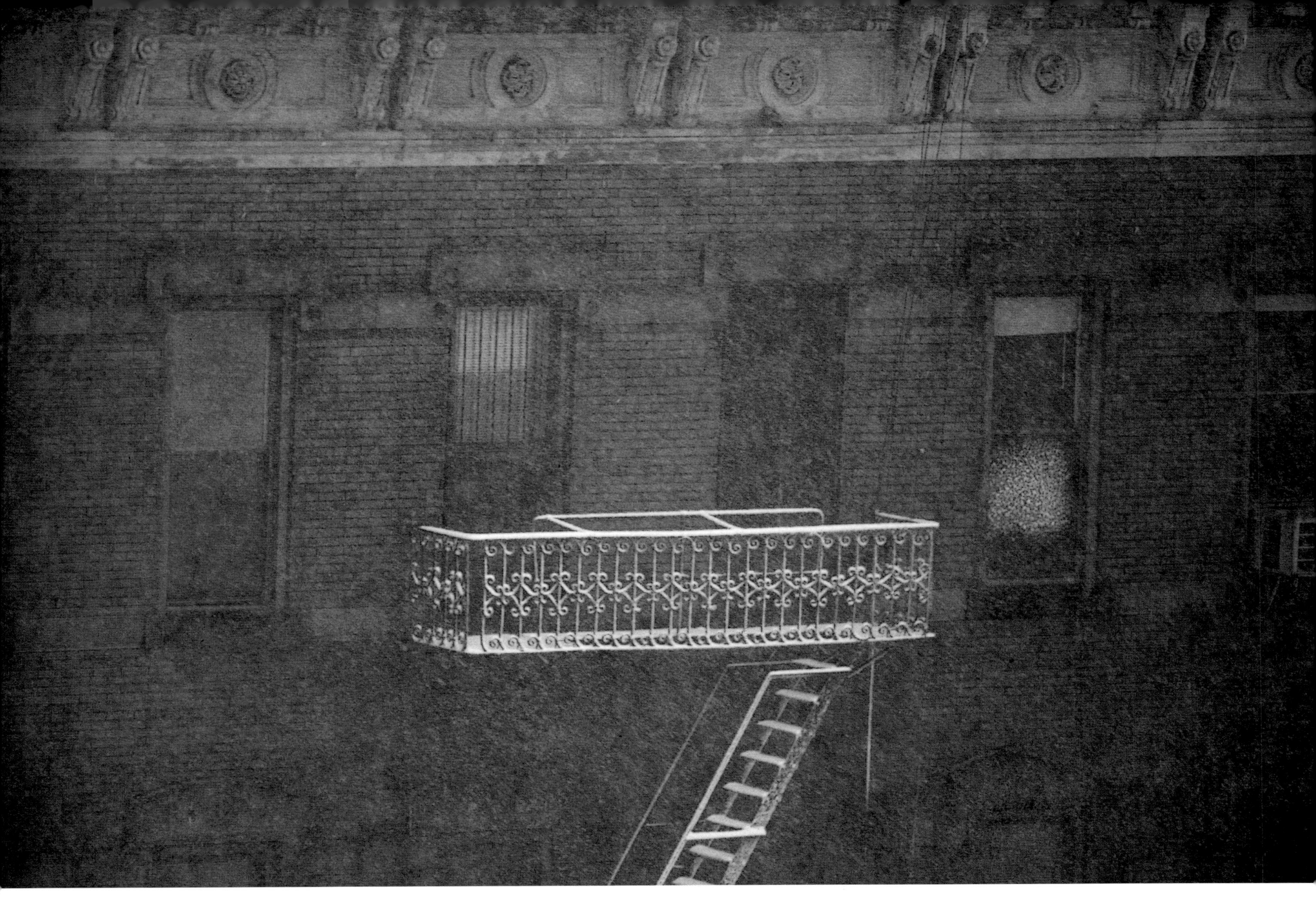

The World Trade Center, before construction of the World Financial Center.

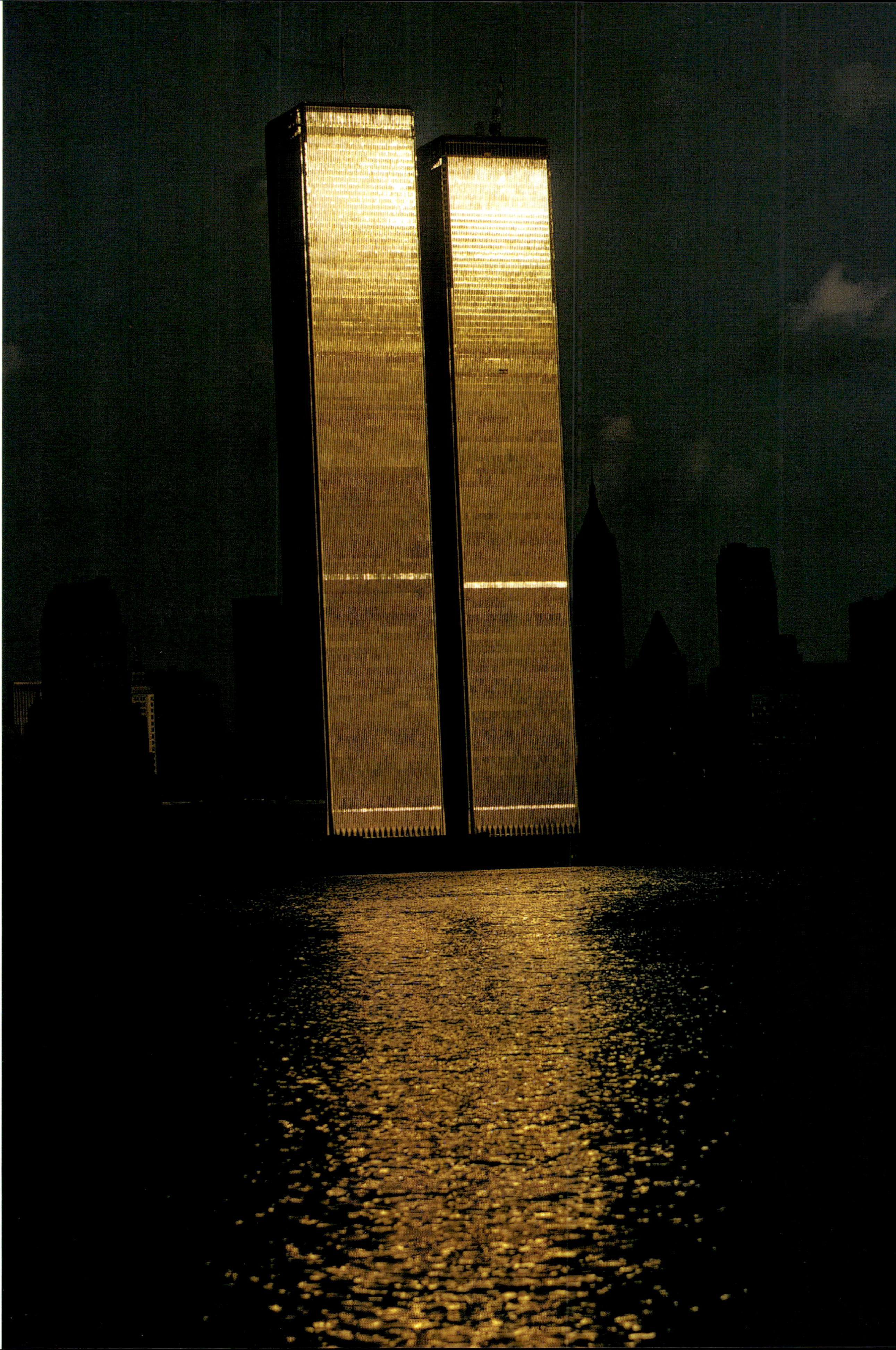

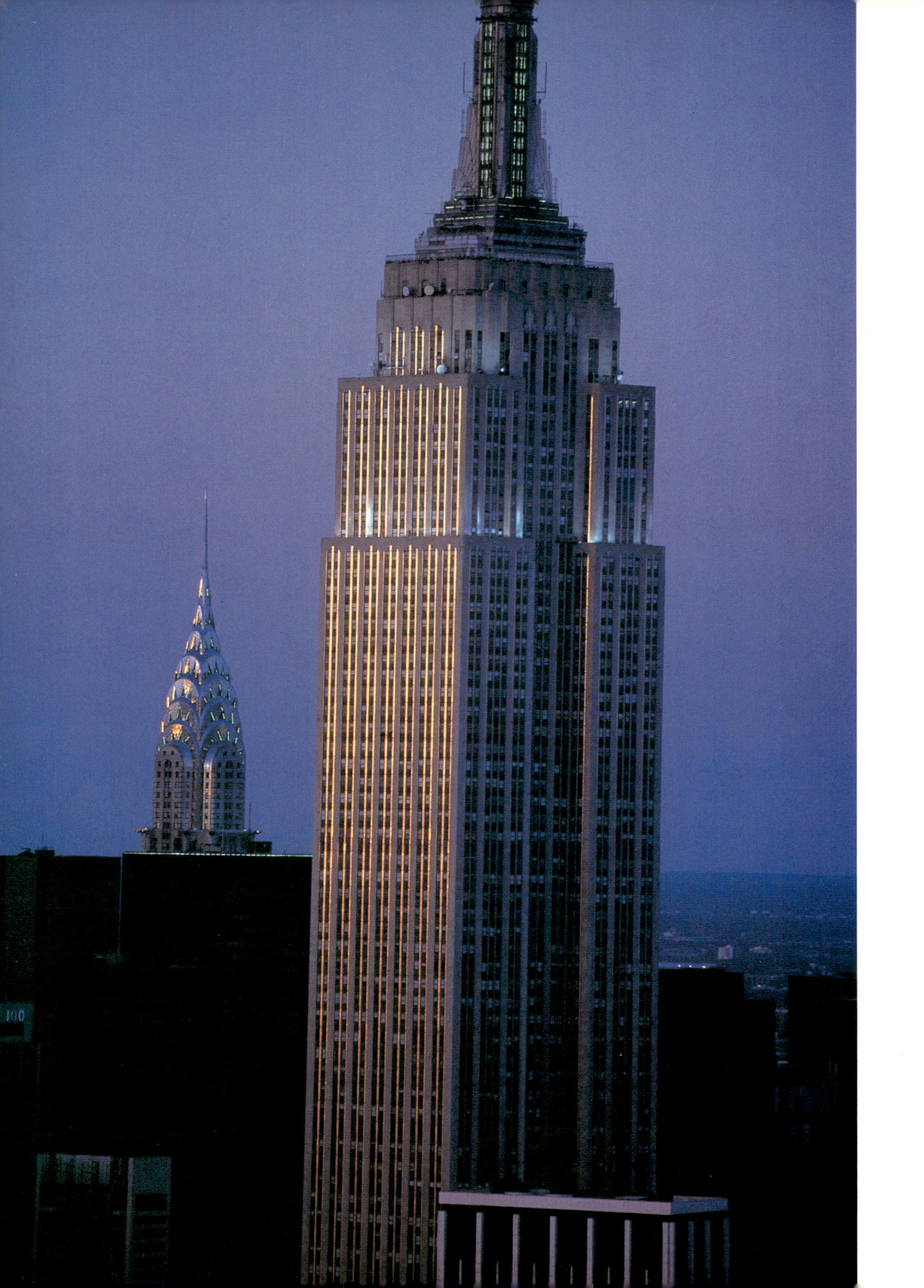

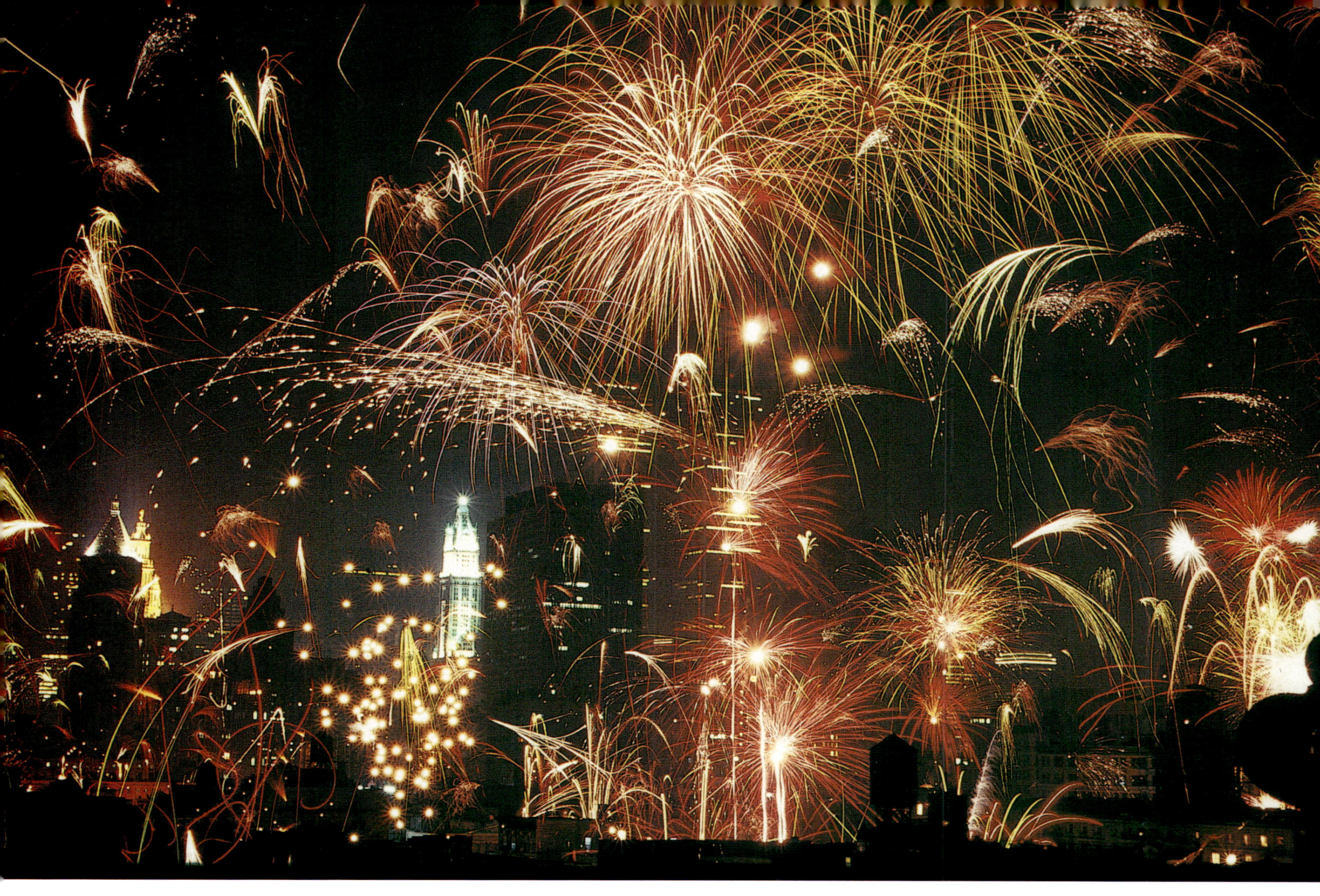

No, these are not the famous Macy's July 4th official fireworks. These are the local fireworks in my neighborhood of Little Italy/Chinatown.